The DEATH of
FREE SPEECH

How Our Broken National Dialogue
Has Killed the Truth and Divided America

JOHN ZIEGLER

CUMBERLAND HOUSE
NASHVILLE, TENNESSEE

Published by Cumberland House Publishing, Inc.
431 Harding Industrial Dr.
Nashville, Tennessee 37211

Cover design: Gore Studio, Inc., Nashville, Tennessee.

Library of Congress Cataloging-in-Publication Data

Ziegler, John, 1967–
    The death of free speech : how our broken national dialogue has killed the truth and divided America / John Ziegler.
        p. cm.
    ISBN 1-58182-441-6 (hardcover)
    1. Freedom of speech—United States. 2. Mass media—Political aspects—United States. 3. Popular culture—Political aspects—United States. I. Title.
 JC591.Z54 2005
 323.44'3'0973—dc22

                                                                 2005009465

Printed in the United States of America
1 2 3 4 5 6 7 8—10 09 08 07 06 05

To Bob-Bob, Janet, and Mom
And for Amanda, Jack, Katie, Bo, and Alyssa

CONTENTS

The DEATH of
FREE SPEECH

INTRODUCTION: WHY I HAD TO WRITE THIS BOOK

> *"If men are to be precluded from offering their sentiments on a matter which may involve the most serious and alarming consequences that can invite the consideration of mankind, reason is of use to us; the freedom of speech may be taken away, and dumb and silent we may be led, like sheep to the slaughter."*
>
> —George Washington,
> first president of the United States

When I was a young boy growing up in the suburbs of Philadelphia, like most good Americans, I believed in a lot of stuff that sounded really great. Among other things, I bought in, briefly, to Santa Claus and thought that if you were kind to people, especially girls, they would in turn be nice to you (yeah right!). Even now, at the age of thirty-eight and having been jaded by the harsh reality that much of what I presumed in my youth to be true was actually utterly false, I am still hoping my badly damaged psyche will eventually heal from these cruel realizations. For the record, I am not holding my breath.

While I long ago accepted that much of what I was taught as a youngster lacked veracity, there are some concepts that I have had a difficult time letting slide away into the realm of just another discredited childhood fantasy. Foremost among those are two principles: that we live in a country where people can say anything they want without fear of punishment, and that the truth usually wins out in the end, or, at the very least, actually matters!

Most of us older than thirty were taught in school that this country was founded largely on the notion that everyone is free to express their thoughts, feelings, and ideas, no matter how unpopular they may be. While the First Amendment to the Constitution really only guarantees us the right not to be punished by the government for the things we say or think, for much of our history our culture has been guided by an even higher authority when it comes to freedom of speech: "Sticks and stones may break my bones, but words will never hurt me."

Much like that childhood adage, up until fairly recently the *real* educator of our youth in the modern age, television, had also led us to conclude that "the truth" was such an extremely powerful force that it was virtually unbeatable. After all, Superman *never* lost in his battle for "truth, justice, and the American way," every episode of *I Love Lucy* ended with the inevitable misunderstanding finally being satisfactorily resolved, and even when the football playbook on *The Brady Bunch* got stolen, truth and integrity prevailed in the end.

Because of what I had been taught, I grew up trusting wholeheartedly that a person could articulate any belief, as long as it was based on truth, and that only good could come of it. I doubt that the real world was ever *exactly* like this, but I am also quite certain that we are much further away from that place now than ever before. Regardless of where we have come from, it seems obvious that we are heading in a wrong and very dangerous direction.

I based this disheartening conclusion largely on my vast personal experience in speaking the truth. Having taken these naïve lessons of my youth to heart, my life has largely been a test study of their validity, or lack thereof.

I should have known very early on that something was amiss with my bedrock doctrines regarding the concepts of free speech and the truth. When I was in second grade at a Catholic school in New Jersey, I was constantly harassed by the class bully. Finally, unable to take it anymore, I decided to express my outrage to the teacher. Unfortunately, as I went to raise my hand to get her attention I inadvertently grazed the face of the offending bully (trust me, he was *much* bigger than me, and I was nowhere near dumb enough to provoke a physical altercation with him).

As fate would have it, all the teacher saw was scrawny little Johnny appearing to strike the big bully. My subsequent pleas and protestations regarding the teacher's misinterpretation of what had occurred seemed only to heighten her resolve to punish me and only me. As I spent the rest of the day in the corner, I should have realized right then that speaking the truth sure isn't what it's cracked up to be. Instead, being rather stubborn, I chalked up the experience to an aberration. I could not have been more wrong.

As I grew up, I developed a reputation for being quite outspoken. In high school, I inadvertently caused the school newspaper to be shut down for the rest of the year because I wrote a column criticizing what I thought was the administration's unfair treatment of athletics. At Georgetown University, I felt the wrath of the athletic department because I had the gall to investigate a basketball player for drug use (the very same athlete who would eventually be kicked off the team because of his involvement with a drug kingpin).

As I began my broadcasting career in local television as a sports anchor and reporter, I quickly (though not soon enough) learned that, much to my surprise, when you call someone on screwing up—even if you are right—it is *you* who is the "bad guy" for just bringing up the incident, and that the first person to complain about an episode will almost always be deemed to be speaking the truth. Needless to say, I was not a very popular guy in a business that favored those who did not care enough about the product to bother trying to find out what went wrong when it inevitably did.

I attempted to become more independent from this brutal business for which I was poorly suited by pursuing an entirely different career endeavor. I spent a year with a high school football team in Steubenville, Ohio, while writing a book about the experience. Unfortunately, the coach of the team decided that the book was too honest (interestingly, he never claimed any of it was remotely false and in fact acknowledged that most of it was actually very positive), and he persuaded then Notre Dame head football coach Lou Holtz, who had previously agreed to write the foreword for the book, to back out of the project. While reneging on his promise, Holtz told me he did not want to be involved in any "controversy."

After the book-writing disappointment, I made the poor decision (just days after my mother had been killed in a car accident) to get back into TV sportscasting. In 1995, at the start of the O. J. Simpson trial, I was an anchor/reporter at WLFL-TV in Raleigh, North Carolina. While introducing a Bears/49ers playoff game in which the Super Bowl champions-to-be 49ers were the heavy favorite, I joked, "Anybody who believes that the Bears have any chance in this game must also believe in Santa Claus, the Tooth Fairy, and O. J. Simpson's innocence."

The next day our main female news anchor (who also happened to be black), took me to task in the middle of the newsroom for making such an "outrageous" statement. When I politely asked her why she thought that it was so inappropriate for a *sports* person to say such a thing when it was so obviously true, she responded that black people do not believe that O. J. is guilty. When I told her that it was not my fault that a segment of the population was choosing to remain "ignorant" about the facts of this case, she stood up and, in front of several coworkers, called me a "fucking asshole" and left the room in tears.

The next day, without any discussion about what did or did not transpire, I was suspended for the newsroom "altercation." Oddly, the black female anchor was not even reprimanded.

Then a black columnist (Barry Saunders at the *Raleigh News and Observer*), who never even saw the show in question and who did not bother to talk to me before publication, wrote an editorial in which I was misquoted and my comment was made into a racial issue.

Even though O. J.' s race had *nothing* to do with what I said or why I said it, and I am the *furthest* thing from a racist, the die was cast and I was eventually fired from my job for supposedly breaking the adverse publicity clause in my contract. Just to top off the whole absurd affair, Saunders, with whom I had subsequently become shockingly friendly, wrote another column bashing the station for firing me and caving in to political correctness. As notorious boxing promoter Don King might say, "Only in America!!"

Deciding that I had had enough with sports television (and vice versa), I figured if TV could not handle my version of the truth, maybe issue-oriented talk radio could.

After being let go at a general talk station in Raleigh, ironically because I told the scathing story of my TV firing (after being directed to do so by the station's consultant, who was apparently as unaware as I was that the TV station he told me to criticize was on the verge of a cross-promotional deal with the radio station for which I was working), I got a gig as the evening host at the FM talk station in Nashville, Tennessee.

In 1997, I was fired from WWTN-FM because I used the word *nigger* in *EXACTLY* the same context that black comedian Chris Rock had made famous. I did so in the aftermath of Mike Tyson biting off part of Evander Holyfield's ear. My point was that the vast majority of white people would never discriminate against Holyfield just because he happened to be black, but some might do so to Tyson because they would think of him, thanks to his continually unacceptable behavior, as a "nigger."

I used the actual word (which I fully understand the horrible history of) mostly because I wanted to point out the double standard of blacks using it all the time and whites not being allowed to do so under even the most benign of circumstances. I was also extremely frustrated by the news media treating the public as children during the O. J. Simpson trial by continually referring to LAPD detective Mark Fuhrman's infamous use of the "n-word" (as if we might all turn to stone if we heard the *ACTUAL* word that Fuhrman used, even in the context of reporting an important fact).

Naïvely, I felt rather safe in using the word because just a few months earlier I had employed it several times on the same station the day after my hero, Tiger Woods (for whom I had created a fictitious "church" in his honor and declared myself "Pastor"), had won the Masters. As with Holyfield, my point was that very few, if any, whites would discriminate against Tiger Woods because, unlike Tyson, he was such a classy guy.

Despite all of this, a few days after my on-air comments I was fired from my job without being offered one cent of severance pay.

Eventually, after hanging tough through some very difficult times and finally learning some important lessons, I made my way back to my hometown of Philadelphia. After being fired, rehired, and fired again within a three-week period by an FM station that was going through a major format shift from traditional talk to "All

Madonna, All the Time" (otherwise known as '80s music), I found myself briefly back in sports.

While doing various shifts at the celebrated WIP-AM sports radio station, a very bizarre thing (even by the standards of my tumultuous career) happened. Mike Tyson held a press conference and called *himself* a nigger. Not being able to resist telling the story of having been fired for *sort of* referring to a man by the exact same word he used to describe himself, I went on the air and discussed this wacky chain of events. However, this time, seemingly proving that while I am certainly stubborn I am not a *total* idiot, I was very careful to not *say* the word *nigger*. Instead, I spelled the nasty word that Tyson had used in describing himself.

I thought that *this* time, I was *completely* safe. How could anything happen to me because I *spelled* a word that a sports figure had used at a public press conference? Once again, I was naïve. I was fired by a man who I (as well as many others) strongly believed to be a racist, all because he ludicrously thought that my *spelling* the word indicated that I was probably a racist myself. It was all enough to make one long for a world that made as much sense as Alice's fictional upside-down Wonderland. Disheartened, I got out of radio for a while and took various jobs as a political polling analyst, freelance newspaper columnist, and television commentator/producer.

Partly because I could not find a suitable and stable situation in the "real world" and partially inspired by the precarious state of the country following the events of September 11th, 2001, I decided to get back into radio when I was offered the mid-morning slot at the legendary WHAS-AM in Louisville, Kentucky.

While there I immediately ruffled feathers by having the audacity to state a simple series of undeniable facts. While discussing the local Catholic priest pedophilia scandal, I mentioned on the air that Catholic priests believe that they have the power to absolve original sin and forgive worldly sins, that they are not supposed to engage in any sexual activity of any kind, and that during each mass they claim to fundamentally alter the essence and substance of the bread and wine into the *actual* body and blood of Jesus Christ. I went on to conclude that it seemed to be a strange way to honor one's God—by eating him and then passing him through your digestive system.

One of the reasons I talked about this was that, as someone who grew up Catholic and went to Catholic school most of my academic career, I was always astonished at how few Catholics even knew that their church's official teaching regarding "transubstantiation" was that they were eating the *real* substance of Jesus, not the symbolic body and blood of the man.

Apparently not recognizing the great educational service that I was doing for their fellow followers as well as the general public, both the Catholic League and the local Knights of Columbus bombarded the station with protests for well over a month. Finally, even after my boss told me that I had done nothing wrong and that I would not be forced to apologize, I was indeed required by management to read on the air a written act of contrition. In an indication of my growing realization that being "right" rarely made much difference in such matters, I reluctantly went along.

For quite a while it seemed as if my concession to reality was indeed the proper thing to do. The Catholic groups backed off and my show became such an amazing ratings success that I quickly became a dominant figure in the market. I even became the co-host of my own prime-time TV show on the local NBC affiliate.

After having survived a year in Louisville (defying the predictions of a local liberal columnist after whom I named a golf tournament to celebrate my anniversary), the madness of the media business once again took over my life. I thought I had seen plenty of insanity in my career, but as it would turn out, I had hardly seen anything yet.

Each Friday I would end my radio show with a segment called "Ask John Anything." We would give prizes to listeners who came up with the best and most creative/bizarre questions. No matter what the topic, I promised them a no-bullshit, *completely* honest, answer.

On August 22, 2003, a female TV host with whom I had shared a *very* public and short romance was released from her morning program. Previously she had talked on her show, in the newspaper, and on my radio station about dating me. Since she had also been on my show often to discuss things as varied as our dating relationship and actor Mickey Rourke's fascination with her breasts while she was covering the Academy Awards, I was not surprised that many of the first calls in the "Ask John Anything" segment dealt with her.

In the process of fulfilling the promise of the segment, I erred in answering questions about how natural her breasts were (or were not), why it was that she never wore skirts on the air (by co-incidence she had told me it was because she did not like to wear underwear and, stupidly thinking I was giving her a compliment, I vaguely alluded to how nicely groomed her private area was) and whether or not she was a "lady" or a "slut" (politely as possible I said she was neither). In short, I made the mistake of providing way too much information. I immediately stated on the air that, "Perhaps I have gone too far here, but that is part of what this segment is all about."

Even though I honestly thought that I was being mostly flattering in my comments and I voluntarily apologized on the air (not to mention that everything I said happened to be *entirely* true), less than a week later I was fired by a company that aired the *far* more outrageous *Howard Stern Show* during the same basic time period from the very same building.

Soon after that colossal injustice, the woman in question (for whom I have never had any animus) absurdly sued both my employer and me. Incredibly, as of a year and a half later, even though the case does not qualify under *any* of the many requirements for a defamation suit, it has still not been thrown out, and by the time you read this may have actually gone to trial.

In just a couple of days I went from having a blockbuster number-one show, with my contract being renegotiated to keep me from leaving for a larger market, to being unemployed and about to lose my part-time television show because the TV station suddenly decided not to honor their agreement to extend the show for another year. While it was certainly in large part a self-inflicted wound, it should not have been "fatal." From both a personal and professional perspective, this episode was by far the most crushing of my many bouts with the forces of gutlessness, political correctness, and my own foolishness.

Bizarrely, a few months later I was hired by one of the top talk stations in America (KFI-AM in Los Angeles), which coincidentally is owned by the very same gigantic company, Clear Channel Communications, that fired me in Louisville. In 2005, after some-

how making my 10 p.m. show one of the most highly rated in the
Los Angeles market, I was promoted to the 7 p.m. shift on KFI and
I hope/expect to be there for some time to come.

While I have certainly made many dumb mistakes in my career, I strongly believe that most of the previously mentioned
events (along with several others yet to be cited) have exposed
many of the flaws in our media culture and the weakness of our
once mighty freedom of speech. These experiences form the foundation from which I seek to examine the greater reality that free
speech, as we have known it, may be dead, and that "the truth"
may have been rendered almost completely meaningless.

If accurate, these suppositions say *far* more about the state of
our national dialogue and the future of our country than just the
personal dangers of being someone who makes their living by
expressing their candid opinions. They go to the very heart of
who we are as a country and whether we will be able to defy the
many predictions of our nation's inevitable disintegration or even
destruction.

In these pages, I will revisit some of the most dramatic and important modern examples of Americans being punished for things
they have said, but with new information presented from a perspective that you have not heard before. I will take a hard look at
how even our rights of *legal* speech are under assault from numerous fronts. We will examine how the First Amendment continues
to be diluted by suspect laws, court rulings, and an overzealous
and misguided Federal Communications Commission.

I will also reveal the remarkable and incredibly underreported
role freedom of speech issues played in the 2004 election cycle
and the irony that the winner of the presidential race would use
his inaugural address to champion freedom and liberty around the
world even as those values were being discarded or at least deval-
ued here at home.

I will also expose and explain the many hindrances to truth
that currently exist and seem to be getting stronger, especially in
our current dysfunctional media culture. Finally, we will scrutinize
the remarkable impact all of this has had on our country, predict
where it is likely to lead us in the future, and suggest some ways
for our country to salvage an essential part of what made it the
best nation that humans have yet created.

CHAPTER ONE: THE NATION'S DIALOGUE IS BROKEN

> *"Liberty is meaningless where the right to utter one's thoughts and opinions has ceased to exist. . . . Equally clear is the right to hear. To suppress free speech is a double wrong. It violates the rights of the hearer as well as those of the speaker. . . . Those who profess to favor freedom, and yet depreciate agitation, are men who want rain without thunder and lightning."*
> —Frederick Douglass, abolitionist leader

There is no question that the process of public debate in America is currently as busted and dysfunctional as the typical celebrity marriage or your local DMV. Amid all the ever-increasing clutter and bluster, and with triviality and frivolity now completely dominant over matters of consequence, the national conversation (if there even still is one) has been dangerously corrupted beyond recognition. In this modern age with an unprecedented amount of information (some of it even true) available to nearly everyone almost instantaneously, we have never had a general public as ignorant regarding matters that actually matter. Even on the rare occasions when big events make it possible for the focus of significant portions of the population to be at least temporarily extracted from the personal and inconsequential, conditions have now conspired to distort the discussion to the point that the truth should no longer be predicted to prevail and has instead been reduced to the subservient role of decided underdog.

In this era in which the explosion of media outlets and the evolution of the Internet have exponentially increased the amount of "speech" in the public domain, there is no doubt that the quality and significance of that speech has quickly become even more diluted than what you would likely find at the open bar at an underfunded charity event. As with most major cultural shifts that occur over a relatively short time period, there are numerous reasons and explanations for this development.

With the attention span of the average American now reduced to that of a three-year-old on Christmas morning, it is virtually impossible for the actual facts of any particular news event to be even remotely understood by the public, or even for any particular subject to remain available on the buffet table of the national agenda for more than just a few days. The vast majority of TV newscasts now have unwritten rules that no story—no matter how significant—can be longer than just two minutes, for fear that the viewer will get bored and change the channel. Furthermore, no matter how important, if the story does not lend itself to video we may hardly hear about it at all. (For instance, compare the coverage of the 9/11 attacks on the WTC with that of the crash at the Pentagon or the Pennsylvania field, and consider how even *more* quickly the networks would have tired of the Asian tsunami disaster if the 300,000 people had been killed with absolutely no video of the waves.) With such tight time restrictions it is simply not feasible for most stories to be explained in anything but an extremely superficial manner, especially to an increasingly disengaged, disinterested, and disconnected populace.

The news cycle itself has shrunk from days down to hours, and the vast majority of even major news stories (other than those of a tabloid/soap opera nature that the networks think they can use to get viewers/listeners addicted enough to stick around for the long haul) evaporate from the landscape after only a sunset or two. Since consumers of news have never been busier or had more non-news media options from which to choose as entertainment, this means that huge portions of even the ever-shrinking "engaged" segment of the population are completely oblivious to significant happenings.

The zeal for ratings among "news" organizations has had several other implications on the disintegration of the national conversation. Because news organizations are now so desperate to hang on to every last crumb of audience share, the tail of what people want to hear about is now wagging the dog of what the public needs to know. Even "hard" news has now become "info-tainment," and the "fluff" that used to be the comic relief of the news day has increasingly become the stuff of "serious" top stories (e.g., Peter Jennings doing special reports on UFOs). The lines between newscaster and actor, and newsmaker and celebrity, have now become, literally, blurred beyond recognition (e.g., fake news comedian Jon Stewart not being ruled out as a successor to Dan Rather). In a frantic attempt to remain remotely relevant, broadcast "news," as well as much of the print media, has totally given in to the nation's obsession with celebrity/entertainment/personality and completely abandoned the standards that used to keep some sort of order when it came to setting the national agenda and refereeing the public debate (e.g., Princess Diana, JFK Jr., Chandra Levy, Robert Blake, Kobe Bryant, Michael Jackson, Terri Schiavo, etc.).

Thanks to the "focus grouping" of the news, far more people, even those who are "engaged" in the process, know the details of the Scott Peterson trial than a presidential candidate's background or political positions, and they are far more likely to be able to identify Paris Hilton than their own congressman. Consequently, political campaigns are now routinely reduced to little more than a battle over who can fund the most entertaining thirty-second commercials. If our citizens were forced to pass a simple civics test in order to vote, these realities would simply be amusing, but since these people actually do cast ballots this development is obviously not conducive to the survival of our democratic republic.

The media's fixation with celebrity has also indirectly destroyed the process by which newsmakers get asked and answer questions. Thanks to CNN's longtime lapdog Larry King, "newsmakers" (assuming they are famous or good-looking enough) who get in trouble always have a place to go where they know they will not have to endure a question that may cause even the slightest bit of discomfort. This has caused virtually every program that does interviews to follow King's toothless lead or run the risk that high-profile subjects (and the ratings they bring with them) will never return. This is aggravating enough when those slithering out of scandal are relatively harmless or insignificant, but the death of the tough or even credible interview has had profound implications.

For instance, believe it or not, Arnold Schwarzenegger went from aging Hollywood action figure to governor of the largest state in the union almost literally without being asked a question in a remotely hostile environment. He announced his surprise candidacy on the *Tonight Show* where his buddy Jay Leno (who would later introduce him on election night) was in no position to ask him a difficult question. Schwarzenegger then did only one high-profile, one-on-one TV interview and that was with NBC (the network his wife worked for at the time) morning "infotainment" show host Matt Lauer, who was once considered such a journalistic joke that the news department at the CBS affiliate in Boston where he did a goofy entertainment show in the late 80s would not even let him set foot in the newsroom. Even that easy test went so poorly for the would-be governor that Schwarzenegger had to fake a technical problem to end the interview.

After that, the candidate was able to limit his vulnerability to questioning to only carefully choreographed situations or in front of friendly interviewers. Even the only gubernatorial debate Schwarzenegger agreed to participate in had the incredible stipulation that the candidates know all of the questions *in advance!* After being elected Schwarzenegger still rarely strays beyond the friendly confines of the Jay Leno–, Tom Arnold–, or Larry King–type interview. The only reason Schwarzenegger was able to pull off this astonishing boondoggle is that, thanks to his enormous star appeal, he was able to dictate all the terms because the media outlets knew just how valuable he was for ratings; and since viewers do not seem to punish media that prostitute themselves in such a way, there are no apparent repercussions for making such a dirty deal.

While the Schwarzenegger example is somewhat extreme, it is hardly extraordinary. Similar circumstances occur, though usually on a smaller scale, every single day, and the situation is undoubtedly getting worse. The best (or worst) proof that the unofficial rules of journalism are being bent more and more in the direction of the interviewee is what happened between NBC and O. J. Simpson.

Just days after Simpson was let off the hook in his criminal trial, he agreed to do an interview with Tom Brokaw and Katie Couric. The interview with the former football star and NBC sportscaster was billed as a "no-holds-barred, anything goes" discussion of the murders and the mountain of evidence against him. Apparently, just before the interview Simpson realized that he was not going to be given the Larry King treatment, and he demanded that restrictions be put on the questions. Even though NBC had put a lot into the promotion of the event and it would have gotten humongous ratings regardless of how castrated the questioning was, NBC rightly and courageously pulled the plug on the entire affair.

However, less than nine years later, the very same NBC and Katie Couric agreed to do an interview with Simpson to commemorate the tenth anniversary of the murders, despite Simpson's demand that there be no questions about—get this—the murders! What changed in those nine years? Had Simpson been exonerated? Hardly. Had he answered even a few of the relevant questions to which the public deserved answers? Not even close. All that was different was the lengths to which Couric and NBC were willing to put their toes in the air for an extra ratings point or two. What makes the contrast of these two events so remarkable is that NBC accepted the *identical* conditions that they turned down less than a decade earlier even though *this* time the ratings gain was miniscule in comparison to what they would have gotten had they bent over for Simpson in 1995. Quite simply, when it comes to whoring one's perceived credibility for "access" to notorious figures like Simpson, the choice of tricks has multiplied while the price has dropped significantly.

The O. J. Simpson case is also representative of another aspect of the nation's broken dialogue. Even a cursory glance at the most captivating news stories of our time reveals that, more often than not, the truth has far too tough a time surviving all of the dysfunctional filters our media and culture have created for it. Ten years after Simpson murdered two people, an NBC poll found that at least 22 percent of the public admits to believing that he is totally *innocent* of the crime. Now in most court cases, even those with a clearly guilty defendant like Simpson, such a result could be partially rationalized by virtue of a lack of good information about the nature of the evidence against the defendant. Obviously, because his trial was on live TV and received unprecedented coverage, this was most certainly not the situation here. Instead, somehow, at least 22 percent of the populace believes something that is patently ridiculous and holds a position for which there is no excuse. This is roughly akin to 22 percent not knowing what day of the week it is. As dumb as Americans can be, there is no evidence that 22 percent of us actually *admit* to being *that* stupid. (It should be noted that polls also show that a majority of Americans say they believe that both the biblical stories of "creation" and Jesus Christ's birth in Bethlehem are historical fact when O. J.-like evidence indicates otherwise; however, anything in the realm of religion tends to break all the rules.)

So what accounts for the NBC poll results? Part of it can be explained by people being far more inclined to believe something if they want it to be true, but even most of those intellectual cowards still need at least *some* evidence on which to hang their hat. Here is where the media was all too eager to help. Under the guise of "objectivity," the news media's matrix for covering any event in which there are two competing forces is to essentially report what each side is saying and imply that the truth must be somewhere in the middle. In the case of Simpson, that meant that the prosecution claimed that 2+2=4 or 5 (they did not do a particularly good job) and the defense countered that, oh no, despite what you might think, 2+2=100. Meanwhile, the non-talk radio listening public was left to believe that it was reasonable that 2+2 really equaled something around 40 or 50. Because large portions of the black community had their own media reinforcing to them that 2+2 may very well equal 100, millions of Americans came to a conclusion that was not in any way consistent with the facts, and the racial divide in this country was needlessly allowed to be deepened by the forces of evil.

Who wins under that dynamic? The liars do. They win and the truth loses because the truth is inherently static and cannot be exaggerated. If the referees are unwilling or unable to call "penalties" on the liars when they go too far, then invariably many gullible people will fall for the lie and the truth will be defeated. Unfortunately, the vast majority of our media lacks the guts or, in many cases, the financial incentives to declare what the truth really is and therefore remove any ratings-friendly conflict, mystery, or drama from their coverage.

Obviously there are many situations in which the truth of a story is truly unknown or ambiguous and where no such declarations would be appropriate. However, the O. J. Simpson case was certainly not one of them and, to this day, mainstream talk radio, the last bastion of somewhat "free" commercial speech, is still virtually the only medium where you will hear the O. J. Simpson story told in the way that it actually happened.

As damaging to the truth as this "there are no facts, only opinions" prism through which most news is presented is, there often is, at least in a murder case (*before* the acquittal) like Simpson's, at least *some* logic to the idea of hesitating to convict a person in the court of public opinion by coming to "premature" conclusions. Such is not the situation with other circumstances where this dynamic is also at work. In fact, the true story of nearly every single huge news event in modern American history has been at least partially lost because of this phenomenon.

The most glaring example of this probably occurred during the impeachment saga of then president Bill Clinton. Never has there been so much heat created by a subject and yet so little light of truth shown on what really happened. Bill Clinton was rightfully impeached for having committed perjury and obstruction of justice (and should probably have been impeached on at least two other counts as well). There was zero doubt as to his guilt and almost no question that such crimes are well within the boundary of impeachable offenses. And yet, despite these stark realities, to this day Bill Clinton has never been truly tried, directly punished for, nor even asked numerous important questions about, his commission of these felonies. Even more maddening is that a majority of the public wrongly believe that he was impeached for having oral sex with an intern, or that he was not even impeached at all!

This ignorance on the part of the public is a direct result of the way the news media, in their effort to pursue both political and commercial agendas, distorted the issues in the case to the point of absurdity. Laughably, during Dan Rather's *60 Minutes* interview with Clinton to discuss the release of his autobiography, Rather (who once admitted publicly that he did not really know who Juanita Broaddrick, who credibly claimed Clinton raped her, even was) *never* uttered the words *perjury* or *obstruction of justice* and only said *impeachment* once. Similarly, during a special broadcast to look back on the history-making events of his broadcasting career, Tom Brokaw indicated that he was one of those who wrongly thought that Clinton had been impeached for having inappropriate sex.

While it is amazing that Bill Clinton was able to actually survive his impeachment, what is far more incredible is that he was able to do so without having to endure a real trial and without most of the public ever even knowing what all the fuss was really about. For instance, how many Americans have any idea who Betty Currie (Clinton's secretary whose testimony to the grand jury should have been enough to remove him from office) is? How many Americans saw Monica Lewinsky's testimony (which was largely jettisoned to the cable news networks and not even shown by ABC, the very same network which would endlessly hype her taped interview with Barbara Walters just days later) in front of the sham Senate impeachment trial? Finally, and perhaps most important, how many Americans ever got a chance to know anything about the *real* Ken Starr (whom Clinton and his cronies still demonize as an out-of-control and corrupt prosecutor), who is one of the most sincere and nicest public figures I have ever interviewed and who had no choice to do what he did because Clinton's attorney general *ordered* him to do so?

What was most depressing about Clinton getting away with his crimes was that the vast majority of the public were not at all privy to the right information when they made their poll-driven "decision" to give him a pass. If the populace had *really* decided that they still wanted Clinton as their president after having heard at least *some* of the most relevant facts against him, then the outcome would have been far more acceptable and not nearly as damning an indictment of both our culture and national conversation.

What made the absence of this reality all the more mind-blowing was that these facts were wrapped within the most salacious and entertaining tale in the history of the presidency and yet even that extremely rare honey pot of facts was unable to draw enough bees to prevent massive ignorance on the subject. If Americans are so out of it that we cannot maintain our focus long enough to get to the bottom of a story as juicy as Clinton/Lewinsky, then what possible hope is there for scandals that occur under far less interesting circumstances? The undeniable truth that the system, our politics, and the public all failed miserably during this drama shows that the national dialogue is unquestionably broken.

A similar set of circumstances surrounded the telling of the remarkable story of the Florida recount in the 2000 presidential election. This fast-paced 37-day rollercoaster ride provided a true and important test of strength for many of our public systems, most of which were exposed as being frighteningly weak. Here we had a bizarre series of circumstances that took the decision of who would be the leader of the free world out of the hands of the people and into the clutches of an odd mix of legal, judicial, political, and media forces. The avalanche of news and information that created numerous twists and turns in the unprecedented drama simply overwhelmed the ability of the American people to keep up, and, amazingly, a huge portion of the public appeared to tune out completely. Considering the unprecedented stakes involved, this incredible lack of interest or ability to remain focused on this remarkable story, combined with the flood of seemingly contradictory information, also allowed for numerous myths to become "reality."

Among those many legends is the idea that somehow George W. Bush was "selected, not elected" president and that he was "chosen" by the U.S. Supreme Court in a "partisan" or party-line vote. Many seemingly intelligent people sincerely believe the entire election was "stolen." Despite the fact that tens of millions of Americans truly accept such accusations as fact, they are completely and utterly false. This is not a situation where those beliefs are just their potentially misguided "opinion" (as the news media, on their best day, might portray it). Rather they are flat-out falsehoods, and if every American was privy to just a few small pieces of information they would be almost universally and undeniably seen as such.

First off, how many Americans (or even news media members) could tell you that the *really* critical vote of the U.S. Supreme Court in the case of *Bush v. Gore* was not 5–4, but actually 7–2? Probably a lot fewer than could list for you all the winners of the hit Fox reality show *American Idol*. Even more important than the true nature of the final vote was the fact that it was an absolute scandal that the U.S. Supreme Court ever *got* the case in the first place.

Though there were many events to choose from, by far the most outrageous thing that happened during the Florida recount was the decision by the Florida Supreme Court to order limited recounts to continue after Bush's victory had already been certified by the secretary of state. This is not just the position of someone who voted for Bush. This was also the unquestionable view of the Democratic chief justice of that very court.

In his remarkable dissenting opinion, Justice Charles Wells said of his court's decision which gave the Gore forces new life after even their cheerleaders in the news media had left them for dead: "The prolonging of judicial process in this counting contest propels this country and this state into an unprecedented and unnecessary constitutional crisis. . . . there is a real and present likelihood that this constitutional crisis will do substantial damage to our country, our state, and to this Court as an institution."

In a world where the truth still had power, such an incredibly strong statement from someone in Wells's position would have shot a Howitzer right through the heart of any notion of legitimacy for the bogus theory that the U.S. Supreme Court acted remotely inappropriately when they stepped in to clean up the mess created by the *truly* partisan Florida court. However, the number of Americans who could come close to citing the words of Justice Wells probably could not fill the Rose Bowl.

There was another important factoid regarding this part of the saga that went even more unnoticed than Wells's stinging statement. The first reporter to announce the ludicrous decision of the Florida court was then NBC reporterette Claire Shipman. Shipman was able to breathlessly reveal the dramatic news *before* the court even announced it. This was the first time during the entire process that a court decision had been leaked before the official pronouncement. Why is this important? Because Shipman later revealed that it was her sources in the *Gore campaign* who let her in on the "good" news! Astonishingly, how the Gore campaign was able to get such privileged information from the Florida court and whether that may have been the "smoking gun" to show the partisan nature of their monumentally important and wrong decision never seemed to interest anyone in the leftist media. This remarkable revelation got completely lost amid their joy over both Gore's chances for victory and this grand story suddenly being not only revived but significantly enlarged.

Obviously, despite the best efforts of the Florida Supreme Court, Gore still lost, but the doubts that remained over the legitimacy of the outcome created divisions within the nation that are still being felt today. Without a shred of evidence and without ever being confronted by the news media, 2004 Democratic presidential candidate John Kerry continually referred to "one million disenfranchised black voters" from the 2000 election in an attempt to stir up racial anger and distrust for political advantage. This then led to a largely unrepudiated effort by some in the Democratic Party to officially protest the results by voting not to certify the *totally* decisive 2004 presidential election. When the truth loses, there are almost always important consequences, and thanks to our increasingly dysfunctional information systems, the truth seems to be losing more than ever and our divisions seem to be widening, especially when it comes to our views of the really big stories (do not even get me started on propagandist Michael Moore's post-9/11 embarrassment *Fahrenheit 9/11* or the way "conservatives" embarrassed themselves in the recent Terri Schiavo fiasco).

One of the clearest examples of how broken the national conversation really has become is the fundamentally fraudulent nature of most of the media through which this discussion supposedly occurs. Foremost among them are the cable news television channels whose format is largely dedicated to the alleged "debate" of the issues facing the nation. However, for the most part, thanks largely to the financial and ratings considerations required for them to survive, they have done almost nothing to further real and productive dialogue. Most of the shows on these networks have become little more than frivolous entertainment disguised as significant argument, with the "debates" just as contrived and staged as a professional wrestling match.

As shameless as the hosts often are in their willingness to self-promote while manipulating the same audience they are claiming to serve, the greater problem may be the guests. The way that guests for programs on Fox News Channel, CNN, MSNBC, and CNBC are chosen and the format under which they are asked to commentate is inherently dysfunctional. Because the shows have to remain fresh in a media world with about a four-hour news cycle, most of the time the guests are chosen in an extremely rapid and often haphazard fashion that sometimes borders on being completely random. Because the producers are so deathly afraid of having someone cancel at the last minute or every second of air time not being fought over like the last doughnut at the police station, the programs are usually way overbooked, which virtually prevents anyone from saying anything of substance without being constantly interrupted.

The guests themselves are almost never chosen on their actual credibility on an issue or their knowledge of the facts surrounding the subject. Instead, they are picked based on a combination of criteria that includes their notoriety, attractiveness (especially for women), relationship to the host/producer, location/availability, and willingness to shape their opinion to conform to what the show is looking for.

I personally have been asked to appear several times on all of the networks except for CNN and on the vast majority of those occasions I could easily tell that, if I wanted to be on TV, I would have to provide the producer with the opinion that they wanted to hear, and on several instances I was rejected when I gave the wrong view. While the allure of being on "national" TV is strong, I hopefully never altered my beliefs just to get an invite, but I am positive that many have. (On some occasions when my views did not fit, I have even directed TV producers to guests that I knew would fake their opinions to get on the boob tube.)

During those times when I did appear, I have almost never felt that the subject on which I was asked for my opinion was handled in a credible or remotely productive fashion (the only time it came close was in the early days of MSNBC when they were still devoting entire hours to subjects, which, thanks to the viewers' tiny attention span, almost never happens today). During one particularly bizarre weekend, I was asked by a network to appear live to discuss the capture of a U.S. spy plane by the Chinese, which I turned down because I did not feel qualified to discuss it, and then, two days later, was invited on by the very same network/producer to talk about my parody Web site devoted to the idea that Tiger Woods might be God. How is *that* for versatile credibility?! (As if that were not enough to make you question the booking process, I also happened to be essentially unemployed at the time.)

The fact of the matter is that the vast majority of these "experts" are nothing of the sort and more often than not they know very little about the subject at hand. Even those who do have knowledge usually have almost no credibility. The political topics are almost always a Republican whore against a verbal prostitute to the Democratic side. Even those who are not on to talk politics almost always have something to sell. Whether it is their book, their show, their publication, their organization, or just themselves in hopes of a return invitation, just about every guest on TV talk shows is hawking *something* and telling the truth (or even their sincere version of it) is usually *way* down on their priority list.

If these shows were simply labeled as the meaningless entertainment that they usually are and the guests were clearly identified as having an agenda that is contrary to speaking the truth, this would not be a big deal. However, that is most certainly not the case and sometimes it is not even the fault of the shows themselves.

In fact, in 2005, the issue of guest commentator credibility finally became a major news story when it was learned that Armstrong Williams, a conservative black columnist and talk show host who frequently appeared on cable news networks to discuss various issues, was being paid $240,000 by the U.S. Department of Education to plug the Bush Administration's "No Child Left Behind Act." While Williams was paid for doing a number of duties, one was to appear on various programs (including his own radio show) and tell everyone how great the NCLBA is. Had he let those shows know this in advance, this would obviously not have been a problem. After all, if everyone who had a financial incentive to shape their opinion was disqualified from being a talk show guest, these programs might be reduced to talking to schoolchildren. Since he did not let anyone know of this obvious conflict, it became a rather large scandal and rightfully so. But if what Williams was hiding was really a disgrace, then so should be the appearance of many other regularly seen talk show faces.

The list of those who do not deserve their lofty perch atop what has become known as the "punditry class" is rather long and therefore any attempt to quantify it would inevitably prove inadequate (for instance, a listing of just the radio talk show hosts whose word should not be trusted would require a lengthy appendix). However, providing at least a few of the more prominent examples of these frauds is certainly in order.

Doris Kearns Goodwin, Mike Barnicle, and Joe Klein are among the most undeserving of their charter membership in the "chattering class." All three are still treated as media darlings and yet all of them have blatantly *lied* about things they have written in such ways that they should have fallen so far as to never even be allowed back on local talk radio (now *that* is pretty low). Goodwin, allegedly a noted historian, who is best known for her fetish for baseball and Lyndon Johnson, was revealed as serial plagiarist in 2001, which, for a historian, is pretty much the equivalent of doing an O. J. Simpson. She disappeared from TV for a short time as some sort of probationary period, but she is now back in full form and even was a large part of NBC's live coverage of the 2005 presidential inaugural parade.

In 1998 Mike Barnicle was fired from his job as a columnist for the *Boston Globe* because it was "discovered" that Barnicle had not only plagiarized in numerous columns over a period of many years, but that he had flat-out made stories up and then continually lied about doing so. How Barnicle ever appeared in *public* again after it became fully known what a fraud he really was is a mystery. How Barnicle ever conned his way into another newspaper gig as well as a regular spot as a TV commentator/host is a real outrage. And yet less than a year after his fall from grace, Barnicle was called upon by NBC to do a dramatic reading of Ted Kennedy's untelevised eulogy to his nephew John who had died after crashing his plane in the ocean. The irony of a plagiarist resurrecting his career by reading the work of someone else seemed to be completely lost on the rest of the media elite.

Joe Klein was the author of the bestselling book *Primary Colors*, the "fictional" story of the 1992 presidential campaign of Bill Clinton. The book was also turned into a successful movie that starred John Travolta. Other than the potential problem of being so obviously close to such a controversial political figure as Clinton, such a fact should not have disqualified him from being given a forum to voice his opinions. However, in an attempt to create buzz about the book, it was released as having been written by "Anonymous." Such a stunt in an effort to further a commercial endeavor is fine, but it should come with a substantial cost in credibility. This price should have been amplified when Klein flatly denied that he was the author. At that point Klein's career as a legitimate reporter or even commentator should have been over. If one is willing to deceive to such an extraordinary degree over a matter of such fundamental importance in an effort to make a few extras bucks, how in the world can their word ever be trusted again? Fortunately for Klein (who today is often seen on CBS), and the many like him, credibility is now an almost completely optional attribute for someone who gets paid for the things they say.

Despite all three having committed "death penalty" offenses, it seems as if their places at the top of the punditry class have only been solidified because of these transgressions. Partially because being well known easily trumps any concerns about credibility in our celebrity-driven age and also because all three happen to be extremely liberal in their political views, they have not been made to pay much of a price and are still very much in the "club." In fact, it is difficult to see how anything other than the integrity of the national dialogue has suffered thanks to their sins and the lack of consequences for them.

Thankfully, this subject is finally beginning to get some viability. In late 2004, "fake news" comedian Jon Stewart (whose TV show on Comedy Central at least properly brands itself as farce) made news by excoriating the cable news process while on CNN's *Crossfire*. The show was canceled soon after Stewart's appearance. In 2005 there was a prominent panel discussion in Aspen at the U.S. Comedy Arts Festival on whether TV debate shows were corroding the dialogue because they had become too divisive. Perhaps appropriately, according to the Associated Press, that discussion ended in a pathetic shouting match between liberal radio host Janeane Garofalo and conservative radio host Laura Ingraham. There must have been at least some light generated by the conference since MSNBC host Joe Scarbough admitted to the dysfunctional nature of the format saying, "If we had one and a half hours to debate Iraq, we'd have a more nuanced discussion. How do you debate Iraq in three-and-one-half minutes?"

The problem here of course is that the entire cable news talk show business is such a scam that almost no one in the exclusive club has it in their self-interest to expose it for what it really is. I myself won an Emmy (proving the award to be a complete joke) while working as a commentator/producer for a regional cable talk network that was wrought with ethical problems and conflicts of interest. Shows there were created and political guests were routinely booked for the sole purpose of stroking the egos of those lawmakers who voted on matters related to the company. In one particularly appalling instance, top executives and even the host of the network's election coverage were told to donate lavishly to the campaign of a prominent gubernatorial candidate. Despite these easily revealed circumstances, since many of the reporters and commentators in the area like getting their faces on TV, they have a strong disincentive to tell the story and, hence, no one has.

After I left there I could have told my version; however, in my settlement not to sue them over a hostile work environment, I was pretty much forced to agree not to disclose the sordid details. Trust me, with all I had to reveal, since they were able to continue perpetrating such fraud without anyone else even reporting on it, they got the better end of the deal. Meanwhile, thanks to my own bit of whoring, the truth, once again, lost out.

For all of their many flaws, obviously the cable news networks are hardly the only reason/evidence that our national dialogue is now broken, but they certainly do represent both the most recent and significant alteration in how that conversation is being conducted. However, this reality should not exempt newspapers, magazines, the "major" TV networks, or talk radio from the negative influences on the national conversation that they have also been guilty of cultivating in recent years (for instance, the nature of talk radio heavily influenced by the antiquated way in which the ratings system requires listeners to remember what station they heard and then transcribe that into a diary, which is why so much time is spent endlessly repeating station call letters).

Since the focus of this book is on "free speech," it is important to point out that the problem here is not too much "free speech," but rather that the vast majority of public speech is not really "free" and that there are now so many impediments to the truth ever getting to most people as to rob this democratic republic of its lifeblood: a properly informed electorate.

As with any discussion, the currency or weaponry of our national dialogue is the words that are used to communicate one's thoughts and beliefs. Thanks to numerous societal forces, in recent decades both the official and unofficial rules restricting what kinds of speech, views, and values can be articulated in a public forum have evolved to the point that our national dialogue is now confined by a straitjacket of political correctness and corporate conflicts and where those who dare to express unsanctioned opinions do so at the risk of being severely punished for what they say.

This modern phenomenon of "Speech Punishment," as we will call it, began in an area of life that, at first glance, would seem counterintuitive to what might have been expected.

CHAPTER TWO: THE RULES OF SPEECH EVOLVE THROUGH SPORTS

> *"People demand freedom of speech to make up for the freedom of thought which they avoid."*
> —Soren Kierkegaard,
> Danish philosopher

There are really two basic forms of what we will call "Speech Punishment." For lack of better terms, they are "Public" and "Legal." Public Speech Punishment occurs when communal forces create consequences for someone who says something that others do not like. This type is, at least for now, far more common than the "Legal" variety of penalty that is enforced by the government and is not, strictly speaking, a violation of the Constitution. However, that does not mean it isn't just as wrong or as hazardous to the future of our nation as the type that directly violates the law of the land.

In fact, a strong argument can be made that the dramatic escalation and virtual acceptance of the Speech Punishment concept in our culture has laid the groundwork for *Legal* Speech Punishment. Thanks to the phenomenon of Public Speech Punishment, the idea of allowing the *government* to actually penalize people for what they say—a notion which not long ago would have been completely unthinkable and abhorrent to most Americans—is becoming even more firmly planted into our cultural psyche, and, slowly but surely, into our law itself.

So, how did we find ourselves in a situation where this country, founded on the concept of ensuring freedom of expression for everyone, is now a place where citizens are routinely punished for things they say, and where fear of speaking what is *really* on one's mind runs rampant in nearly every walk of life? Oddly, the answer to that question, while complex, has much of its origins in what would seem to be a highly unlikely arena of American life: sports.

At first glance, the world of sports would not seem to provide fertile ground for the growth of this societal fungus now commonly (and somewhat erroneously) referred to as "political correctness." After all, sports is generally thought of as fairly trivial in the larger scheme of things, and the objective nature of athletics is highly conducive to cultivating a mentality where there is only one truth (i.e., the final score). In short, at least until recently, the sports arena has not been a place where a lot of baloney is tolerated.

Sports has also supplied some of the most dramatic moments of social progress in America, and many of our most important figures in the battle for racial equality have come from the fields of athletics. While sports certainly has its share of bigotry and prejudice, in general, athletics, being one of the few areas where people are judged mostly on what they do rather than who they know, is probably one of the areas of American life with the fewest incidents of discrimination and intolerance.

Add all that to the fact that most high-profile athletes in the modern age are not usually highly educated or even particularly interested in the vast world around them, and have usually experienced far more racial/ethnic diversity in their professional lives than most Americans do, one could easily assume that sports would not be a place from which incendiary controversy and societal debate would ignite.

However, despite these realities (or perhaps partially because of them), sports have indeed, no matter how counterintuitive it may seem, provided some of the most stunning and significant incidents of Speech Punishment in our contemporary culture.

HOWARD COSELL

Like a small tremor before a major earthquake, it is only in retrospect that a *Monday Night Football* game on September 5, 1983, seems to have triggered a series of spectacular events.

It was on that night that Howard Cosell, a man who changed the nature of broadcasting and who, ironically, became famous for his "tell it like it is" style, made an on-air statement that would lead to the conclusion of his association with the most successful sports television program of all time and mark the beginning of the end of his illustrious career.

While describing a replay of Washington Redskins wide receiver Alvin Garrett running after a reception, Cosell referred to the agile Garrett as "that little *monkey*." When Cosell had used the term "monkey" years before to refer to a running back named Mike Adamle, it was not even noticed. Since Adamle was white, no one interpreted anything else behind it other than Cosell trying to use some marginally creative imagery to describe Adamle's running style. Garrett, however, was black, and that changed everything.

Despite having used the word before in his commentary and even though he had an impeccable record on race relations (including almost single-handedly making Muhammad Ali an icon by supporting him through his military draft "issues"), Cosell immediately faced a firestorm of media criticism alleging that his use of the word *monkey* to describe Garrett made him a racist. The irony of this episode would be heightened by the fact that Ali himself, in a very public and clearly manipulative attempt to drum up interest in a fight, demeaningly referred to his black opponent, Joe Frazier, as a "gorilla," without repercussion.

Even without Cosell's work on behalf of black athletes and the fact he used the word *monkey* in the past in reference to a white player and even his own grandchildren, the logic behind condemning someone as "racist" for using that word is dubious at best.

The presumption would seem to be that using the term "monkey" to refer to a black person is racist because blacks are somehow lower on the evolutionary tree and therefore inferior to other races. However, in order to be offended by that word, does one not already have to have that faulty/racist premise in his mind in order to interpret it as having anything to do with race? In a sense,

Cosell's use of the word monkey to describe Garrett actually showed that it never even occurred to him that the word could be interpreted as a racial slur (which is exactly why he had used it before to describe a *white* player).

Clearly, blacks have every reason to be sensitive about the use of such language because some cretins have used animal and evolutionary references in the past to justify their hateful racism. However, the circumstances of this situation clearly did not indicate any ill intent or motive on Cosell's part and should have been ignored, especially after he apologized for any misunderstanding.

Since the "rules" of forbidden speech in the modern media had not yet been firmly established, Cosell was able to hang on to his job until the end of the 1983 season, but he was not renewed for the following year and his career was never the same. Cosell, by then far removed from the limelight he once craved, died in 1995, a lonely and somewhat bitter man.

If the Cosell incident was indeed a tremor, the earthquake came later in the form of another highly unlikely suspect in what would become a dangerous and destructive game of media "gotcha."

AL CAMPANIS

On April 6, 1987, ABC's *Nightline* devoted an entire broadcast to the 40th anniversary of Jackie Robinson playing with the Los Angeles Dodgers and breaking baseball's notorious color barrier. As part of the program host Ted Koppel interviewed the Dodger's vice president and general manager, Al Campanis. Campanis had played with Robinson and been a part of the Dodger organization since 1943, so it appeared that he would be the perfect guest for a show that did not figure to create much disagreement. What happened instead has indirectly had a profound impact on the nature of speech and expression in America.

Following is an excerpt from their live conversation (with Campanis at a remote location unable to see Koppel):

Koppel: Mr. Campanis . . . you're an old friend of Jackie Robinson's, but it's a tough question for you. You're still in baseball. Why is it that there are no black managers, no black general managers, no black owners?

Campanis: Well, Mr. Koppel, there have been some black managers, but I really can't answer that question directly. The only thing I can say is that you have to pay your dues when you become a manager. Generally, you have to go to the minor leagues. There's not much pay involved. Some of the better known black players have been able to get into other fields and make a pretty good living in that way.

Koppel: Yeah, but you know in your heart of hearts . . . you know that that's a lot of baloney. I mean, there are a lot of black players, there are a lot of great black baseball men who would dearly love to be in managerial positions, and I guess what I'm really asking you is to, you know, peel it away a little bit. Just tell me, why you think it is. Is there still that much prejudice in baseball today?

Campanis: No, I don't believe it is prejudice. I truly believe that they may not have some of the necessities to be, let's say, a field manager, or perhaps a general manager.

Koppel: Do you really believe that?

Campanis: Well, I don't say that all of them, but they certainly are short. How many quarterbacks do you have? How many pitchers do you have that are black?

It was immediately evident to Koppel and nearly everyone watching that Campanis appeared to have given a clearly racist answer. In fact, it was so obvious that when they came back from the next commercial break an admittedly "flabbergasted" Koppel actually provided Campanis one more chance to lift himself out of the hole he had created. Instead, Campanis just kept digging. He went on to compare the lack of blacks in baseball management to the dearth of black swimmers being caused by their lack of "buoyancy."

While there certainly *is* a noticeable lack of competitive swimmers who are black, there is no known physical reason for that phenomenon. But regardless, the obvious implication was that potential black managers lack "brains" the same way that potential black swimmers supposedly lack "buoyancy." By any measure, *that* is a racist statement.

The irony here was that it came from a man who nobody thought was remotely racist and who was making an appearance on the show *because* he had befriended and supported Jackie Robinson when few whites were willing to publicly do so. As Koppel's ABC colleague sportscaster Al Michaels would say years later, "I knew Al Campanis pretty well. Al was not a racist."

Another mitigating factor in evaluating what Campanis said is that Koppel certainly manipulated the seventy-year-old man, who was doing the interview from a baseball park over a thousand miles from the studio. Despite Koppel's assertion that Campanis's initial answer to his question was "baloney," what the old man said was not only highly defensible, it was probably very true. Had Koppel bothered to think about it, blacks did not begin to become a significant percentage of the baseball playing population until the 1970s. This interview was done in 1987. Most baseball managers were in their 50s and 60s at the time. Exactly how many former black players in that age group had indeed "paid their dues" by that point? Obviously, far fewer than Koppel implied in his heavy-handed attempt to get a juicier answer from his guest.

Despite all that (as well as the requisite apology), the decision two days later by the Dodgers to fire Campanis was *absolutely* justified, if not also unfortunate. Because he had essentially said that blacks were inherently and fundamentally mentally inferior, Campanis had to go. Expressing such thoughts should *not* put a man in jail, but they should disqualify him from holding a position of such public prestige and importance to the community, especially one in which he was in charge of hiring and firing employees.

With the Campanis controversy, a standard had been set. The first modern rule of Speech Punishment had been established. If a public figure makes a comment that clearly indicates he or she views a particular minority group as being mentally or intellectually inferior to others, then that person can and will be severely punished. While proponents of free speech may be understandably uncomfortable with there being *any* such standard of punishing people simply for things they say, as long as the government is not providing or deciding the penalty, some such standard is certainly within the boundaries of a just society. As a precedent-setting case, the Campanis affair was not necessarily a bad one.

With most "standards," the rules act much like a bar in a high-jump competition. Anything "over" that bar "qualifies," while anything below it does not. Had the Campanis comments been used (as they should have been) in this manner, then the domino effect that would eventually transpire would not have occurred and its impact on free speech would have been minimal and perhaps even profoundly positive. Instead, the Campanis controversy was used more as a *lasso* than as a *bar*, with the forces of political correctness using it to snag nearly anyone (at least those they did not like) who dared come remotely close to making similar statements.

The first and most dramatic example of someone being unjustly caught in the "Campanis Effect" involved yet another aging sports figure long past his prime.

JIMMY "THE GREEK" SNYDER

Jimmy "the Greek" Snyder was once the world's most famous (and overrated) oddsmaker. For over a decade he was part of the original "NFL Today" team that made up CBS's extremely popular football pre-game show.

On January 15, 1988, on Martin Luther King Jr.'s birthday, a local television reporter approached Snyder in a restaurant. Despite having had a few drinks, the self-absorbed Snyder, never having seen a TV camera he didn't like, agreed to answer some questions about why black athletes are so dominant in certain professional sports. Snyder, a high school dropout, suddenly transformed himself into Charles Darwin.

Snyder explained, "The black is a better athlete to begin with because he has been bred to be that way. This goes all the way back to the Civil War. During slave trading, the slave owner would breed his big black to his big woman so that he could have a big black kid."

He then, clearly at least partially in jest, added about blacks in sports, "They've got everything. If they take over coaching like everybody wants them to, there's not going to be anything left for the white people. I mean all the players are black. The only thing the whites control are the coaching jobs."

The historical accuracy of Snyder's claim regarding the breeding of slaves has certainly never been fully substantiated. However, neither has it been completely discredited. Some historians (both black and white) believe that what Snyder said is actually true, or, at the very least, quite possible.

Certainly the concept that genetics play a role in athletic success is hardly controversial. Barry Bonds, Kobe Bryant, and Peyton Manning, among many others, are all the unquestioned beneficiaries of great genes from their famous fathers. Commentators routinely cite great genetics as a reason for an athlete's success and do so completely without incident.

What is also indisputable is that blacks *have* dominated football, basketball, and track in numbers that are *dramatically* out of proportion with their percentage of the population. Social and cultural factors cannot possibly be the only explanation for 15 percent of the populace making up vast *majorities* in these sports, particularly in a nation where nearly every able-bodied American boy has both at least a passing interest in sports as well as ample opportunity and incentive to test one's potential skill. So to claim that there is no *physical* component to why there are so many blacks at the top level of sports is kind of like pretending that the only reason that most sports TV sideline reporters are attractive white females is that they just happen to be the most qualified to ask the coaches what they need to do better in the second half.

Jon Entine's comprehensive and acclaimed work *Taboo: Why Black Athletes Dominate Sports and Why We Are Afraid to Talk About It* ended any serious debate about the reality of black athletes, particularly those with genetic ties to West Africa, having a significant physical advantage when it comes to certain types of athletic endeavors.

So the black dominance Snyder spoke of is a *fact*. So is the truth that there is a genetic component to this success. But is stating this reality *insulting* to black people? Does it somehow *demean* black athletic achievement?

Well, if it does, you should tell that to the thousands of black athletes who rightly take great pride in a heritage that, for whatever reason, makes them better suited to excel at certain games. Just go to any urban playground and ask the black players if they automatically presume that they can "take" any white guy even before they see him play. Their answers would be nearly unanimous in the affirmative, and without a hint of shame.

NBA star Shaquille O'Neal actually wrote in his book that it was *embarrassing* for him to be dunked on by a white guy. As a "white guy" myself, I have always marveled at the insanity of black men being supposedly saddled with the "degrading" stereotype of possessing great athletic and sexual prowess. Gee, sounds like a rough deal to me!

Can you imagine what the response would be if a white golfer said it was humiliating to lose to Tiger Woods because he is black? Obviously that would create a hue and cry akin to a female nipple being exposed during the Super Bowl halftime show. O'Neal's statement, however, was barely even noticed.

Black athletes like Carl Lewis, Charles Barkley, and the late Arthur Ashe have routinely acknowledged the reality of black superiority in certain sports. Ashe, who was a liberal media icon even before he got AIDS, said it best when he admitted, "Sociology can't explain it. Until I see some numbers [to the contrary], I have to believe that we blacks have something that gives us an edge. . . . My heart says no, but my head says yes."

So what did Snyder say that was so awful? Well, he gave an *opinion* about history that *may* not be completely substantiated in fact. If such speculation is considered a "speech crime," then it follows that *all* commentators have committed countless "felonies." To say that such a "rule" would have a chilling effect on free speech would be as obvious as observing that people tend to stay indoors when it is cold outside or are more apt to get fat when they eat a lot of ice cream.

Snyder also joked about blacks taking over an entire sport because of their dominance. Was his prediction accurate? Well, the 2004 Olympic Basketball team had *zero* white *players* and several white *coaches*. Maybe if they had a white player who could shoot and a black coach who could relate better to the players they would have won more than just an embarrassing bronze medal.

Did Snyder have malice or hatred in his words or manner? Not even close. What about his personal history? Everyone who knew him said that his life indicated that he did not have a racist bone in his oversized body, and he had gone out of his way to help people of color whenever possible. Did he apologize? Of course. Was he, like Campanis, in a position to hire and fire people? No. Unlike

Campanis, was his job to give controversial opinions? Yes. Were the circumstances of the interview mitigating? Absolutely.

Despite all that, the Campanis "rule" was significantly dumbed down and Snyder was fired almost immediately by CBS. His former on-air partner, Brent Musberger, made a very strong on-air statement supporting CBS's firing of Snyder (with whom Musberger had shared a contentious relationship). Musberger would be rewarded for his misplaced loyalty by being fired by CBS just a couple of years later.

If based on Snyder's supposedly "racist" comments (and not his age and fading prediction proficiency), his firing was, quite simply, totally and completely unjust. It also had real and destructive public and personal consequences.

To say that his firing crushed Snyder would be a gross understatement. For anyone, but especially for a man, losing one's job is about as dehumanizing an experience one is likely to endure. But, as I know from personal experience, losing a high-profile gig in the media, especially in a publicly embarrassing firing, is particularly emasculating. When your persona is so closely tied to your work and you lose your job, it is easy to feel that you are no longer a person at all. It requires an enormous amount of resolve to overcome this type of personal devastation, and not everyone has it in them to rise from such demoralizing ashes.

Snyder never really even got the chance. He never again held a serious job and suddenly found longtime "friends" no longer wanting to be seen with him or even willing to return his phone calls. He quickly gave up attempting a comeback and retreated, reluctantly, from public life. The once gregarious "Greek" became a sad and broken recluse who had lost his grip on reality.

I know this because I was one of the last people to interview Jimmy "the Greek" Snyder. In January of 1995, as a TV sports anchor/reporter in Raleigh, North Carolina, I was able to find, and talk my way into, Snyder's pleasant home on a nice golf course in Durham.

As I was waiting that afternoon for Jimmy and his wife to return from running errands, I found myself alone in the Snyders' living room. I quickly noticed that there was something strange about all of the stacks of magazines and newspapers that were piled on the coffee table and by the fireplace. Even though this was 1995, *none* of them had dates on them past 1988. It was as if time had literally stopped the day Snyder was fired. As if his life had ended. In many ways it had.

As eerie and haunting as witnessing that was, it was nothing compared to when I finally got to meet with Snyder himself. The first time I saw him, he was staggering into the house being helped into the kitchen by his devoted, but clearly demoralized, wife. Even though it was well after noon and he had just been out in a car, he was still in his pajamas and looked as if he had not shaven his face or brushed his once signature curly hair in several days.

As awful as he looked, he sounded even worse. It happened to be the week of the Super Bowl and, as a way of initiating conversation, I asked who he thought would win the big game. Jimmy "the Greek" Snyder, the man who once *was* the Vegas line when it came to professional football, did not even know which teams were *playing* in the Super Bowl!

The only time I saw even a hint of the old sparkle in his eye and energy in his voice was when I told him the game in question was between the 49ers and the Chargers, and that the 49ers were heavily favored. It seemed as if some long-forgotten instinct kicked-in as he gave me his emphatic opinion that the spread was too large. For the very last time, Jimmy "the Greek" Snyder was wrong about a football spread.

I came to Snyder's house hoping that I could persuade him and his wife to agree to an on-camera interview with him. I left more convinced than ever that his story was worth telling, but also that, for better or worse, I lacked the heart to do what it would take to force it out of them.

Snyder died several months later. His funeral in Steubenville, Ohio (where he grew up to become the town's second most "famous son," behind Dean Martin) was poorly attended. All his obituaries mentioned the incident that lead to his firing in the first paragraph. They should have also cited that ill-fated controversy as his cause of death, because clearly it killed him.

Ever since this "Greek tragedy" bastardized and confused the rules of Speech Punishment, the floodgates have been opened and many innocent victims have been wrongly caught in the ensuing wake.

Since then, Fuzzy Zoeller, Ben Wright, Rush Limbaugh, Paul Hornung, Gary Barnett, John Rocker, Marge Schott, and Dale Earnhardt Jr. are among the many sports figures that have been substantially and (I strongly believe) unfairly punished for things they have said. What is *really* frightening about their stories is not only that they were inappropriately disciplined for expressing their opinions, but also that (at least until now) almost *no one* even bothered to publicly come to their defense.

FUZZY ZOELLER

After Tiger Woods took the world by storm with his historic twelve-shot victory at the 1997 Masters, former Masters champ Fuzzy Zoeller was asked what he thought about the young phenom dominating the game's most prestigious tournament. Zoeller, extremely popular with the media because of his penchant for wisecracks, attempted to make a joke about the tradition of the defending champion determining the menu for the next year's Champions Dinner.

With an alcoholic drink in hand, Zoeller said, "That little boy is driving well and he's putting well. He's doing everything it takes to win. So, you know what you guys do when he gets in here? You pat him on the back and say congratulations and enjoy it and tell him not [to] serve fried chicken next year. Got it?"

Then Zoeller smiled, snapped his fingers, and walked away. He then turned and, from a distance far from the microphones, added, "or collard greens or whatever the hell they serve."

Interestingly, Zoeller's comments did not even make air until almost a *week* after he made them. It was not until a CNN producer happened to review a tape and someone decided that a controversy could be created that the public was even made aware of Zoeller's statement. Of course, that says more about the often corrupt nature of the news media and the arbitrary nature of human events than the appropriateness of Zoeller's attempted joke.

It is certainly easy to comprehend why some who did not understand the context of the statement might have been offended. Calling a black man "little boy" (Tiger, who is technically more Asian than African, was twenty-one years old at the time) was obviously unnecessarily demeaning. While the use of the words *hell* and *they* were obviously unfortunate, joking that Tiger may serve fried chicken and collared greens was *not*.

Unbeknownst to the vast majority of the public or the national news media that jumped all over the late-blooming story was the reality that it had become a tradition of sorts to predict and ridicule the menu of the next year's dinner based on the nationality of the winner. When Germany's Bernhard Langer won, bratwurst was expected; when Spain's Jose Maria Olazabal was victorious, tapas and spicy chicken dishes were joked about; and when Englishman Nick Faldo donned the green jacket, everyone simply dreaded *anything* that might be served.

Zoeller merely attempted to fit Tiger into a type of category which, to him, was no different from other past champions. However, he clearly forgot that stereotyping about what Germans might like to eat is, unfortunately, completely different from doing the same about African Americans (even those of mixed race who actually refer to themselves, as Tiger does, as "Cablinasian").

Zoeller quickly apologized profusely, but Tiger, supposedly too busy to respond publicly (though more likely urged on by his racially militant father), allowed Zoeller to twist in the wind for several days. Only after Zoeller was publicly ravaged by the media and fired by several sponsors, including Kmart, did Tiger issue a statement calling Zoeller's remarks "unfortunate" and expressing his "shock" and "disappointment" while also "accepting" his apology.

Zoeller quickly slid dangerously close to the same type of personal destruction that claimed Jimmy "the Greek." Apparently very depressed, Zoeller uncharacteristically withdrew not only from the limelight, but also from much of life. According to producers at WHAS radio in Louisville, Kentucky (near where Zoeller lives in Indiana and where I once worked), Zoeller attempted to call in to talk shows several times after the incident, but was seemingly too drunk and too bitter to risk putting on the air. By all accounts Zoeller felt betrayed and used. Feeling understandably burned, it took Zoeller a couple of years before he slowly returned fully to public life and, while, in many ways, he has made a remarkable "comeback" from the edge of the abyss, he has never truly been the same lovable "Fuzzy" since.

When I met briefly with Zoeller in 2003 while at a party at his expansive and rustic Indiana retreat, it was clear that the wounds of the Tiger episode had understandably not yet fully healed. Despite the fact that he was well aware of what a huge Tiger Woods fan I am, he expressed unquestionable anger at Tiger, but had even more animosity for his father, Earl, whom he blames for exploiting and exacerbating his troubles. Zoeller made it very clear that he felt that the *real* racist in this situation was not him, but rather Tiger's dad.

Zoeller refused a formal interview for this book, but not before adding this juicy irony: When Zoeller saw Tiger face-to-face for the first time since the controversy, Tiger happened to be eating. Yes, Tiger was munching on *fried chicken*.

BEN WRIGHT

Golf was also the setting for an earlier episode that said a lot about the nature of free speech and the evolving media culture. CBS television announcer Ben Wright gave a newspaper interview while covering the LPGA Championship in 1995. He apparently told the female reporter that the women's golf tour was being hindered by the prevalence of lesbians in the game.

Wright was quoted as saying, "Lesbians in the sport hurt women's golf. When it gets to the corporate level, that's not going to fly. They're going to a butch game, and that furthers the bad image of the game." He also added, "Women [golfers] are handicapped by having boobs—it is not easy for them to keep their left arm straight—their boobs get in the way."

At first, Wright vehemently denied making the comments. Since there was no tape of the conversation, Wright's employer, CBS, decided to stand behind him and thanks in part to support from some prominent LPGA players he temporarily survived a media firestorm. Then, several months later, after Wright had reportedly bragged to friends that he actually *HAD* made those comments, he was fired.

In a sense, Wright got in trouble for telling the truth, saved his job by lying about it, and then got fired for telling the truth about lying about telling the truth. I cannot think of a better illustration of how endangered the value of truth is and how absurd the game of punishing a person for their opinions has become than this silly scenario.

The reality is that Wright was right. Corporate America has no interest in supporting butch-looking lesbians who play golf. Not because they are homophobic (necessarily), but because it does not sell to their audience. It is no secret that, until recently, the LPGA tour has been, for better or worse, dominated by lesbians who had little or no interest in marketing their game to a broader audience.

Is it sexist for men to demand women show some heterosexual appeal in order to sell their game? Well, if the top women could play golf nearly as well as the top men, it would be, but they clearly do not, so the reality is that they need something *else* other than just playing ability to attract attention. The American women in the 2004 Summer Olympics used an unprecedented amount of sex appeal to draw notice to their sports and were rewarded with extremely good television ratings as well as lucrative endorsements. There is no doubt that heterosexual sex still sells better than the homosexual variety, and the LPGA, like all pro leagues, is in the business of selling their game and their players.

As much as it may bother some social-engineering liberals, those are the facts of human nature. For the same reasons that no one would (or at least should) ever require advertising agencies to use only fat/ugly people in their commercials, a pro sport should be free to market itself in whatever way they think is best for business. If Wright was wrong about homosexuality being adverse to that goal in most situations, so is the vast majority of our society, not to mention the human genetic hard drive.

Wright did *not* say that lesbians are bad people, or that they should not be allowed to play on the tour. He did not even express any personal animosity toward them. He was simply giving his more-than-legitimate opinion about the impact of that truth on the ability of the tour to sell its self and on the preferences of potential sponsors. Wright did not create or even really endorse that reality; he simply exposed it. While one could legitimately argue that he should have been fired for *lying* about what he said, the actual statement should not have put him in a proverbial sand trap to begin with.

As for the comment about boobs, there are very few top female golfers in today's game who would be considered even remotely "endowed." Ironically, the best "stacked" player of all
time, Jan Stephenson, got herself in trouble in 2003 for saying in a
magazine interview that "the Asians are killing our tour" because
of their "lack of emotion" and "refusal to speak English." She did
not happen to mention that one of the many reasons that Asians
are now so prominent on the LPGA tour may very well be that,
unlike Stephenson, they are not hindered by big boobs.

RUSH LIMBAUGH

The year 2003 also saw radio talk show host Rush Limbaugh
become a lightening rod for free speech issues involving sports.
Limbaugh, the most successful talk show host in history and a
man who almost single-handedly saved AM radio, decided to expand his horizons and, seemingly just for fun, joined ESPN's NFL
pre-game show as a commentator. He was clearly hired to bring
his massive radio audience to the cable show and to stir things up
with his controversial perspectives.

After just a couple of weeks on the air, Limbaugh created way
more attention than even he intended by saying that he felt that
the quarterback for the Philadelphia Eagles, Donovan McNabb,
was being overrated by the media because he is black. Limbaugh
said, "I think what we've had here is a little social concern in the
NFL. The media has been very desirous that a black quarterback
do well. There is a little hope invested in McNabb, and he got a lot
of credit for the performance of his team that he didn't deserve.
The defense carried this team."

Much like Zoeller's statements about Tiger Woods, Limbaugh's comments made almost no immediate impact. Even two
of his black cohosts did not make anything out of what Limbaugh
said on the air. It was not until the Philadelphia sports media
latched onto the story and then the comments absurdly made their
way into the debate among Democratic presidential candidates
(who clearly had a political agenda in making a perceived "Republican mouthpiece" look like a racist) and the NAACP jumped
on the bandwagon that it quickly exploded into a major issue in
the national news media.

When one of Rush's previously silent black cohosts reportedly threatened to resign if Rush was not fired, Rush did ESPN a huge favor (and himself and his cause a potential disservice) by resigning from his position. ESPN, after releasing a massive sigh of relief, gladly accepted the offer. Bizarrely, they decided to get rid of Rush for doing exactly what they had wanted from him when he was hired just weeks before.

What Rush said was incorrect, but it was not remotely racist. He did not say that McNabb was only playing because he is black. He did not say that McNabb would be a better player if he were white. He did not even say he disliked McNabb. All he did was give his *opinion* about why it is that McNabb seemed to be getting a lot of positive publicity.

The reality is that McNabb was the focus of a lot of attention because he happened to be by far the most *entertaining* player of a team that had been a game away from the Super Bowl each of the previous two seasons and which would end up finally going to the Super Bowl in 2005 (where McNabb's poor performance would be blamed for his team's defeat). The media loves stars, especially those who are fun to watch. While McNabb is not nearly the best quarterback in the league, his style is exciting. Is he overrated? Perhaps. But it is *not* because he is black. Plus, much like U.S. presidents during times of peace and prosperity, quarterbacks of winning teams are *always* overrated.

It is also important to point out that, at one stage, Rush would have been correct about the media being especially "desirous" of a black quarterback to do well. But that novelty wore off at least a decade before he made his comments. In fact, when the Eagles drafted McNabb, the selection was booed by the fans in attendance. They had been urged to do so by a white radio talk show host (with whom I once worked) who wanted the team to draft a running back who also happened to be black. Ironically, that talk show host works for the same radio company that airs Rush's radio show on many of its biggest stations, including one in Philadelphia.

When it comes to race and the sports media overrating players, it still does occur, but usually only when a player's race makes him an exception to the rule. Often, that means the beneficiaries happen to be white, not black. The definitive example of this is former NFL defensive back Jason Sehorn. Sehorn was one of the most recognizable faces in the league, but he was at best a mediocre player. However, he was a white guy playing a "black" position and that, combined with the fact that he is good looking enough to marry an extremely attractive TV star (Angie Harmon), makes for great copy.

Rush, who has made a tremendous career largely out of bashing the forces of political correctness, correctly admitted later that he had probably made a mistake by resigning and making life too easy for those trying to destroy him. By resigning he may have actually allowed the rules of Speech Punishment to be even further bastardized without there ever being a full "vetting" of the issues to determine if a new line really had been drawn by society.

Now the precedent has been set that commentators (at least if they are conservative) cannot give televised opinions about the media providing favorable treatment to a black person without risking their jobs. Since the news media *does* go easy on black leaders all the time (as long as that "leader" is a liberal like Al Sharpton or Jessie Jackson), this "rule" is a huge victory for political correctness and a massive defeat for the truth.

If this new rule holds, it would be the most ridiculous and least substantiated speech tenet we have inadvertently created to date. Make no mistake; this result was exactly the intention of liberals who saw the Limbaugh episode as a chance to advance their agenda by trying to diminish one of their most potent foes. But perhaps even more valuable than their failed attempt to weaken Limbaugh was the creation of yet another layer of protection against eliminating the news media's unofficial but clearly real and offensive prohibition on criticizing liberals of color, a ban that is insulting to black people, has exacerbated racial divisions, and allowed numerous injustices to be committed.

PAUL HORNUNG

Football, race, and political correctness collided once again in 2004 when former Heisman Trophy winner and NFL Hall of Famer Paul Hornung caused a stir by suggesting that his alma mater, Notre Dame, for whom he had been working as a radio announcer for four decades, needed to lower its academic standards for football players so that it could get more of the top black athletes.

In an interview with a Detroit radio station, Hornung said, "As far as Notre Dame is concerned, we're going to have to ease it up a little bit. We can't stay as strict as we are as far as the academic structure is concerned because we've got to get the black athlete. We must get the black athlete if we're going to compete."

At first glance, Hornung's comments (which he had essentially made publicly many times before, including on ESPN and on my Louisville radio show) might seem to belong in the same category as those made by Al Campanis. After all, it sounds like he is saying that blacks are too stupid to get in to Notre Dame on their own so the standards have to be dropped. However, with just a little common sense, one can easily see that this is not what he meant and that his assertion is not remotely racist and is, in fact, absolutely accurate.

The problem the notoriously outspoken Hornung ran into is that his argument was based on the assumption that everyone recognizes the *fact* that the vast majority of the top football players happen to be black. If one cedes that most of the top high school football recruits are indeed black, then what Hornung said makes perfect sense and is not at all objectionable. Does anyone seriously deny that the average top football prospect (largely because they have not had to be academically proficient in order to be perceived as successful and treated as special) is far less academically qualified than the average Notre Dame student? Of course not.

What Hornung was saying was that in order to have access to a larger pool of the top high school recruits (most of whom happen to be black) Notre Dame needed to lower its academic requirements. While one can certainly argue (as I would) that such a strategy would not be good for Notre Dame as an institution, it is unquestionably true that if Notre Dame did what Hornung suggested they would indeed be able to recruit more of the top high school football players, and since most of them happen to be black, Notre Dame would therefore end up with more black players on their team. Interestingly, at the start of the Lou Holtz era at Notre Dame the school *did* lower its standards for football players and, shockingly, ended up with both a better and "blacker" team.

Frankly, I do not see what is so complicated about understanding what Hornung meant here. However, such nuanced reasoning was apparently beyond the grasp of the news media which arbitrarily decided that this time Hornung should be "hung" for saying essentially the same thing he had said numerous times in the past. Hornung agrees, telling me, "If I had said the same thing ten years ago, nothing would have even been said. But we live in a different world now."

Hornung, exasperated and hurt when Notre Dame made no effort to back him up and convinced that they were not going to renew his radio contract, ended one of the longest associations in sports broadcasting by resigning his position.

However, unlike others who have been personally devastated or even destroyed by their bouts with the new rules of free speech, Hornung seems surprisingly at peace with what happened. While he is not bitter, he does not hesitate to add that he will leave it up to his younger wife to decide whether his alma mater will still get any of the large allotment of his fortune he had previously planned on willing to them.

As fate would have it, at the end of their first season without Hornung, the Fighting Irish fired their football coach Tyrone Willingham (who just happened to be black) even though the team's academic performance was exceptional. Then, as a final, perhaps fitting, twist to the Hornung story, Notre Dame was turned down by its first choice as a replacement for the popular Willingham largely because the prospective head coach was concerned that the university's academic standards were too stringent to allow enough top athletes into the school.

While I was not there to witness it, the gleam from Hornung's smile could probably have been seen from his office in Louisville all the way to South Bend.

GARY BARNETT

In 2004, college football saw another episode of Speech Punishment, but this one dealt with the issue of rape, not race.

Katie Hnida, a woman who had once tried to be a kicker on the University of Colorado football team, went public with allegations that she had been raped by a teammate almost four years earlier.

Colorado's head coach, Gary Barnett, was asked by a reporter specifically about her *playing abilities*. Barnett responded, "It was obvious Katie was not very good. She was awful. Katie was not only a girl, she was terrible. OK? There's no other way to say it."

Barnett's statement immediately exploded into a national news story as feminist groups expressed outrage that the coach would have the gall to disparage an alleged rape victim. The next day Barnett held a press conference and apologized "for answering that question in a manner where I must have come across as insensitive."

The university's president, Elizabeth Hoffman, was not impressed. Claiming the coach was "not apologetic" when she discussed his remarks with him, she suspended Barnett for over two months while a committee investigated the sexual allegations of Hnida and several other women who had also come forward to claim that Colorado football players had raped them. Hoffman made it clear that Barnett was being put on paid leave because of his comments about Hnida. She said, "It was my feeling . . . that he did not understand the seriousness of the comments he had made the day before."

What Barnett said was indeed pretty stupid considering the general climate of political correctness and the specifics of the firestorm that the multiple allegations of sexual assault had suddenly created around his program. However, his comments should not have been remotely close to reaching the standard of causing him to be suspended and almost fired from a job at a *state*-run college where academic freedom of thought is supposedly celebrated and protected.

There is absolutely *no* doubt that what Barnett said about Hnida was true. She *was* terrible. After she transferred to the University of New Mexico she made "history" by being the first woman to play in a bowl game. In her lone play in the game she attempted an extra point that did not even get past the line of scrimmage. The reality is that Barnett, probably fearing a backlash if he cut Hnida, had done her a favor by even allowing her to be *on* the team in the first place. When asked how she was as a *player*, Barnett simply told the unquestionable truth.

Barnett was *not* the one who was accused of rape. He did *not* say she was a liar, call her a slut, or claim that the allegations were not to be taken seriously (as, for instance, criminal defense attorneys now routinely get away with doing in rape cases). He just said that she was a lousy kicker. What could possibly be wrong with that? Does coming forward with rape allegations somehow make a person immune from being criticized in *any* way, even when several years had passed since the alleged assault?

The suspension and near firing of Barnett would seem to come perilously close to setting that absurd precedent. (This was not the first time a college coach had gotten heat for a rape-related comment. Then Indiana basketball coach Bobby Knight once told Connie Chung that "when rape is inevitable, relax and enjoy it." Knight, then at the height of his power, was not disciplined for his remark.)

The extreme injustice of the Barnett case would be illustrated by two related episodes that would occur in the ensuing months. First, his boss, President Hoffman, testified under oath that the word *cunt*, which had allegedly been used by a Colorado player to describe Hnida, could be used as a "term of endearment." Later, while defending her benign historical view of the incendiary word that most women abhor, Hoffman broke down in tears. She did not punish herself for expressing such an "insensitive" view (though one year later she would be forced to resign thanks to a series of other scandals).

Secondly, while Barnett was fighting for his career because he called a possible rape victim a terrible placekicker, Los Angeles Laker superstar Kobe Bryant was defending himself against charges that he *actually* raped a teenage girl. Far from being suspended from his team, Bryant was regularly flown by a private jet from court proceedings so that he could make it back in time for games. After the season, the coach (who was dating the owner's daughter) was fired and the extremely popular Shaquille O'Neal was traded, reportedly because Bryant wanted them gone.

Since one can strongly argue that Bryant should not have been punished by his team until he was found guilty in criminal court (which he was not), the real parallel to the Barnett situation is in the treatment of the alleged victim. Bryant unleashed his defense team in a nearly unprecedented assault on his accuser's life and reputation, which eventually intimidated the accuser into not testifying against him and the criminal charges being dropped.

While Bryant did lose some endorsements because of the episode, when one considers what Bryant did both physically and verbally to his accuser and compares it to Barnett's truthful evaluation of Hnida's kicking ability, it is ridiculous to the point of absurdity that their punishments were so similar.

Oddly enough, that was not the only aspect that the two cases shared. Both Bryant's accuser and Barnett got screwed in the state of Colorado.

As a postscript to this episode, after barely surviving the firestorm Barnett ended up coaching the next season and winning his conference's "Coach of the Year" award while making plenty of money for his school by taking their team to the conference title game and winning a bowl game.

Soon after those events, it was "discovered" that Ward Churchill, the tenured chairman of the University of Colorado Ethnic Studies Department had written an essay three years earlier arguing that the 9/11 attacks were in retaliation for the Iraqi children killed in a 1991 U.S. bombing raid and that the hijackers were "combat teams," not terrorists. He went on to say that those killed inside the Pentagon were "military targets," and "As for those in the World Trade Center, well, really, let's get a grip here, shall we? True enough, they were civilians of a sort. But innocent? Gimme a break."

These statements are obviously outrageous and so wrong as to hardly be worthy of rebuke. The governor of the state called for his firing, and the university board of regents apologized to the public. However, while forced to endure a heated controversy, Professor Churchill, as of this writing, has not been officially disciplined by the University of Colorado (though his detractors, fueled by a crusade by conservative commentators, appeared to be plotting his demise by investigating every "non-speech" aspect of his highly suspicious past).

Since he is a tenured professor at a state university, not being fired for something he wrote would be the outcome any true advocate of free speech would support. While it appears as if Churchill will not be fired (at least not directly for his words), he did voluntarily resign his chairmanship—perhaps because it had been quite a while since his Ethnic Studies Department had won their division or qualified for a bowl game.

JOHN ROCKER

One of the strangest and most alarming episodes of Speech Punishment came in the seemingly unlikely form of a pitcher for the Atlanta Braves named John Rocker.

In late 1999, when he was then arguably the best relief pitcher in baseball, Rocker gave a long, rambling interview to *Sports Illustrated* as he drove the reporter around Atlanta. During the discussion he said a lot of very angry and ill-advised things. Much of his rage was focused on New York City, which just happened to be the site of a series of recent incidents where, during the playoffs, New York fans had chanted obscenities at him, thrown bottles and batteries at his head, and dumped beer on his girlfriend. Clearly Rocker had good reason to have some resentment toward the city that never sleeps.

When asked if he would ever play for a New York team, Rocker unloaded: "I would retire first. It's the most hectic, nerve-racking city. Imagine having to take the [Number] 7 train to the ballpark, looking like you're riding through Beirut next to some kid with purple hair next to some queer with AIDS right next to some dude who just got out of jail for the fourth time right next to some 20-year-old mom with four kids. It's depressing."

Rocker went on to explain his dislike for New York this way: "The biggest thing I don't like about New York are the foreigners. I am not a very big fan of foreigners. You can walk an entire block in Times Square and not hear anybody speak English. Asians and Koreans and Vietnamese and Indians and Russians and Spanish people and everything up there. How the hell did they get in this country?"

The reaction to Rocker's tirade was somewhat slow, but universal. Condemnation came from all corners. From gay and immigration activists, to New York Mayor Rudy Giuliani, to the commissioner of baseball, anyone who was asked for an opinion called for Rocker to be punished for what he had said. Since Rocker's comments had been fairly lengthy, they were usually simply referred to by the media as some derivative of "Rocker's offensive, hate-filled, racial and ethnic slurs."

But what exactly had Rocker specifically said that put him over the transient line where free speech becomes publicly punishable? To my knowledge, amidst the massive amount of slanted media coverage of his statements, that question was never even asked and certainly was not properly answered.

When Rocker's comments are looked at objectively, it is difficult to pinpoint exactly what he said that even began to reach the "Campanis" standard. Using the word *queer* would appear to be the most egregious speech infraction Rocker committed, but no one has ever established that using *that* word is "actionable." In fact, a smash hit TV show in 2003 even used the word in its popular title, and later spawned another show that did the same.

As for the use of the word in association with AIDS, does anyone seriously dispute that there is a correlation between homosexuality and the dreaded disease that has slowly faded from the top level of the public consciousness?

When it comes to the accuracy of Rocker's description of passengers on the #7 train, CBS late night talk show host and New York icon David Letterman said it best when commenting on Rocker's observations saying, "Well, at least we know he *has* ridden the #7 train."

The response to Rocker's comments regarding New York "foreigners" is perhaps more interesting and important. Rocker said that he is not a fan of foreigners, that he wants them to speak English, and he expressed confusion about how these "foreigners" got into the country in the first place. What exactly is so inherently horrible about any of those beliefs?

Rocker did *NOT* say he *hates* "foreigners" or that they should be harmed in any way, or even that they should be deported; he just said that he does not *like* them. Have we really lowered the standard for "hate speech" to the point that if you do not have *affinity* for a group it is the same as expressing *abhorrence* for them? If so, with the rising tide of unconstitutional hate crime legislation, we may soon all be drowning due to such nonsense.

At least equally alarming to every American should be the idea that wishing that all people who live in this country could speak English is somehow a racist or even inappropriate notion. Think about just how outrageous, not to mention contrary to our founding principles, that is.

Whether English should be the official language of the United States is certainly an issue over which reasonable people can disagree. At the very least, a strong argument can and should be made that our national unity is threatened when millions of Americans do not even have the ability to communicate with the vast majority. To suggest that there is something *racist* about wanting all Americans to be able to speak to one another would be laughable if it were not also extremely treacherous.

Much like the Limbaugh situation where simply exposing the media's soft treatment of certain blacks was prematurely and inappropriately reprimanded, the forces of the Far Left took advantage of the opportunity to intimidate anyone who might dare suggest that immigrants have an obligation to learn English. This is one of the many examples of how the "speech rules" established in the sports world have transcended athletics and have far-reaching ramifications.

Finally, as for Rocker's confusion about how "foreigners" get into this country, it is important to note that it is unclear if Rocker was referring to legal or illegal immigrants. This is another trick that liberals try to pull with the help of their willing accomplices in the news media. By lumping the two *extremely* different groups into one in the public's consciousness, illegal immigrants can benefit from the affection and sympathy that most Americans have traditionally had for those who have migrated to this country legally.

The self-censorship in most of the news media with regard to illegal immigration is staggering. In Los Angeles, where illegal immigration is by far the issue that most impacts the lives of its residents, the local TV newscasts rarely dare to utter the words *"illegal alien"* or even "illegal immigrant" for fear of being perceived as politically incorrect. The liberal *Los Angeles Times* almost always follows suit. Instead of using the terms mentioned above, the far more benign (not to mention inaccurate) "undocumented worker/migrant" is usually used to describe those who are in the country illegally.

Bizarrely, though somewhat predictably, Latino activist groups are actually taken seriously when they accuse certain members of the media (usually radio talk show hosts) of being racists because they have the gall to say the words *illegal alien/immigrant*. We have actually reached the point where to refer to someone by the two words that simply best describe their legal status makes one vulnerable to the ultimate speech charge of racism (which is laughable on an entirely different level because the same activists who make the accusation of racism also absurdly claim that there is no racial correlation to those who tend to enter this country illegally).

Once again, the goal of liberals is to frighten those who are against *illegal* immigration from expressing their opposition. Since defending people who come to this country illegally and cost American taxpayers billions of dollars is not a debate that liberals can win with logic (especially in a post-9/11 world), scaring the opposition into silence is the only way they can triumph. That, in part, was what the crucifixion of John Rocker was *really* all about.

Rocker was also victimized because he is a white man from the rural south. Because of his background, it was automatically (and, ironically, prejudicially) presumed that Rocker could have no motivations other than racism and homophobia for saying what he said. Had he been black or even just from the north, his comments likely would have been taken more lightly or simply ignored as the irrelevant ramblings of an ignorant baseball player.

While Rocker may in fact be an idiot as well as a "complete jerk" (as he described himself during his apology) who is not worthy of society's respect, he also did not deserve the type of punishment he received. Rocker was ordered by baseball to undergo psychological testing before his sentence was determined, as if *that* embarrassment were not penalty enough for simply stating some fairly reasonable, though easily misunderstood, opinions. All in all, this treatment was roughly akin to subjecting someone to torture and then wondering why he is in such a lousy mood.

After determining Rocker's sanity, or lack thereof, saying his racial and ethnic remarks "offended practically every element of society," Commissioner Bud Selig forbade the reliever from attending spring training, suspended him for the first month of the season, imposed a $20,000 fine, and ordered Rocker to undergo sensitivity training. The suspension was longer than the average sentence of most *repeat* offenders of baseball's drug policy and harsher than that received by a player who had *punched* his *manager* (not to mention those who mocked the game and destroyed its record book via rampant steroid use). Furthermore, Selig set the precedent that it is acceptable to fine and suspend a player because he offends people. Strangely, Selig never defined exactly what Rocker *said* that was so terribly offensive. After an appeal by the players association, Rocker was finally allowed to attend spring training, his suspension was cut in half, and his fine reduced.

When Rocker returned to play he was greeted by a standing ovation from his hometown crowd and, with some notable exceptions, even the road fans were far less hostile than the New York mob that had ignited Rocker's rage to begin with. It was obvious that, in general, there was a disconnection between the manner in which the media reacted to his comments and way in which the "people" saw things.

Despite even more controversy when he severely and inappropriately confronted the writer of the original *Sports Illustrated* piece, Rocker managed to have a successful 2000 season. However, after somehow surviving the initial wave of condemnation, the pressures of his infamy finally took their toll. In short order, Rocker, partially because of numerous behavioral issues, quickly faded from All-Star status and was sent to the minors, where he was traded multiple times and was reduced to a fringe player. In 2004 John Rocker did not even appear in a major league baseball game. In what some may see as a cruel but fitting twist of fate, by 2005 his last two baseball assignments were in Venezuela (where he was booed with chants of "racist") and Long Island, New York, which is just forty miles from where his downfall started.

MARGE SCHOTT

Perhaps the saddest and most legally problematic example of "Speech Punishment" in baseball occurred in the case of a person who never even played the game.

In 1985, Marge Schott became the owner of the Cincinnati Reds. To say that she was eccentric is kind of like describing Michael Jackson as weird—clearly an understatement. A widow who was a notoriously cheap, chain-smoking recluse more devoted to her St. Bernhard "Schottzie" than to any human being, Schott was well known for acting in strange and peculiar ways. Many people, especially the old white men in baseball's establishment, did not care for her and wished that the elderly woman would just go away.

In 1992, a former Reds employee testified in support of another former Reds worker in a wrongful firing lawsuit filed against Schott (in which she would eventually be cleared of any wrong-doing). In his deposition he said that Schott had referred to former Reds Eric Davis and Dave Parker as "million dollar niggers." Yet a third former employee also testified that he had heard Schott use racial slurs. Also divulged was that Schott owned a swastika arm-band, which she displayed in her home.

Schott quickly issued a statement saying, "I am not a racist." A few days later she released another statement in which she said her use of the word *nigger* and the owning of a Nazi armband were not intended to offend. Schott then gave an interview to the *New York Times* in which she said that Hitler was "initially good" for Germany, that she was kidding when she used the word *nigger*, and that she couldn't understand why the word *Jap* was offensive.

At that point, Major League Baseball (MLB) announced the formation of a committee to "investigate" Schott. Two weeks later she apologized to her fellow owners for making insensitive re-marks. Two months after that the league announced that Schott was being fined $25,000 and was banned from the day-to-day operation of the Reds for a year.

In 1994, after her return to the helm of the Reds, Schott created more controversy by saying she did not want her players to wear earrings because, in her view, "only fruits wear earrings." Schott later clarified her comment by saying she was "not prejudiced against any group, regardless of lifestyle preferences."

In 1996, Schott's words once again got her in trouble when she said that Adolph Hitler "was good in the beginning, but went too far." Two days later Schott issued another apology for seeming to have praised Hitler. A month after that MLB declared that Schott was once again being forced to surrender day-to-day control of her team—this time for a year and a half. A little over a year after that Schott was essentially forced to *sell* her beloved Reds at a re-duced price. In 2004, Schott passed away, apparently alone and far from the spotlight she simultaneously seemingly loved and loathed. Upon her death, former baseball commissioner Fay Vin-cent said of Schott, "I always thought of her as a tragic figure."

Much like the John Rocker case, it seems as if Schott was castigated and punished not for any particular trip over the "line" of "acceptable" speech, but rather for numerous excursions close to it. Clearly, the most serious allegation against her was that she was accused by two former employees of using the word *nigger* in reference to two of her players during private conversations.

Even though it is at least theoretically possible that Schott was indeed, as she claimed, using the word as a joke and was not fully aware of the power of that slur, obviously it was wrong for her to use it in that context. However, at least three factors greatly mitigate this transgression.

First, the word was in no way intended for public dissemination. If everyone who had ever privately used the word *nigger*, even in jest, was automatically disqualified from owning a business, then the GNP would be a small fraction of what it currently is. Second, both of the men she used the slur in reference to (Dave Parker and Eric Davis) had *glowing* things to say about their actual experiences with Schott as well as her many noble philanthropic efforts. Third, Schott was the *owner* of the team and not simply an employee. In a country whose economic system is based on the sacred nature of personal property ownership, there must be an extremely high threshold surpassed before we start taking property away from people who have committed no crime just because we do not like them or their words.

Our Founding Fathers would be absolutely dumbstruck by the fact that an American citizen lost control of her property just because she used words that offended some people. Of course they also would be quite shocked that a woman owned a business whereby she paid black men millions of dollars to play a game they'd never even heard of!

Much has also been made of Schott's apparent praise of Hitler and her owning of Nazi paraphernalia. Here is where her saga far transcends the fairly minor issue of whether a business owner should be able to get away with using the word *nigger* in private. While it is obvious that Schott had some sort of fascination with Hitler, since when does an *interest* in a major historical figure in any way imply *approval* of that person? By that logic, one could easily conclude Rush Limbaugh really loves Bill Clinton and that Michael Moore feels the same way about George W. Bush.

Are we really so immature as a people that owning a historical artifact of evil dictatorship is somehow an indication of support for the ideas of that regime? Is this really enough justification to have personal property essentially taken away from a law-abiding citizen? At least when that person is as unpopular as Marge Schott, this is apparently the case.

Of course, Schott also made and then later repeated some comments that seemed to some to suggest that she endorsed the way Hitler ran Germany. What she *really* said was that Hitler was "good" at the start and then went "too far." What is possibly remotely wrong with having that view of history? Former Los Angeles Laker basketball coach Phil Jackson once publicly praised, without incident, Mussolini and Hitler for the "sense of order" that they created, saying, "It was what people needed at the time." Even American hero Charles Lindbergh, among others, would have strongly agreed with Schott's perspective on Hitler. In fact, one can legitimately argue that any *other* perception of Hitler's reign would not only be inaccurate, but actually extremely dangerous.

Why is it that we insist on having such a childlike, one-dimensional view of Hitler? Do we really believe that Hitler told the German people, "Look, I am evil. Horribly wicked. I am going to kill millions of innocent people. But trust me, it will all be worth it in the end." And that the entire country responded, "Sounds good to us!"

Even if one possesses such an infantile outlook, the word *good* can still be accurately and appropriately used in some contexts, regardless of one's political persuasion, to describe Hitler's early reign. For better or worse, for millions of dispirited and economically ravaged Germans, Hitler *was* "good" in at least some respects. To suggest otherwise denies what makes the specter of Hitler so truly scary.

The *real* Hitler is far more frightening than the cartoon character we have forced ourselves to swallow by severely penalizing people who dared to even mildly suggest a different version of history. Laughably, a 2003 TV movie entitled *Hitler* was reworked because the producers were afraid that Hitler was coming off as too human. Such absurdity is not only an insult to history, but a denial of the reality that part of what makes the

Hitler tale so important was that Hitler *was* human and, as such, did not possess only repugnant characteristics. How else are we to understand and learn from Hitler's fooling of British Prime Minister Neville Chamberlain into infamously concluding he had achieved "Peace in our time," if we do not at least allow people to publicly ponder this probable explanation for his early popularity?

The point here is not to rewrite the record with regard to Hitler and his horrifying reign of terror or even to defend those who may support his awful legacy. When a justifiable and essential view of history is so roundly repudiated to the point that people are punished for even mildly proposing it, it is not only freedom of speech that lays in ruin, but also, perhaps even more destructively, the fortitude of future thinkers who will inevitably be less likely to dare to challenge the conventional wisdom.

Do we really want to live in a country where our citizens are afraid to speak out in defiance of what the vast majority accepts as "true"? The dangers of such a society where citizens are reticent to present a view of reality that differs from the establishment were outlined long ago in what is commonly referred to as the "Big Lie" theory. Ironically, the man most often credited with creating this concept is Adolph Hitler.

It would seem obvious that our irrational fear of stating anything other than the most negative aspects of Hitler actually *increases* the chance that history could see his horrible likes again.

DALE EARNHARDT JR.

While some may argue that NASCAR racing is not really a "sport," there is no denying its popularity as well as its impact on American culture. The tragic death of racing legend Dale Earnhardt was one of the most underreported stories in the modern history of the mainstream media (especially in comparison to the grotesque over-coverage of the deaths of Princess Diana and J.F.K. Jr.).

Earnhardt's son, Dale Earnhardt Jr., found himself embroiled in one of the biggest sports controversies of 2004 when, after winning a race at Talladega, he was interviewed live on NBC and in his excitement over the victory let loose with the word *shit*. In response to Earnhardt's use of one of the Federal Communications

Commission's "forbidden" words, NASCAR not only fined him $10,000, but also deducted 25 points from his total in the annual Nextel Cup standings.

Fining athletes for things they say that either their management or the league does not like is not uncommon. For instance, the PGA tour routinely silently fines golfers for the use of profanity on the course. In most of these cases the issue is one of insubordination or of creating an unbecoming image, rather than strictly one of "free speech." But the fact that Earnhardt was also punished in a way that actually took him out of first place in the sport's most important standings, made this affair far different from the normal situation.

What also made this episode remarkable was that NBC (fearful of being fined by the FCC for airing "obscenity") immediately initiated a five-second delay for NASCAR broadcasts so that any future use of profanity could be extracted from the "live" broadcast.

All of this created the bizarre specter of a "sport" where its participants "curse" more than any other, and where spectators watch hoping to see someone get in a spectacular (not to mention life-threatening) high-speed car accident, finally being motivated to institute a delay so that viewers will be spared the horror of ever having to hear a "bad" word. There was no indication that pictures of people being killed (which are not currently vulnerable to government fines) will also be extracted from future broadcasts.

THOSE WHO GOT AWAY

While the sports world has provided far more than its share of sacrifices to both the gods of political correctness and the "Thought Police" in recent years, those who have somehow managed to escape a public execution for things they have said also provide insight into the evolving rules of acceptable speech.

Charles Barkley, the unofficial "patron saint" of politically incorrect speech, has literally made a career out of defying the normal regulations of public dialogue. As a member of the Philadelphia 76ers basketball team, Barkley once told a reporter after hearing a question he did not appreciate, "See, that's why I hate white people." The still largely beloved Barkley would even later write a book with the ironic working title *Why Do White People Hate*

Me?, which would be released under the title *Who's Afraid of a Large Black Man?*

Contrast Barkley's "I hate white people" statement to *any* of those that have been discussed so far in these pages. Quite simply, there is no comparison. Barkley's statement, made on videotape, was theoretically *much* "worse" than anything, for instance, Fuzzy Zoeller said.

To draw an analogy between Zoeller and Barkley is extremely revealing because in both instances an enormously popular and gregarious athlete, known for joking around, made an apparent racially insensitive comment on camera to a reporter. Even though on its face Zoeller's statement was nowhere *near* as blatantly racist as Barkley's, Zoeller was castigated and severely punished, while Barkley emerged unscathed and today is the most acclaimed TV commentator in basketball, as well as Tiger Woods's best buddy and commercial endorser costar. As a big fan of the man, I am *not* suggesting that Barkley should have been disciplined for his attempted joke, but rather simply pointing out that the arbitrary nature of our unsanctioned speech rules is staggering and that double standards run rampant with regard to their enforcement.

Obviously Barkley was not held accountable for this and other racially charged comments because he is black and, to a lesser extent, because he is lovable. However, I thought that the "black exception" to the rules only applied when a black person was talking about his *own* race (thus the astounding double standard regarding the use of the word *nigger*). It is truly difficult to tell if Barkley has paved the way for further exemptions from the rules, or if he has simply found a way, much like Bill Clinton did in the political realm, to defy convention.

Philadelphia is also the home of another basketball icon who was able to dodge the speech bullet mostly because of his race. In 1994 longtime Temple University coach John Chaney stormed into an opposing white coach's videotaped press conference and, while being physically restrained, screamed, "I'll **kill** your fucking ass! You remember that! I'll kick your ass! Kick your ass!"

Despite the fact that his tirade against then University of Massachusetts coach John Calipari could easily be perceived as a crime, Chaney was never in any danger of being fired. Had the much maligned Bobby Knight done the same exact thing to a black coach and also had Chaney's history of racially questionable comments, it would seem that his firing would have come quickly and without controversy. Instead, protected by the urban nature of his school, the high density of blacks in his city, his relative success as a coach, and the color of his skin, Chaney remained Temple's coach, even long after his team had fallen from the game's elite. However, his job security finally came into question in 2005 when he was suspended for ordering a player to purposely injure an opponent, which led to a key player breaking his arm and being lost for the season.

In 2003, the manager of the Chicago Cubs, Dusty Baker, did his impression of Jimmy "the Greek" when talking to reporters about the challenges of playing baseball during the dog days of summer. Baker said, "Personally I like playing in the heat. Most Latin people and minority people do. You don't find too many brothers from New Hampshire or Maine, or the Upper Peninsula of Michigan, right? We were brought over here [in slave ships from Africa] because we could work in the heat . . . isn't that history? Your skin color is more conducive to heat than it is to lighter-skinned people. I don't see brothers running around burnt. That's a fact. I'm not making this up."

Like Snyder, Baker was attempting to make an evolutionary argument, tied to slavery, that people of color have a physical advantage when it comes to athletics. Unlike Snyder, there is no actual historical foundation for what Baker said. No one has ever suggested that slave owners went to all the trouble of getting black people from Africa simply because their skin color allowed them to work better in the heat, and everyone knows that dark colors absorb light/heat, which is why most people wear white when they are trying to keep cool.

However, despite the remarkable similarity between Baker's comments and Snyder's, and the fact that what Snyder said made a lot more sense, was made under far less dubious circumstances, and was not made by a man in a management position, Baker walked away unscathed. I believe it was perfectly proper for Baker not to be punished, but there is no doubt that the fact that he was not illustrates just how blatantly hypocritical and contradictory the mangled system of speech rules we have created really is.

Oddly, in a sense, maybe Baker *was* correct about his theory regarding skin color and enduring high temperatures. After all, if Baker's skin had not been black, he undoubtedly would have found himself unable to absorb the oppressive heat of the media firestorm that would have surely come his way.

Baker, Chaney, and Barkley are hardly the only sports figures who have managed to get away with saying things that a white person could not have said.

Warren Sapp, then of the Tampa Bay Buccaneers, ripped the NFL for its "slave system," and in response to the Limbaugh/McNabb flap, said that "there are way more scrubs in this game that are Anglos than are black ones that are being pumped up." Sapp, who is black, was then rewarded with a more prominent role promoting the league.

Reggie White, a future NFL Hall of Famer who was also a black minister before his sudden death in late 2004, once gave an address to the Wisconsin state legislature that included deliberate stereotyping of virtually every ethnic group imaginable in a manner that was perceived by many as bigoted and homophobic.

While White was not hired for a commentator job with CBS for which he had expressed an interest, it is doubtful that his willingness to publicly assign certain qualities to particular groups was a large part of that decision. Again, there was no reason White should have suffered consequences for his words, but there is also very little doubt that if he were not black, he certainly would have.

Strangely, even *that* double standard does not always hold in the situational ethics of Speech Punishment. Former NBA star Larry Bird, who is white, somehow got away with saying in 2004 that the NBA needs more white superstars. During a round table discussion on ESPN, Bird concluded, "I think it's good for a fan base because as we all know the majority of the fans are white America. And if you just had a couple of white guys in there, you might get them a little excited. But it is a black man's game, and it will be forever. I mean, the greatest athletes in the world are African-American."

Bird happens to be right and the concept is one that goes far beyond the trivial realm of professional sports.

What Bird was saying was that white people, who make up the vast majority of NBA ticket holders and television viewers, prefer watching games with at least some players with whom they have *something* in common. Since most NBA players are much taller and richer than the average fan, and come from very different cultural, geographic, and economic circumstances than they do, there are *very* few commonalities with which the customers can connect with the entertainers. Race can certainly be a source of "bonding" between the two.

There should be nothing wrong with feeling a kinship with someone because you share the same race. It is universally accepted that most members of minority groups benefit from role models of their own race. No one would ever think to criticize a young black boy for admiring Tiger Woods simply because he is a "black" man in a white man's game. Conversely, why would anyone think any differently about whites hoping for someone who looks like them to succeed in what has become a sport dominated by black men? To assert that there is anything inappropriate about white people rooting for other white people is to create an absurd division and needless obstacle to our ultimate goal of *true*, not *fake*, equality.

Bird actually did not go far enough. He should have said the NBA needs more white *American* players. Polls have shown that whites are far more likely to embrace a *black* professional athlete than they are a foreign born player with a name they cannot even pronounce. Currently, American-born white players in the NBA are as rare as unattractive women in television news.

Again, there should be nothing wrong with Americans wanting to have other Americans for which to root. Just ask those who run tennis what they would do for a few more top players who are American. Or ask NBC's executives how important it is to their Olympic ratings that Americans (preferably physically attractive ones) are in medal contention.

So why did Bird escape unharmed with a comment that could easily be interpreted as an extreme violation of the speech "rules"? Well, there are a couple of explanations. One, Bird is a true legend and the news media tends to give more slack to those with stature (Jack Nicklaus survived a controversy when he correctly observed that one of the reasons that there are so few black golfers is that they tend to have more fast-twitch muscles, which are not conducive to playing a game that requires such precise timing).

Secondly, Bird had been the "victim" of race speech in the past when fellow NBA star Isaiah Thomas told reporters that if Bird were not white he would be considered "just another good player" (several years later Bird would fire Thomas as coach of the Indiana Pacers). In the mind of the sports media, this sort of evened things out.

Finally, Bird made his statements in the presence of several black players, including Magic Johnson, who did not object to what he said. While it makes no logical sense, making racially questionable comments while hanging out with prominent black people seems to have some sort of mollifying effect on how the remarks are perceived (radio "shock jock" Howard Stern has made a career out of this reality by using a black female sidekick). Of course, *that* circumstance did not help Rush Limbaugh at all!

While I predict that a similar situation involving whites hoping to promote people of their race will rear its head again in the future, it would seem that the circumstances of the Bird affair, while certainly interesting and important, are so unique as to not actually establish any significant new rules of acceptable speech.

That would also appear to be the case with a situation that involved another NBA player and so many conflicting forces of political correctness that the news media became so confused that it just dropped the whole thing.

In 2001, Charlie Ward, another former Heisman Trophy winner, while playing for the New York Knicks basketball team, said, "Jews are stubborn . . . There are Christians getting persecuted by Jews every day . . . They had blood on their hands."

While it is certainly understandable why a Jewish person might find these comments offensive, the dueling categories of "PC protection" involved in the situation is what is truly fascinating. Ward is black, and the "rules" say black people can't be punished for making racially/ethnically insensitive statements. But this was not a "racial" issue, but rather a religious one. However, the "religion" in question was Judaism, which is not only a religion, but also a culture and, some would claim, a race. Add that to the fact that Ward was playing for a *New York* team and the media there was faced with the specter of the Jew card "trumping" the black one. But even further complicating matters was that Ward made his comments in a private Christian Bible study group, creating the nasty problem of criticizing a huge sect of *that* religion for their seemingly plausible interpretation of the scriptures.

After filtering the controversy through their complex maze of speech rules, the perplexed New York media just finally gave up and Ward was let off the hook. He played a couple of more years in New York before being traded to two Texas teams where his comments were highly unlikely to cause a problem with the fan base.

The Ward case illustrates the absurdity and folly of the un-elected members of the news media trying to create these unwritten speech rules. Inherently, when it comes to judging speech there are *always* going to be issues of context that are crucial to a proper interpretation. This is why it was ridiculous to ever begin going down this treacherous slippery slope in the first place. Such a slide has not only proven to be extremely destructive to our formerly free society, but also such arbitrarily contrived rules make it nearly impossible to climb back up the oily incline.

Unfortunately, the silly and nonsensical rules of free speech largely created in the world of sports have not only devolved over time, but have also spread like a virus into more substantial and significant areas of American life.

CHAPTER THREE: POLITICS CATCHES THE SPEECH VIRUS

"In America the majority raises formidable barriers around the liberty of opinion; within these barriers an author may write what he pleases, but woe to him if he goes beyond them."

—Alexis de Tocqueville,
Democracy in America (1840)

The way that "speech rules" have been implemented in the political arena is significantly different from the manner they have become imbedded in other areas of American life. Because, by definition, politicians are usually elected, statements made by a candidate or an officeholder have generally been judged by the electorate itself and not just by the news media and corporate management. Since we the people are supposedly the "bosses" of those that we elect, we are the ones who get to decide if an elected official should be "fired" for saying something we deem inappropriate.

This manner of punishing politicians for their improper statements is perfectly reasonable and well within both the spirit and the law regarding free speech in this country. Even the most fervent advocate of free speech would argue that if an elected official (or a prospective one) says something that the voters do not like that it is not only absolutely acceptable but perhaps even mandatory that this person be rejected at the polls. Obviously, what an officeholder or candidate says should always be considered more than legitimate fodder for supporting or rejecting that person on Election Day.

However, the rules of Speech Punishment in politics have moved far beyond that standard in recent years, and this has not only had a chilling effect on what our elected leaders feel they are allowed to say publicly, but has also created an array of double standards regarding how these rules are being enforced. Later, during an examination of how our speech rights are under assault by the law of the land, we will fully discuss the dramatic impact that "Campaign Finance Reform" has had on how we elect our leaders. For now, we will scrutinize how political speech is being restricted not by law but by society, usually through the self-appointed thought police in news media and politicians that are too intimidated by them to stand up for what is right.

Comments made by political appointees is one of the areas of political life that has produced numerous examples of Speech Punishment. The history of officials either being removed from or never getting jobs in government because of things they have said is fairly long. However, often these are not really issues of free speech, but rather of politics. In many cases, the official's statements indicate a political belief that is either unpopular or in contrast with the views of his or her boss. While such cases are usually unfortunate and often indicate how constrained our national dialogue has become (not to mention expose the laughable gutlessness of the vast majority of our leaders), they are typically not, strictly speaking, examples of Speech Punishment.

For instance, it is virtually accepted now that no one who hopes to someday become a justice at the federal level can *ever* make a public statement that could be construed as remotely "pro-life" on the issue of abortion. While this may seem to be a restriction on free speech, it is really a political calculation. Because the news media crucifies anyone who is openly "pro-life," it would not be possible to get such a person's nomination through the U.S. Senate. While such a political computation is certainly a bastardization of the nomination process as it was originally intended (and also probably not an accurate assessment of public opinion), it is also not *really* an issue of free speech.

JOCELYN ELDERS

One notable example of the treatment of an appointee that does cross over into that formerly sacred area is the case of former U.S. Surgeon General Jocelyn Elders. On December 1, 1994, at a United Nations–sponsored conference on AIDS, Elders declared that masturbation "is a part of human sexuality, and it's a part of something that perhaps should be taught—perhaps even as part of our sex ed. curriculum."

In an act of colossal irony that would only grow over time, then president Bill Clinton fired Elders for suggesting that masturbation be taught in schools. This despite the fact that as surgeon general she had absolutely no power to actually order schools to tutor students in the art of self-pleasure.

Such a reality was just a small part of why the firing of Elders was beyond ridiculous. Elders is a person of obvious limited mental capacity who is also clearly more than a bit "off." She had also previously made many far more bizarre comments without incident. After she was fired almost no one bothered to point out the absurdity of a dumb person being canned for actually saying something smart that was, at worst, a perfectly legitimate issue for the surgeon general to offer up for public discussion.

Similarly no one cared to consider the ridiculous precedent or the profound implications inherent in creating a culture of fear among public officials and how such fear would serve as a dramatic disincentive for them to propose reasonable, though potentially offensive, solutions to important problems. This would seem to have a particularly dangerous impact in the area of science and medicine where freedom of thought is integral to taking the chances often necessary to crack difficult dilemmas.

Of course none of this even begins to touch the matter that *far* more American children ended up learning about nonintercourse-related sex acts (in a much less constructive manner) from her boss Bill Clinton than Jocelyn Elders ever dreamed of. In case you have already forgotten, even though inadvertently introducing America's youth to oral sex (after lying about it) was one of the *least* damaging charges against him, Clinton did not get fired or even seriously consider resigning.

NIGGARDLY

While Charles Barkley may have the title when it comes to escaping Speech Punishment, the "patron saint" of all politically oriented *victims* of Speech Punishment *has* to be David Howard. In 1999, as a top aide to Washington, D.C., Mayor Anthony Williams, Howard used the word *niggardly* during a meeting with two city employees to describe how the city was going to need to handle its resources in order to fix its budget crisis. The word niggardly means "miserly," but apparently at least one of the African Americans in attendance did not understand what he meant by "niggardly" and thought that Howard was using a racial slur.

Rumors quickly began to swirl that Howard, who is white, had used the dreaded "n-word," and Howard was asked by the mayor to submit his resignation. This despite the fact that it had become obvious to everyone, including the mayor, that Howard had most certainly not used the "n-word" but instead had employed a word that was perfectly appropriate in context. The mayor, acknowledging that there was nothing inherently wrong with using the word *niggardly*, still justified the decision to accept Howard's resignation on the grounds that using the word in the presence of black people showed a lack of judgment, and that the sensitive racial climate of the city warranted exercising extra care when it came to choosing words that even *sound* like racial insults.

The unprecedented absurdity of essentially firing a government official because some around him did not understand the definition of a legitimate word quickly became national news. Within days, even numerous black leaders came forward to say that they were embarrassed by the situation and that they felt as though the truth was being punished and ignorance rewarded. Even Julian Bond, the chairman of the NAACP, mocked the acceptance of the resignation and suggested that it made black people appear petty and stupid.

Finally, partially because of the backlash, partially because Howard handled the situation in a remarkably graceful manner, partially because he also happened to be active in gay causes, but mostly because there was no ambiguity about who was right or wrong in the situation, the mayor offered to take Howard back. It was decided that Howard would return to work for the mayor, but in a different capacity so that he did not have to work with those who apparently did not possess a simple dictionary.

There was no word on whether Mayor Williams was niggardly when he renegotiated Howard's salary.

TRENT LOTT

The most spectacular and misunderstood modern episode of political Speech Punishment occurred in December of 2002 after then Senate majority leader Trent Lott praised Senator Strom Thurmond at a party celebrating Thurmond's 100th birthday. Lott, a white man from Mississippi, said of the former "Dixiecrat" 1948 presidential candidate, "I want to say this about my state: When Strom Thurmond ran for president, we voted for him. We're proud of it. And if the rest of the country had followed our lead we wouldn't have had all these problems over all these years either."

Though several members of the media were there for the celebration of Thurmond (or at least what was left of him) hitting the century mark, Lott's comments were largely ignored in the initial news accounts of the event. Much like the Zoeller and Limbaugh situations, almost no one who was actually there seemed to think there was anything wrong or even noteworthy about Lott's flattering statement.

Several days later, liberal newspapers with an agenda against the Republican leader Lott started to create controversy about his statements and began the drumbeat for repercussions. The fact that the story broke late and was lifted into the public consciousness on the backs of those who had an incentive to diminish Lott would not be so relevant if the incredibly overblown coverage was based on logic or truth, but that was most certainly not the case.

To fully understand the Lott/Thurmond incident, you must first know the history of Thurmond's career and presidential run. Thurmond was a Democrat who broke with the party to run for president as a "Dixiecrat." Among the most prominent elements of the Dixiecrat's campaign was a "segregationist" platform. When Thurmond ran in 1948 he won four states, got over one million popular votes, and received 39 votes in the Electoral College.

Thurmond then switched to the Republican Party where he became and remained a U.S. senator almost up until he died in 2003.

When the leftist elements of the news media began to smell blood and sense that they could get away with scoring points with Lott's comments honoring Thurmond's long-ago presidential bid, they almost universally referred to what Lott said as having praised racial segregation. Many news accounts soon began dropping Lott's quote from stories altogether and instead just referred to Lott's "racially insensitive remarks."

Let us assume for a moment that *had* Lott *actually* extolled the virtues of maintaining segregationist polices fifty-four years ago, that this indeed would have been worthy of condemnation and perhaps even punishment. Even the leader of Lott's party, President George Bush, after Lott had apologized to "anyone who was offended" by his statement, said, "any suggestion that the segregated past is acceptable or positive is offensive and it is wrong." However, Lott *never* came close to doing what the president and others charged him with.

What Lott *did* do is defend his state's vote for president in 1948 while giving tribute to a 100-year-old man at a nongovernmental function. Had Lott said, "If Strom had won, then we wouldn't have had all these problems with *Negroes* over all of these years," then *that* would have clearly been inappropriate and worthy of the repudiation Lott eventually got for his birthday speech.

But no matter how hard the forces of the Left want to make it so, Lott did *not* do that. It seems that in order to justify their inherent belief that conservatives are racists, anything that can be even vaguely interpreted as revealing racially discriminatory thoughts on the part of a conservative must be an illumination of their racist "dark side," which is presumed by the media elites to exist in the first place. If you "Google" the term "circular argument," this kind of logic would likely be exactly what you would find.

Even if you grant that a conservative white male from the Deep South (like John Rocker) is considered guilty until proven innocent when it comes to issues of race, a closer look at the Lott situation reveals that what he said did not necessarily have much to do with race at all. At the very least, to come to the conclusion that Lott was longing for an America where whites and blacks remained legally separate requires enough mind reading to make even a carnival psychic uncomfortable.

For Lott to be "convicted" in this case it *must* be a fundamentally racist endeavor to even mildly commend Thurmond's presidential bid. If that is in fact the case, then that means that there were four states and over one million voters that were complete racists in 1948 (interestingly, a cursory examination of Mississippi's vote totals in 1944 and 1948 proves that virtually all of Thurmond's votes came from Democrats). Does anyone *really* believe that? There were certainly plenty of other reasons to consider a Thurmond candidacy that had nothing to do with racial prejudice. Although the Left has done an excellent job of morphing and distorting being in favor of "states rights" into somehow being indistinguishable from racism, that is just simply not the case.

In fact, there were many other reasons having nothing to do with race that Lott may have had in mind when he made his comments. Lott himself claimed after the controversy, "When I think back about Strom Thurmond over the years, what I have seen was a man who was for a strong national defense, economic development and balanced budgets and opportunity, and that's the kinds of things that I really had in mind."

Was this simply the desperate attempt by an embattled politician to rationalize and warp what he really meant? Well, as fate would have it, the record clearly showed that Lott had made *extremely* similar public statements about Thurmond at least twice in the past. While the news media used these incidents to try to show that Lott really *did* mean what they claimed he meant and that he had not simply misspoken, in reality those prior comments, which the media portrayed as "aha!" moments, should have unquestionably *exonerated* Lott.

On both of the previous occasions that Lott publicly praised Thurmond's presidential bid (once at a Ronald Reagan rally in 1980 and years later at the signing of a military appropriations bill) Lott was obviously and unambiguously referring to Thurmond's strong positions on national defense. The issue of race never came close to coming up in the context of either of the previous Lott statements.

To further understand the absolute absurdity of making a "speech rule" that it is forever fundamentally "racist" to commend someone with a commendable personal record on race relations (including supporting a child he fathered with a black woman) who has been in the U.S. Senate for over a half a century, consider the legacy of Abraham Lincoln.

Would anyone ever be remotely criticized for praising Lincoln's views on race? It would be far more likely for Larry King to ask Bill Clinton about credible rape allegations, Dan Rather about "unimpeachable sources," or John Kerry where he was during Christmas of 1968. Obviously no one would *ever* be questioned for supporting Lincoln's position on the rights of blacks.

But what would happen if an American politician supported the racial policies of a presidential candidate who had previously said the following?

> I am not nor ever have been in favor of bringing about in any way the social and political equality of the white and black races. . . . I am not nor ever have been in favor of making voters or jurors of Negroes, nor of qualifying them to hold office, nor to intermarry with white people; and I will say in addition to this that there is a physical difference between the races which I believe will for ever forbid the two races living together on terms of social and political equality.

Abraham Lincoln made that now stunning statement during the famous Lincoln-Douglas debates, which were held just ninety years before Strom Thurmond began his run for president. Are we really to believe that the country changed so much in less than Thurmond's lifespan to justifying the "rules" having been altered from no praise being high enough for Lincoln's run on the issue of race, to absolutely no tribute at all being allowed for Thurmond's, even in the most general sense?

Despite the overwhelming evidence in Lott's favor, his fate was sealed when Anne Northup, a Republican congresswoman from Louisville, Kentucky, went on national television to denounce his pro-Thurmond statement and call for him to step down. One of the more twisted rules of modern American politics is that there really is not a *true* scandal unless someone on your "team" says there is (unless of course you are Bill Clinton and several members of your own party vote to impeach you and it is still reported as a "partisan witch-hunt"). Northup's betrayal of Lott officially opened the floodgates against him, the waters of which reached their high point the next day when the president referred to Lott's remarks as "offensive."

Just moments before the president made his anti-Lott announcement I interviewed Congresswoman Northup on WHAS-AM in Louisville. Among the highlights of the discussion were that she claimed she did not react to Lott's comments sooner because she had been on vacation and had not read about them until just the day before (about a week after the original statement had been made). I also asked her why, if he was such an obvious racist, she and her party had supported Thurmond for Senate for over half a century and how she could speak well of Abraham Lincoln considering his previously mentioned declaration on race.

Congresswoman Northup did not have much of an answer for either inquiry.

Even more important than the obvious holes in the logic of Northup's argument was *why* she decided to stab Lott in the back. Nowhere in any of the many national news accounts that reported Northup's call for Lott to step aside as majority leader of the Senate was there any indication that, despite being a Republican, Northup herself had a political agenda in coming out so publicly against him. Northup is a Republican in a majority Democrat district that also has a very high percentage of black voters. She had just narrowly won reelection because she had successfully taken the fire out of the Democratic black vote in Louisville, largely by aligning herself with some black religious leaders for whom she had arranged federal funding.

Whether she was speaking out of perceived political necessity or because of real conviction (or perhaps some combination) only Northup knows, but the circumstances of her recent reelection should have greatly diminished the impact of her anti-Lott position. Instead, partially because the liberals in the news media were all too happy to have a Republican jump ship, Northup was suddenly afforded enormous national credibility, the type of which she could never have dreamed of had she criticized a Democrat.

With his numerous attempts at apology failing, a Republican member of Congress calling for him to step down, and the president also being highly critical of what he had said, Lott had no choice but to withdraw from the most powerful position in the Senate. While I have no love for Trent Lott because I strongly believe he sold out the country when he personally reduced the impeachment trial of Bill Clinton to a sham, it is also obvious to me that what happened to him was an extreme injustice that set yet another peculiar and perilous precedent in the realm of Speech Punishment.

Or did it?

CHRISTOPHER DODD

One of the most sinister aspects of the modern rules of Speech Punishment is that the enforcement of these nonsensical laws is insidiously inconsistent, with those deciding who is "guilty" and who is not clearly biased in their seemingly arbitrary judgments. While the issue of media favoritism has appropriately received infinitely more attention in recent years, having the light shone on the indisputable reality that the vast majority of news media outlets are extremely prejudiced against conservatives has certainly not changed that actuality. In fact, it may have even exacerbated it.

There may be no better (or worse) example of the truth of this notion than comparing what happened to Trent Lott to what did *not* occur in the case of Connecticut U.S. Senator Christopher Dodd.

A little over a year after Lott stuck his foot in his mouth while praising Strom Thurmond, Dodd took to the floor of the U.S. Senate to mark the 17,000th vote of West Virginia Senator Robert Byrd (why this odd number was considered noteworthy is not apparent). Dodd stood next to Byrd and with great passion declared that "Robert C. Byrd . . . would have been *right* at any time [in our history]. He would have been *right* at the founding of this country . . . he would have been *right* during the great conflict of civil war in this nation. I cannot think of a *single* moment in this nation's 220-plus-year history where he would not have been a valuable asset to this country."

When I first heard about what Dodd said I thought for sure it was a joke. I was convinced it had to be an urban legend or a fake news item from the parody Web site The Onion. After all, one could not concoct a series of circumstances to create a more strik-ing comparison with the Lott situation if they simultaneously pos-sessed Lance Armstrong's legendary desire and Dan Rather's suspect standard of memo verification.

What Dodd said about Byrd was obviously a far stronger en-dorsement of the totality of his career than Lott apparently ever considered providing for Thurmond. Lott just praised Thurmond's presidential bid, while Dodd not only honored Byrd's entire life, but also said that Byrd would have been great for the nation long before he was even born. What is truly amazing about Dodd's statement (and one of the reasons the story originally smelled like a fake) is that he actually went *out of his way* to mention that he thought Byrd would have been great during the *Civil* War.

If Dodd had been speaking about the career of Strom Thur-mond, his reference to the former segregationist as being the ideal leader during the Civil War and our nation's founding would have been at least highly questionable. But the fact that he was actually talking about Byrd (on the floor of the U.S. Senate no less, not at a private party) makes those comments not just inappropriate, but absolutely bizarre, if not politically suicidal.

What most Americans are blissfully ignorant of (because he is a powerful Democrat and therefore protected by most media out-lets) is that Senator Byrd, unlike Thurmond, is a former member of the Ku Klux Klan.

In fact, Byrd was not just a member; he was the official "Klea-gle," or recruiter, for the West Virginia Klan. While Byrd claims he "retired" from the Klan in 1943, in 1964, while leading a filibuster of the Civil Rights Act (which he led twenty Senate Democrats in opposing) Byrd, who never served in any form of the armed serv-ices, said, "[I would never fight] with a Negro by my side. Rather I should die a thousand times . . . than to see this beloved land of ours become degraded by race mongrels, a throwback to the blackest specimen from the wilds."

As late as 2001 Byrd was still getting away with the type of public speech that would have instantly ended the career of any Republican, even one who did not have Byrd's racist past. In an interview with the Fox News Channel Byrd said, "There are white niggers. I've seen a lot of niggers in my time. I am going to use that word." The Dean of Democratic Senators using the same word that has resulted in harsh punishment for numerous public figures (including myself) caused barely a ripple on the media's biased pond.

So, without a doubt, Byrd's history of questionable positions on race was far more egregious than Thurmond's (even before it was revealed that Thurmond fathered a black child whom he supported for life). Plus, Dodd's remarks were much more complimentary, were far more connected to the actual issue of race, and the setting of the event was far more formal and public than in Lott's case.

But wait! That's not all!! As "luck" would have it, Dodd just happened to have made a very interesting statement during Lott's troubles. Senator Dodd ludicrously claimed, "If a Democratic leader had made [Lott's] statements, we would have to call for his stepping aside, without question, whatsoever."

Again, this is *not* an urban legend. Despite the nature of the facts that seem scripted as part of some sort of media social experiment, they are all very true. Remarkably, it is also accurate to say that Dodd not only avoided punishment, but also that the story barely eclipsed the meager attention garnered by Byrd's use of the word *nigger*. Then, to top it all off, when former Minority Leader Tom Daschle lost his Senate seat in 2004, Dodd was surreally mentioned as a possible successor. It is not known whether his pro-Byrd remarks played a part in his not being promoted to the post most similar to the one from which Lott was demoted.

This bizarro world came full circle when, as the newly re-elected President Bush walked down the steps of the Capitol to take the oath of office, he was immediately followed by two Senators who represented each party on the Inaugural Committee. Believe it or not, the two that were chosen were Trent Lott and Christopher Dodd.

The point of the Lott/Dodd comparison is not that Dodd necessarily should have suffered consequences for his strange praise of Byrd. Rather, it is to confirm, beyond any doubt, that one of the biggest problems with the entire concept of punishing people for the things they say is that if there is even *theoretically* a way for such penalties to be meted out with any semblance of logic or fairness, that we most certainly have not come close to implementing, or even finding, it.

The Dodd situation is hardly the only evidence of this reality in the realm of politics. The list of politicians who have avoided punishment for potential "speech crimes" due to the arbitrary nature of enforcement is both long and distinguished.

How many Americans are even aware that in 2003 Senator Ted Kennedy referred to President Bush's judicial nominees as "Neanderthals"? Such a comment would have been simply stupid and worthy of an apology if the nominees in question were all white men, but what would have happened had a Republican made the same comment about a small group of people that included a Hispanic and an African American? I can assure you that such a Senator would likely soon be unemployed.

The same goes for another Democrat, then Senator "Fritz" Hollings, using the term "wetbacks" (roughly the equivalent of the "n-word" for Mexicans) during a Senate floor speech. The blip *that* episode made on the news media radar was much smaller than even the latest contestant from a poorly rated TV reality show being dropped early on from the program.

Or how about Senator Patty Murray (yes, another Democrat) lying to a group of Washington state schoolchildren in 2002 about why Osama bin Laden is worthy of praise? Oh, you mean you never heard that she lamely claimed, "We've got to ask, why is this man [bin Laden] so popular around the world? Why are people so supportive of him in so many countries . . . that are riddled with poverty? He's been out in these countries for decades, building schools, building infrastructure, building day care facilities, building health care facilities, and the people are extremely grateful. We haven't done that."

Compare her patently false view of why bin Laden is worthy of admiration (there is ZERO evidence that he has done anything that she claimed and ample substantiation that the United States, on the other hand, has) with Marge Schott's view of Hitler, which was far more historically accurate. Now contrast the reaction over a baseball owner saying things about a long-dead enemy and a U.S. Senator telling schoolchildren blatantly inaccurate things about a current one. Are you beginning to understand the utter insanity at work in this stupid and treacherous game?

RICK SANTORUM

Sometimes even situations in which the suspect manages to escape the speech noose still show the unfairness and danger intrinsic to the current "system." Such was the case of prominent Republican Senator Rick Santorum, who in 2003 came within the circumference of Ted Kennedy's head of becoming a victim of unjust Speech Punishment.

On April 22, 2003, CNN's Web site reported under the headline SANTORUM UNDER FIRE FOR COMMENTS ON HOMOSEXUALITY: "Top Democrats and gay rights advocates blasted comments by Senator Rick Santorum in which he appeared to compare homosexuality to incest, bigamy and adultery, and they called on the Pennsylvania Republican to repudiate the remarks. One prominent Democratic group also called on Santorum to resign his leadership post in the Senate."

My gosh! What on earth did Senator Santorum say? Comparing two adult men having sex in private with a father having relations with his daughter? Saying that two women making love was like a man having multiple wives? Claiming that engaging in homosexuality was the same as breaking the bonds of marriage? That seems clearly outrageous! Of course, that also is not close to what Santorum "appeared" to do.

The controversy exploded out of an Associated Press interview in which Santorum was prominently quoted as saying in regard to an anti-sodomy law in Texas then being debated before the Supreme Court:

> If the Supreme Court says you have the right to consensual sex within your home, then you have the right to bigamy, you have the right to polygamy, you have the right to incest, you have the right to adultery. You have the right to anything. Does that undermine the fabric of our society? I would argue yes, it does. It all comes from, I would argue this right to privacy that doesn't exist in my opinion in the United States Constitution, this right that was created . . . And now we're just extending it out. And the further you extend it out, the more you—this freedom actually intervenes and affects the family. You say, well, it's my individual freedom. Yes, but it destroys the basic

unit of our society because it condones behavior that's antithetical to strong, healthy families. Whether it's polygamy, whether it's adultery, where it's sodomy, all of those things, are antithetical to a healthy, stable, traditional family.

While as a libertarian, I vehemently *oppose* much of Santorum's statement as well as the underlying premise that the government should have an inherent role in outlawing behavior that someone might deem to be in conflict with the formation of a "traditional" family (by that standard, allowing both parents to work outside the home would have been outlawed long ago), what Santorum said is not remotely anti-gay or worthy of anything more than honest disagreement.

What Santorum was doing was simply making the "slippery slope" argument when it comes to judicial rulings. He was saying that if the government does not have the right to ban sodomy (as the Court would eventually rule), then on what basis does it have the legal right to ban any *other* private sexual behavior? Here, he happens to be exactly right and in no way shape or form was he *comparing* homosexuality to any of the other sex acts that he listed. Interestingly, he left bestiality off the list but mentioned it later in the interview. Even though it would have been perfectly legitimate to have included bestiality in his slippery slope argument, had he chosen to have done so it may have sealed his fate.

This despite the fact that all he was doing was making a fairly complex but very important legal case that changing the law with regard to homosexuality may have profound unforeseen and unintended consequences. Plus, he actually went out of his way not to slam homosexuals by saying, "I have no problem with homosexuality. I have a problem with homosexual acts."

Again, while it is easy to disagree with Santorum's view on homosexuality and the government's role in legislating against it (as I do), it seems absolutely impossible to twist Santorum's comments into anything other than a legitimate position over which reasonable people can disagree. This, if I am not mistaken, is pretty much what politics is supposed to be all about.

Had Santorum been a Democrat his remarks would not have even been deemed worth mentioning by the press, but because conservative Republicans are presumed to be anti-homosexual, they are again considered guilty until proven innocent. Fortunately, Santorum was eventually exonerated (barely), but his brush with destruction illustrates just how broken our national dialogue is. When it is politically perilous to even mention a sensitive subject while making a legal argument, there can be no doubt that things have gotten completely out of control.

JIM MORAN

Just for the record, it *is* apparently possible for a Democratic politician to suffer real consequences for what they say, but oddly, only when they do not really deserve them. In 2003, Virginia Congressman Jim Moran, then a powerful member of the Democratic leadership and a frequent guest on cable news talk shows, was addressing an anti-war forum in his home district when he had the audacity to say, "If it were not for the strong support of the Jewish community for this war in Iraq, we would not be doing this. The leaders of the Jewish community are influential enough that they could change the direction of where this is going, and I think they should."

For some strange reason, Moran felt compelled to apologize for his remarks, but that did not keep him from being castigated by House Minority Leader Nancy Pelosi (no stranger to odd and exceedingly questionable comments herself) who called his remarks, "irresponsible," "inappropriate," and "offensive," while announcing Moran's demotion within the party.

What no one bothered to point out was exactly which part of Moran's statement had caused a problem. Does anyone seriously doubt that our support of Israel, which had previously been fired on by Iraq, had at least *some* role in why we decided to invade? Does anyone doubt that, if for some reason, Israel and the American Jewish leadership had requested that we *not* go into Iraq that there would have been at least a reasonably good chance that we would have reconsidered—and with good reason? Does anyone seriously object to the idea that if you are against a war, as Moran was this one, that it would be legitimate to wish that a group that may have the influence to tip the scales in your direction join you in your cause?

It would appear that the answers to those questions are self-evident and that what was *really* happening here was simply the Democratic Party being hypersensitive to the American Jewish community's perception that they have extreme influence over American foreign policy, which, for better or worse, they absolutely do. In short, Moran got hung for simply stating a truth that even many strong supporters of Israel (like myself, for instance) would, without hesitation or equivocation, agree with. Once again, it appears that bringing Judaism into any free speech situation seems to act as some sort of demagnifying force rendering most of the usual rules either reversed or ineffective.

What must make Moran particularly confused and frustrated over his treatment is that his political party continues to constantly appease Jessie Jackson despite his far more infamous and inflammatory anti-Semitic description of New York City as "Hymie Town" during his 1984 presidential campaign, as well as other black "leaders" who obviously harbor far more animus against Jews and Israel than Moran could ever possibly be accused of.

ARNOLD SCHWARZENEGGER

The issue of Jewish sensitivity again exposed the hypocrisy of the Speech Punishment process during the infamous 2003 recall election of California Governor Gray Davis. During movie star Arnold Schwarzenegger's eventually triumphant run to the governorship, a controversy arose about comments that the extremely liberal "Republican" had allegedly made in the mid-1970s during the filming of a documentary on bodybuilding.

The statements attributed to Schwarzenegger were not even on camera but were instead part of the film director's book proposal. According to a full transcript of the long-ago conversation, the former Austrian citizen, whose father was a member of the Nazi party, had supposedly said, "I admired Hitler, for instance, because he came from being a little man with almost no formal education, up to power. I admire him for being such a good public speaker and for his way of getting to the people and so on, but I don't admire him for what he did with it."

Either because of political bias, a desire for sensationalism, or plain old incompetence, the way the story was reported largely left *out* the part about Schwarzenegger *NOT* admiring Hitler for what he did with his power. Bizarrely, despite the incredibly benign nature of the comments, the mitigating circumstances and context of the "interview," as well as Schwarzenegger's well-documented financial support for Jewish causes, the nearly ancient off-camera interview dominated the campaign for days and threatened to torpedo the star's election hopes (even stranger was that his *words* from that bodybuilding film made far more news than his illegal *act* of using steroids during that same time period).

Meanwhile, Schwarzenegger's main rival for the governorship, Democratic Lieutenant Governor Cruz Bustamante, was able to run without his use of the word *nigger* just two years earlier creating even the slightest roadblock for his campaign. Perhaps you are thinking that I am referring to some sort of private slip of the tongue where someone simply alleged that Bustamante used the forbidden "n-word" (like Bill Clinton is said to have done routinely while Governor of Arkansas). Hardly. Believe it or not, Bustamante dropped the "n-word" in public, as the *keynote* speaker at an event honoring Black History Month in front of a gathering of black trade union members.

After about 100 shocked members of the audience walked out, Bustamante profusely apologized and later held a press conference where black "leaders," citing his past support of minority causes, forgave him for his "slip." The news media, apparently checking their Speech Punishment rulebook and seeing no "violation," hardly ever mentioned the incident again.

So apparently the rule here is if you have the "correct" *beliefs* or at least *positions* and the self-proclaimed "leaders" of the potentially offended group provide you with an unofficial "pass," then everyone else is just supposed to "move along" and pretend as if it never really happened.

All of this happened in the very same state where O. J. Simpson—clearly guilty of double murder—was allowed to go free largely because one of the many detectives on the case used the "n-word" during a private taping for his creation of a *fictitious* movie character for which he was, at least temporarily, personally destroyed. If this whole situation were not so blatantly unjust it would actually be pretty funny.

AL SHARPTON

Humor, or at least entertainment value, can be an important weapon in the fight to maintain one's viability after making statements that might otherwise end a career. Of course it is usually only enough to keep one alive if it is augmented by other factors, such as being a black liberal. No example is more illustrative of the absolute ridiculousness of the Speech Punishment process in the political arena than that of the continuing saga of black activist "Reverend" Al Sharpton.

It is difficult to overstate just how absurd Al Sharpton's rise to national prominence has been. In 2004 Sharpton was given an important speaking role at the Democratic National Convention and was paid $87,000 as a "consultant" to the Kerry campaign. This after a primary election season during which, despite being allowed in all of the televised debates, he garnered no serious electoral support.

So why was Sharpton even allowed in the debates in the first place? Only because the Democrats were afraid that he would raise a fuss with black voters if he were excluded as he should have been. Why did he have the leverage to make that threat? Not because he had any real evidence of genuine support among blacks, but rather because Sharpton has access to the news media (especially the cable news TV talk shows) whenever he desires. Why do the cable news shows love having Sharpton on? It is not because he has ever actually won anything, accomplished anything, written anything, or become an actual expert on anything. It is simply because Al Sharpton is a celebrity and an entertaining guest.

If Sharpton's brand of celebrity and the source of his entertainment value were based on something relatively benevolent (like, for instance, Arnold Schwarzenegger and his career of killing fictitious bad guys in action movies), the credibility he is erroneously granted by the news media would simply be yet another sad indication of how Americans seemingly value fame and amusement over almost anything else. However, the treatment of Sharpton proves that we have officially eliminated any perceptible difference between fame and infamy, and any distinction between being noteworthy and notorious.

How is this the case? It is because the foundation of Sharpton's "fame" is built of one of the most egregious and real speech crimes that one can possibly commit in this country.

In 1987 Al Sharpton first became known to the general public by jumping on the bandwagon of an African American teenage girl named Tawana Brawley, who claimed to have been raped by a gang of whites, including a prosecutor and law enforcement officials. Sharpton quickly became her media spokesperson and immediately began spewing charges of rape and racism to anyone who would listen. As it turned out, the whole thing was an elaborate hoax. If that had been the end of the affair, it would have been reasonable to presume that, like a much more serious and dangerous version of the former lip-synching pop group Milli Vanilli, Sharpton would have been properly branded a fraud and never heard from again.

The exposure of Sharpton as the promoter of a cruel deception was only the beginning of what should have been the funeral for his public persona. Stephen Pagones, the assistant district attorney whom Sharpton continually accused of rape, actually sued Big Al for libel. Despite the fact that the standard for proving libel is rightfully *extremely* high (one must be shown to have made statements that one knew to be false, and which had to have been made with malice and which have been shown to have created damage), a jury of Sharpton's peers found him guilty of libel and fined him $65,000, which Sharpton refused to pay.

Now considering the catastrophic fate of many of those we have already documented in these pages (none of whom came remotely close to breaking the law in their statements), one might think that being found guilty of libel in *any* case, especially one as heinous as Sharpton's, would provide a definite "death penalty" for someone's credibility and public stature. If there is a "speech crime" from which one should not be allowed to recover, the libel verdict against Sharpton should have provided it, especially since the "Rev" had absolutely no other positive accomplishments upon which to fall back or base a comeback. Once upon a time (not too long ago), the Tawana Brawley case would have been the end of Al Sharpton. Instead, it actually marked the beginning of his rise to prominence and power.

Sharpton somehow was permitted by the news media to use the notoriety (or notoriousness) that he gained from his Tawana Brawley lies to launch an extremely successful career as a professional race-monger. In incident after incident Sharpton was allowed to take to the microphones to spew his special brand of racial hatred and division. Soon, it was just accepted that Sharpton was a "black leader," even though he had never been close to being elected to anything and his organization was virtually nonexistent (not to mention corrupt). The media covered whatever he did seemingly based only on the notion that he was well known. Why was he well known? Well, because the media had covered him in the past. Why? Almost entirely because of his role in the Tawana Brawley case.

As Robin may have said to the Caped Crusader, "Holy circular argument, Batman!"

I personally witnessed a classic example of Sharpton's genius at media manipulation during the Florida recount after the highly contested 2000 presidential election. After holding court outside of the base of operations for the recount in Palm Beach County, Sharpton slowly waddled his way across the highway (blocking traffic as he did so) while being taunted by several dozen rabid Bush supporters. Apparently completely oblivious to the jeering, Sharpton appeared to actually slow down as he crept closer to his final destination of the lunch buffet down the street. It was clear that he knew exactly what he was doing as the media hoard of photographers grew larger along his rather innocuous journey.

Here was a man who had been long ago completely discredited by a court of law, with absolutely zero standing in the situation (he was not a Palm Beach or even Florida resident, nor an elected or even party official), where there was no evidence of race playing any role whatsoever, being covered as if his trip to the buffet was a major news story. Sure enough, that night and the next day the news pictures indicated that Sharpton had created quite a ruckus during one of the slower periods of the recount. Sharpton had gotten exactly what he wanted. His celebrity, legend, and, in the media's eyes, credibility had all grown, like his waistline, just a little bit more.

It should be noted that while he may be severely lacking in character, Sharpton is an *extremely* intelligent fellow. In fact, when I briefly interviewed him amid the mob during his journey to lunch that day he provided me with the most constitutionally sound explanation for the Gore legal challenge that I had heard articulated to that point (regarding the Fourteenth Amendment issues inherent in counting votes differently county by county), one which the Supreme Court would ultimately cite in the opposite direction in the election-concluding case of *Gore v. Bush*. However, further revealing him as a charlatan, since that memorable afternoon I have seen Sharpton on numerous occasions take to the airwaves to raise race in the 2000 Florida election in a manner directly in contradiction to what he told me that day on his way to the buffet.

One of the keys to Sharpton's scam is that he fully understands the first rule of television talk shows: never be boring (for female guests that rule replaces the word *boring* with unattractive). So, free to say absolutely anything (after all, if vicious libel *helped* his career, what could he possibly say to hurt it?), Sharpton is able to be constantly entertaining, even if often at the cost of creating further divisions between the races. But heck, in the world of cable TV talk, a tenth of a ratings point or two is considered well worth any potential damage done to the country.

With almost every TV talk show gladly willing to make that cynical exchange, Sharpton is a prized guest on programs where he almost never even has to face his past and unsuspecting viewers are given the impression that he is a real and serious political force without a heinous history that goes way beyond just the libel verdict against him. (It is important to note here that, similarly, boxing promoter Don King, who among other transgressions, has *killed* at least two people, was granted numerous TV appearances to bizarrely promote the 2004 reelection of President Bush, without his past ever being mentioned, or probably even known, by the host or the audience he was supposedly attempting to influence.)

Sharpton has even been able to turn his outrageous persona into his own post-election reality show on Spike TV (a network small enough to withstand any potential anti-Sharpton boycotts because it is already routinely being "boycotted" by at least 99 percent of the nation) called "I Hate My Job." Sharpton has also played himself during guest spots on the popular ABC show *Boston Legal*.

The multi-faceted problems and conflicts inherent in the Al Sharpton phenomenon were best illustrated by MSNBC's coverage of his rancorous and incendiary speech to the 2004 Democratic Convention. The host of the coverage, Chris Matthews, actually pulled MSNBC out of the speech before its grand finale while asking the extremely relevant question of whether it was a good thing for the Democratic Party to have someone whose career was "based on a lie" making the case that the president had misled the American people into war.

There were at least two major problems with Matthews' exceedingly important point. The first is that Matthews himself had done more than any other member of the news media in creating Sharpton's viability by having him on as a guest numerous times before, during, and after his ludicrous campaign for president. I asked Matthews via e-mail whether he had ever brought up the incident to which he referred in his convention commentary during any of Sharpton's many previous appearances. Despite having done so numerous times in the past on other matters, Matthews did not respond.

The second problem with this scenario was that Sharpton had already been hired by MSNBC's sister network (CNBC) to do commentary for both political conventions and later would be in discussions with him for both a radio and TV talk show possibility. It is not remotely a stretch to suggest that without Matthews and the NBC family's support, Sharpton would never have been in a position to make the speech that Matthews cut out of while fearing that it might be harming the Democratic Party.

In a sense, Matthews' legitimate point being made by him on an NBC network was not much different from a defense attorney complaining about his clearly guilty former client getting away with yet another crime because his law firm loaned the criminal the money with which he purchased the getaway car.

Or at least something like that.

CHAPTER FOUR: EVERYTHING IS ENTERTAINMENT, BUT IT'S NOT ALL FREE SPEECH

"We live in oppressive times. We have, as a nation, become our own thought police; but instead of calling the process by which we limit our expression of dissent and wonder 'censorship,' we call it 'concern for commercial viability.'"
—David Mamet, actor, director, writer

While there are two basic forms of what we have been calling Speech Punishment, there are at least three types of *restrictions* on free speech in modern America. The first, which we have already been documenting, comes from society punishing those who say things that some of us do not like. The second, which represents the only true form of "censorship" or potential violation of the Constitution, is when the government actually penalizes people for expressing themselves or prevents from doing so. The third, and perhaps the most prevalent, is when a person or group self-censors for fear of retribution from society, their employer, or the government.

The field of "entertainment," which seemingly encompasses nearly every form of communication in our increasingly trivialized culture, has recently seen a greater variety of free speech restrictions than any other element of our society. From performers complaining that they have been forced to pay a price for expressing their political opinions, to corporations being fined by the government for allowing certain words to be uttered or body parts to be seen, to broadcasts being canceled or curtailed because of various forms of intimidation (real or perceived), there is an unquestionable epidemic of expression constriction in the world of entertainment.

"There's an atmosphere of fear in America right now that is deadly," said singer Elton John in 2004, referring to the "censorship" of performing artists. When someone as important and credible as Elton John says there's a problem, we all need to take notice.

Much like the sports world was an odd place for the anti–free speech virus to originate from, the arena of entertainment would seem to be the most unlikely of places for it to gain momentum. And yet it has.

Proof of this is best illustrated by examining the last bastion of real free speech in this country, the purest and most basic form of entertainment: stand-up comedy. Armed with nothing but a microphone, the stand-up comic, whose only mission is to make a live audience laugh, may very well be the only person in America that can say virtually *anything* he or she wants to. The only check on their free speech is whether their routine is compelling enough to draw an audience large enough to pay the bills of the club that booked them. Other than that, *everything* is fair game.

Similarly, other than stand-up comedy (and perhaps on some very rare, self-sustaining Web sites), *every other* public form of commercial speech in this country, is, for better or worse, at least partially restricted by various forces of suppression.

What makes stand-up comics apparently immune from the virus? It has much more to do with what they do *not* have than what they do. Because club comics usually work only for themselves, they are not concerned with corporate sponsorship and therefore need not worry about the prospect of frightened backers withdrawing financial support over potentially offensive speech (a luxury that radio talk show hosts, unfortunately, do not share). Because what stand-up comics say isn't usually communicated over the "public airwaves" (at least not until they get popular enough to make it to broadcast television), they are, at least for now, safe from governmental interference in their content. And because their audience has usually paid for the privilege of hearing what they have to say, there is a presumption that, at least at some level, the audience knows what they are in for.

Take, for example, Robin Williams at the 2005 Academy Awards. Williams was scheduled to sing a comedic number about, of all things, the forces of *censorship*. Had he been performing in a club, there would have been absolutely no problem. The Oscars, however, are broadcast on ABC with a vast/diverse audience and the advertisers are so "mainstream" (gutless) that the level of sensitivity towards controversy is exponentially heightened. Despite the pre-show hype that, with the edgy Chris Rock hosting, this telecast would be anything but toothless, the censors edited the piece to the point that Williams and his writers refused to present it. Instead he came on stage with a piece of masking tape over his mouth and proceeded to do a watered-down "stand-up" version of the intended song. Remarkably, this "censorship" story was almost completely lost amid the media's fascination with the female stars' designer dresses.

No one career has experienced more of the "Baskin Robbins" variety of free speech flavors than comedian/actor/author/ commentator/talk show host Dennis Miller. Miller has gone from being a stand-up comedian with almost no restrictions, to a *Saturday Night Live* cast member with FCC and NBC corporate considerations to constrict him, to an HBO talk show host with the almost comedy club–like freedom of pay cable TV, to an actor who usually only says what someone else has written, to an author with only a large corporate publisher to worry about, to the straitjacket of a *Monday Night Football* analyst on "over the air" ABC-TV, to the somewhere-in-between ambiguity of basic cable (CNBC) as a sometimes serious, sometimes not, talk show host.

His varied and almost unique experience with the various legal and perceived public standards of free speech have apparently given Miller a strong understanding of both the importance and vulnerability of that once sacred right. "No First Amendment [at all] produces Hitler," observes Miller. "A healthy First Amendment produces David Duke. There's a big difference there . . . The one muscle we should be developing right now is the one that helps us make the right choice. If some governmental bureaucracy steps in and makes those choices for us, then that muscle will become weaker than a mixed drink in a strip club."

Interestingly, Miller is also distinctive in the free speech arena because he happens to be one of the very few "Hollywood" celebrities (and by far the most outspoken) who is not extremely liberal in his political views. But Miller is part of a species that is even rarer than the Hollywood Conservative. He is a Hollywood Conservative who is not afraid to let that world know what his views are. For all the bluster from the entertainment left that somehow they have been recent victims of speech suppression, one of the many dirty little secrets of Hollywood is that there are *many* conservatives who are afraid to voice their opinions at all for fear that they will not be able to get work from the very stars on the Left who are complaining about alleged "censorship" of their own views.

Most Hollywood figures are afraid of even just *appearing* on KFI-AM, the top talk station in Los Angeles, because they are frightened of somehow being seen as approving of the station's perceived anti-illegal immigrant "agenda." As someone far outside the Hollywood scene, even I personally know a conservative commentator who suddenly stopped expressing political opinions when he started working as a consultant on a big movie.

That being said, the last couple of years have produced numerous incidents where celebrities have claimed to be bitten unfairly by the "Speech Punishment" bug. In what, at first glance, would seem to be a reality counterintuitive to what might be expected (considering the normal bias in the media favoring liberals and against conservatives), the vast majority of them have indeed been very liberal. However, upon closer examination it appears obvious that, in the end, most of these episodes actually confirmed rather than denied what has only recently finally become the semi–conventional wisdom regarding media bias.

THE DIXIE CHICKS

"I disapprove of what you say, but I will defend to the death your right to say it."
—Voltaire, eighteenth-century
French philosopher

In March of 2003, the country music industry was rocked by a controversy involving their most talented and promising young act, the Dixie Chicks. While performing in London on the eve of the Iraq war, the Chicks' lead singer, Natalie Maines, apologetically told the crowd, which she presumed to be antiwar because of the perceived political climate in Great Britain,

"Just so you know, we're ashamed the president of the United States is from Texas."

Just a few years before this incident, Maines's comment would likely have gone almost completely unnoticed. After all, the statement was made on foreign soil, at a live concert with limited media access, without any official TV coverage of the event. However, in an age when almost anything that happens in public is recorded in some shape or form and where the Internet allows for virtually everything to be reported, often without credibility, Maines's statement almost immediately reversed the rotation of the entire country music world.

There were several important and somewhat uncommon factors that contributed to the brushfire created by the Chicks' comment. The first was that it was made in foreign country, just before a war, in a nation that the United States was relying on as its chief ally in that war and where the prime minister was under enormous political pressure to withdraw his support from the pending invasion. There was little doubt that largely because of the Dixie Chicks' persona and background the anti-war movement in the UK was considered a huge public relations victory.

After all, if even a popular U.S. *country* music band from *Texas* thought the president was a dope, then the rest of the world could feel justified in believing the worst about him. So the timing of the statement, either by accident or design, could not have been chosen to have more of a negative impact on the world's perception of both the president and U.S. policy toward Iraq.

Had the statement been made by one of the usual "suspects" from the entertainment world's liberal elite in New York or Los Angeles, then it likely would have made almost no impact. But because the Chicks were from *Texas* and not only played *country* music, but *real* country music, the comment took on the feel of desertion or even treason. It is widely known that most country music stars tend to be as conservative in their views as other entertainers tend to be liberal. But more importantly for the Chicks themselves, so is the country music fan base.

When Madonna, Bruce Springsteen, and the rock group Pearl Jam made statements about the president that could easily be deemed far more offensive than what Maines said, there was not only no international impact, but their fans were largely unaffected

as well. This was mostly because the vast majority of these entertainers' supporters were either in agreement with, ambivalent to,
or completely ignorant of the significance of their anti-Bush/war
position (as well as not being from Texas). The same was not true
with the Chicks, whose average fan was a big supporter of both
President Bush and the war, and probably had at least some affection for Texas.

From a pure free speech perspective, the only thing remotely
"actionable" about Maines's original statement (which was enthusiastically supported by the rest of the band), was that she was
so personally critical of the president on foreign soil just before a
decision to go war. Based only on precedent, it is difficult to argue
that the ladies should have been punished solely for the content
of the comment. However, that does not mean that the harsh reaction they received was unjust, but rather only that it had very
little to do with free speech and everything to do with selling a
product.

Almost immediately, to varying degrees and for different reasons, country music radio stations stopped playing the records of
the Dixie Chicks. Contrary to numerous published reports, there is
no evidence of a corporate conspiracy (by, for instance, the allegedly pro-Bush Clear Channel Communications) causing the
"bans" or boycotts. Instead, in the vast majority of cases, *individual* radio stations, often after soliciting listener input (which ran
exponentially against the Chicks), decided to reduce or eliminate
the Chicks' airplay, at least temporarily.

One of the reasons that leftist elements of the media presumed
that there had to have been some sort of decree from the moun-
taintop of one of the radio giants like Clear Channel is that so
many country music stations acted so similarly in such a short period of time. However, this had to do with the fact that, as shown
by the results of our last two presidential elections, "Red State"
America, which tends to be overwhelmingly dominated by country music stations, still tends to think and act at least somewhat
homogeneously. In other words, the country music fan in South
Carolina is likely to have the very same reaction to a particular
situation as one in South Dakota (kind of like the similarity of
thought among the liberal media elites of New York, Washington
D.C., and Los Angeles).

So radio stations stopped playing their music and there were sporadic protests that included destroying their CDs and burning tickets to their still-packed concerts. But the momentum of the anger against the Chicks may have been quickly stifled had they not handled the situation in such a peculiar manner. While she did apologize, claiming that what she said was only a joke, Maines seemed to be begging for more retribution when she opined, "I realize now that I'm just supposed to sing and look cute so our fans won't have anything to upset them while they're cheating on their wives or getting into drunken bar fights or driving around in their pickup trucks shooting highway signs or small animals."

Putting aside for a moment Maines's shocking (though potentially at least partially accurate) view of her audience, it is interesting that, at least on some level, she seems to understand the problem. Yes, Natalie, that is *exactly* why people pay to hear you sing; because it makes them feel good. And because you make them feel good, they like you. And because they like you, they buy more records, tickets, and merchandise with their hard-earned dollars. But when you say something with which they strongly disagree, at a really inappropriate time, in a particularly poor place, they have every right to no longer like you and then to stop buying your stuff, especially when you later strongly imply that they are nothing but white trash.

Did Natalie Maines have the right to say what she did? Absolutely. But her fans had just as much of a right to express their dissatisfaction with her comments by holding her and the band financially accountable. Such a reaction is not a violation of the concept of free speech; it is actually a validation of it. It is also a far more legitimate and democratic means by which to enforce Speech Punishment than the usual method of allowing just a few media elites to enforce the inconsistent and nonsensical rules. But in this case, it turned out that there was no real punishment.

Ironically, though not surprisingly, in the end the Chicks "affair" probably helped their careers immensely. Partially because we now live in an age where celebrity trumps almost *everything*, any "scandal" that makes an entertainer better known ends up being, bizarrely, *good* for their career, even for "stars" like Paris Hilton who do not even have a career to begin with. Thanks to numerous factors, there is no doubt that the Dixie Chicks became bigger stars with a broader reach *after* the London incident.

Suddenly, the Dixie Chicks, who previously been largely ignored by the national news media and treated as little more than an up-and-coming country band, found themselves worthy of a *Primetime* special with Diane Sawyer on ABC. Complete with the obligatory filtered cameras, softball questions, and crocodile tears, the TV appearance was a publicist's dream.

Almost overnight, the Dixie Chicks, who had already been trying to cross over into more mainstream music, were huge *national* figures who were provided martyr status by a more than sympathetic press. Now, instead of just being viable in the "Red States," the Chicks would be welcomed as bona fide stars in the "Blue" ones as well. While there are undoubtedly still pockets of anger and resentment against the Dixie Chicks among their old fan base, there is no question that, when it was all said and done, they suffered no long-term consequences for what Maines said and likely have experienced a significant net gain from the whole episode.

BILL MAHER

"If liberty means anything at all, it means the right to tell people what they do not want to hear."

—George Orwell, author of *1984*

A similar, though elongated, series of circumstances surrounded the first major post-9/11 incident of Speech Punishment. Recent media history has shown that whenever something huge and tragic happens in America, some commentator (usually a radio DJ or talk show host) is going to lose his job for talking about it in an "insensitive" manner. In fact, I have often joked on the air that a story has not truly reached its apex until someone gets fired for commenting on it.

Obviously the epic tragedy of September 11th, 2001, needed no further verification of its massive significance, but it was still inevitable that someone would get swept away in the maelstrom of confusion, fear, and anger that gripped the country in the days following that fateful Tuesday morning.

That happened one week after the attack when Bill Maher, then host of the paradoxically titled *Politically Incorrect*, objected to President Bush's description of the terrorists as having engaged in "cowardly acts." Maher told his ABC audience, "Staying in the airplanes when it hits the building, say what you want about it, it's not cowardly. . . . We have been the cowards lobbing cruise missiles from 2,000 miles away. That's cowardly."

Calling the U.S. military "cowardly" would never be a particularly good idea for the host of a network show that relies on advertising dollars from mainstream corporations. Doing so a week after 9/11 was *really* dumb. Doing so in a manner that strongly implied that those who had just attacked the U.S. were *LESS* cowardly than our own military was simply an apparent attempt at career suicide (no pun intended).

In a written statement Maher immediately apologized, saying his views "should have been expressed differently. In no way was I intending to say, nor have I ever thought, that the men and women who defend our nation in uniform are anything but courageous and valiant, and I offer my apologies to anyone who took it wrong."

That did not stop advertisers like Sears and FedEx from canceling their commercials on the program and some ABC affiliates from eventually dropping the show. While *Politically Incorrect* remained on the air for several more months, the stench of death quickly enveloped the program and no one was surprised when ABC finally canceled it and essentially fired Maher.

The significance and irony of a show named *Politically Incorrect* being dropped because its host said something that was deemed to be *politically incorrect* should not be lost amid all of the other issues that its demise illuminated. In a sense, if only symbolically, it was a watershed moment in the diminishment of the value of free speech. After all, if you cannot say something highly controversial (even if poorly timed) on an *entertainment* program called *Politically Incorrect*, then obviously there is a massive volume of media outlets where speech is even far more restricted.

For those, like myself, who despise the entire concept of "political correctness," because it is really just a weapon of the "thought police" in their war to intimidate those who disagree with them into keeping silent, the show by the same name provided plenty of friendly fire. Under the guise of rejecting political correctness, Maher's former talk show, largely because it was dominated by the liberal Hollywood mentality, was actually *extremely* politically correct. It is nearly impossible to separate political correctness from liberalism because "PC" has become a tactic of that dying philosophy to help them "win" arguments by making it against the "rules" for the other side to use all of their artillery.

Interestingly, as the host of *PI*, Maher himself did an excellent job of apparently pretending or "acting" as if he was a *real* "independent" who was an equal opportunity offender. As it turned out, when Maher needed a new gig and no longer had to appeal to a broad audience on a major network, he revealed himself to actually be extremely liberal and a true-blue Bush-hater. In 2004 on his HBO show *Real Time*, Maher joined Michael Moore for an on-air stunt in which they both literally got on their knees to beg guest Ralph Nader to get out of the presidential race so as not to jeopardize a Kerry victory. Was Maher faking his political independence previously or is he just lying now?

With Maher it is impossible to know what his real political convictions are (assuming he has any) because his words appear to be motivated only by what will get him the most laughs, women, attention, women, money, and, yes, women. Of course there is nothing inherently wrong with those motivations dictating what someone says, as long as the person whose words are based on such trivial concerns is not taken seriously. Unfortunately, that has not been the case with the post–ABC firing version of Bill Maher.

While early on Maher had to fight through the normal depression of a Speech Punishment victim (at one point engaging in the most despondent interview on Howard Stern's radio show that I have ever heard a public figure give), much like the Dixie Chicks, he is actually in a better place now than he was before committing his "crime."

When he was the host of *PI* he was considered by the mainstream media to be nothing but a buffoon whose show was based around the usually embarrassingly ignorant opinions of C- or D-list "celebrities." About the only social significance given to the program was that it helped create the destructive notion that it is acceptable to let anyone voice their opinion on TV and then give that view credence simply because the person giving it has some measure of fame.

Today, despite his post-9/11 comments, and even though his current TV show reaches a much smaller audience on HBO than it did on ABC, and in spite of his dramatic and rather curious change of political persuasion, Maher is treated in many corners of the media word as a respected political commentator.

Maher has somehow become a regular one-on-one guest on *Larry King Live*, *Hannity and Colmes*, and *Hardball with Chris Matthews*. He is even allowed to write frequent editorials in the ultraliberal *Los Angeles Times*. For the record, these are not appearances where he just cracks jokes about the news of the day and is treated like the semi-amusing court jester; instead, he is mostly asked for his straight opinion on political matters, as though he were Henry Kissinger.

Why is it that Maher is treated with *more* respect even though he has become a smaller star, and after his career has provided numerous reasons for his integrity/authority to come into question? Well, part of that has to do with the almost inherently fraudulent dynamic in which TV talk show guests are chosen on the basis of their appearance, notoriety, and relationship with the host/producer rather than because of their knowledge or credibility, but it also may not be a coincidence that his career resuscitation coincided with his sudden hard turn to the left on the political spectrum.

This is *not* to suggest that there was some sort of massive liberal media conspiracy whereby a "meeting" was called to let Maher back in the "club" if he agreed to mostly bash conservatives. However, there is a fairly long and growing list of commentators/celebrities who have, with varying degrees of success, suddenly moved their opinions further to the left, or at least decided to expose how liberal they "really" are, only after seeing their fame fade or fail to ignite. To varying degrees and in different ways, Alec Baldwin, Ben Affleck, Arianna Huffington, Rosie O'Donnell, Margaret Cho, Janeane Garofalo, Chevy Chase, Keith Olbermann, David Brock, Ed Shultz, Jim Jeffords, Geraldo Rivera, Linda Ronstadt, Carl Bernstein, and Walter Cronkite immediately come to mind as public people who have either consciously or subconsciously engaged in opinion modification for the purpose of career enhancement and/or the regaining of attention (it should also be noted that figures like Zell Miller, Dick Morris, Bernard Goldberg, Glenn Beck, and Dennis Miller have been very successful at pulling off the same maneuver in the opposite direction).

Whether Maher intentionally switched his political views as a career move is not particularly relevant. What *is* important is that we have such a dysfunctional media culture in this country that giving *your* real opinions can cost you your job, while making them up can actually help you get a better gig, or, in Maher's case, the gig and the girls.

As Maher found out when ABC refused to take the heat caused by his "cowardly" comment, one of the great misconceptions about the modern media is that "controversy sells." Most people I meet who have never been in the business of giving one's opinion think that the more outrage you provoke the better it is for your ratings and, therefore, your career. In most cases, this is simply not true. The reality is that only certain types of controversy (as well as whatever ratings that may garner) are good for business in the world of media commentary. Ironically, it is actually far easier and safer from a business perspective when the opinions that create the controversy are contrived, calculated, and counterfeit. Quite simply, when it comes to creating a storm with your words in America, we tend to reward those whose bluster generates a wind that is phony, while punishing those who really do mean what they say.

As a radio talk show host (by far the most vulnerable of opinion-based occupations) it frustrates me that those who get in the most trouble in my business are usually those who are punished for giving highly controversial but usually legitimate and, at the very least, *real* perspectives on the news/issues of the day. Conversely, it amazes me that if a remark is made by, say, a "character" as opposed to a "real" person (even when everyone in the audience knows it is the host doing the impression), that it is almost impossible for that host to be reprimanded or punished for what he said.

Two hosts I used to (sort of) work with have literally based their entire careers on this concept. One national and one local, both have used the same cast of tired old character voices for years, and are able to offend just about anyone and everyone without fear of repercussion. Why it is that they are allowed to regularly say things that would ordinarily be deemed highly inappropriate just because they are doing so while hiding behind a made-up voice has been a source of mystery to me for which I simultaneously admire and revile the hosts.

As dubious as it is for someone to hide behind a make-believe persona to construct their points, it may not be as insidious as a similar trend. As a result of fake opinions being safer than real ones, an entire genre of "talkers" has been created where their broadcast views are as carefully crafted and contrived as those of the politicians they so love to skewer.

With this variety of commentator, controversial perspectives that may offend their target audience/advertisers are discarded, while those that they think will make them more appealing to their "constituency" are amplified or exaggerated. This is one of the many reasons why the only opinions you will likely ever hear on "conservative" talk radio about religion (especially Christianity) are extremely positive and almost never derogatory. In a fragmented media world where one only needs a loyal sliver of the audience to survive, it can, literally and figuratively, pay to preach to the choir.

One of the more interesting examples of this fake/real phenomenon comes from an extremely unlikely duo that *made* their living from completely mindless and filthy gags, and then almost *lost* everything when they did something that may have actually had value as legitimate social commentary in the area—believe it or not—of Christianity.

OPIE AND ANTHONY

"If we don't believe in freedom of expression for people we despise, we don't believe in it at all."

—Noam Chomsky, educator and linguist

The notorious radio team "Opie and Anthony" became well-known in the northeast for their bawdy brand of humor which was spiced with sexual escapades. Early in their careers they were fired several times for crossing the nebulous line of appropriate on-air discussion. On at least one occasion they actually got canned on purpose because they figured, correctly, that the publicity would further their image as the "bad boys" of radio and that it would help advance their career.

They quickly became syndicated on numerous FM music/talk stations and, like Howard Stern before them, they got big ratings by taking a genre (talk radio) known for being very serious and mostly political, and turning it on its head by focusing on anything and everything that had previously been forbidden—usually graphic sexual content.

In one of their more notorious features, they actually sponsored a contest called "Sex for Sam" in which couples could earn points based on which public places they could get away with having sex as well as which sex acts they could engage in while being part of the broadcast. The stunt obviously raised eyebrows, but, mostly because their ratings were good, largely created no real repercussions for the dangerous duo.

That changed on August 15th, 2002, when they found an apparently horny and attention-starved couple seemingly willing to do what would initially seem both unthinkable and completely unsuitable for broadcast content. Their plan was to have sex in a church. Not just any church, but St. Patrick's Cathedral in New York City.

Opie and Anthony had a reporter on the scene to describe what sounded like two adults going into the back of St. Patrick's Cathedral and attempting to engage in some sort of sexual activity. As it turned out, the security on hand quickly ended the escapade and apprehended the couple. There was no indication that the "deed" was actually done and none of the allegedly "forbidden" words that usually trigger an "indecency" complaint to the Federal Communications Commission were used. From a pure content standpoint, the incident was no different from the many other installments of their on-air sex contest "Sex for Sam." The reaction however, was as dissimilar as a nuclear bomb is from a firecracker.

The ensuing inferno was immediate and ferocious. Faced with universal condemnation led by various outraged Catholic groups, the show's owners, Infinity Broadcasting, immediately took Opie and Anthony off the air (they were not technically fired since they were paid through the remaining two years of their contract).

Considering the breadth and level of indignation over the incident, there is *no* doubt that the decision to fire Opie and Anthony was a legitimate business decision. However, there were probably hundreds of other equally inappropriate moments that occurred previously on their program (as well as other Infinity properties, such as Howard Stern's show) that could have previously triggered the guillotine.

In fact, it is very possible that had Howard Stern done exactly the same thing for the very same parent company, that he might have gotten away with it. The reality is that because Stern makes Infinity far more money than Opie and Anthony, he gets a much longer leash. When the U.S. Supreme Court famously pronounced that "money equals speech" (in a landmark campaign finance decision) they could have just as easily been referring to the entertainment/commentary industry. Quite simply, the more money you make the company, the more freedom of speech you possess.

Much like getting called for "holding" in an NFL football game, Opie and Anthony could have been declared in "violation" almost anytime the authorities decided the time was right. This is why they and their brethren are, usually derisively, referred to as "shock jocks." The audience is supposed to be "shocked" that anyone would have the guts/stupidity to get away with saying and doing such things on the formerly tame medium of radio.

But while the fact that Opie and Anthony could have been fired at virtually any time, after any one of their constant excursions over the "line," does not diminish the nature of their speech "crime," it does illustrate, once again, how almost impossible it is to determine, prior to the fact, where that imaginary boundary actually is.

The dismissal of Opie and Anthony also reveals a far more dangerous aspect of Speech Punishment, because this was a case in which the *government* actually got involved. The Federal Communications Commission, which is an unelected government body that is suppose to regulate the over-the-air broadcasting industry, voted to fine Infinity Broadcasting the statutory maximum of $357,000 for the incident (later to be part of a record $3.5 million settlement between Infinity and the FCC).

The fine was based on "the egregious nature of the material" as well as "Infinity's recent history of indecent or *apparently* indecent broadcasts." One of the commissioners, a frighteningly nutty Democrat named Michael Copps, actually dissented from the decision because he thought the punishment was far too *light* and that the offending stations should be given the "death penalty" by having their licenses *revoked*.

Let me get this straight. . . . Because a broadcast is "egregious" and because it follows other broadcasts that were "apparently" indecent, a station should be fined by the government the maximum and come within two votes of being permanently taken off the air?! The reality is that, as "egregious" as the "Sex at St. Pat's" broadcast may have been, there is little evidence that it was technically "indecent." In fact, a convincing argument can (and shortly will) be made that the definitions of potential FCC violations were essentially *created* in order to *protect* exactly the type of program Opie and Anthony did that day.

There are three basics forms of FCC "no-nos" for radio and television stations that use the "public airwaves" as their primary channel of broadcast. They are profanity, indecency, and obscenity.

"Profane" speech is defined by the FCC as language that "denotes certain of those personally reviling epithets naturally tending to provoke violent resentment or denoting language so grossly offensive to members of the public who actually hear it as to amount to a nuisance."

What the heck does *that* actually mean?!

It would appear that this provision could be read to indicate that anything short of screaming over the airwaves of a station with a black audience: "Kill all the niggers!" does *not* qualify. Or, just as easily, it could be interpreted to suggest almost *anything* someone finds objectionable or a "nuisance" could meet the criteria. This is by far the most poorly written of the FCC definitions and thankfully, at least for now, it is rarely used to prosecute anyone. However, assuming the current trend of FCC overreach continues, I predict that its inherently vague nature will eventually be used as a hammer for the government to further punish speech (outside the realm of sex) that it or vocal members of its populace does not like.

The most commonly "violated" broadcast restriction is that over "indecency." The FCC has defined broadcast indecency as "language or material that, in context, depicts or describes, in terms patently offensive as measured by contemporary community broadcast standards for the broadcast medium, sexual or excretory organs or activities."

Because even the most activist of courts have consistently held that "indecent" material is protected by the First Amendment (it must be that nasty "Congress shall make no law . . ." wording), it cannot be banned entirely. So the FCC has decided that "indecency" is only banned between the hours of 6:00 a.m. and 10:00 p.m., which is the same rule as for "profanity."

Does that last sentence seem strange to you? The First Amendment unambiguously protects free speech, the courts have said that means that even "indecent" speech is perfectly legal, and yet an unelected government commission arbitrarily decides that this type of speech is legally punishable during the most popular 67 percent of the broadcast day? And almost no one sees a problem with that?!

The FCC has actually had the audacity to make up a variety of speech that is *NOT* protected by the First Amendment. According to the FCC, "obscene" broadcasts are prohibited at "all times." Speech is deemed "obscene" if the "average" person finds the material appeals to the "prurient" interest, and it describes sexual conduct in a "patently offensive" manner, and it "lacks serious literary, artistic, political, or scientific value."

That last provision is *most* interesting. The FCC says that certain types of speech, which would otherwise somehow magically be exempted from First Amendment protection, are apparently completely free from government restriction if they have serious value as commentary. Like most FCC edicts, it is rather ambiguous and unclear if this means that otherwise "obscene" speech would then automatically fall under the category of "indecent," or if possessing "serious value" allows such material to be broadcast at all hours.

Regardless of how that apparent contradiction is interpreted, there is no doubt that, despite how the Opie and Anthony episode was portrayed in the news media (except for one appearance by some guy named John Ziegler on the Fox News Channel), it could easily have been deemed to have "serious value" as commentary.

While at first glance that last statement may appear to be absurd, consider *when* the Opie and Anthony stunt took place. In the summer of 2002 the Catholic Church in America was fully embroiled in by far the greatest scandal of its history. Hundreds of Catholic priests were being credibly accused of having sex with their parishioners, usually young boys. Many Catholics felt, with great justification, that there was a stunning lack of outrage or willingness on the part of the Catholic Church leadership to bring those guilty to justice.

Whether this was their intention or not (that part is almost irrelevant), within *this* context the "Sex at St. Pat's" stunt unquestionably provided important commentary that unquestionably should have been judged to have provided the broadcast with "serious value." After all, did not Opie and Anthony expose the massive hypocrisy of the Catholic Church by creating a situation where their leaders expressed *far* more indignation over a radio broadcast of two *consenting adults* attempting to have sex in a church than they did over numerous allegations of *child molestation* actually occurring there? Whether you agree or disagree with that conclusion, there is no question that it is a valid and "serious" issue for discussion.

While there certainly may have been many other effective and far more tasteful ways in which to make this point, there is almost no doubt that this context easily exempts the episode from being declared "obscene." While that still potentially (depending on how one interprets those convoluted definitions) leaves the issue of "indecency" on the table, if that particular broadcast is a violation of FCC rules, then so is a massive portion of radio and television programming. (Has the FCC ever *seen* "soap opera" or "reality" TV where sex scenes are routinely *viewed* and heard, rather than just described?)

Essentially, for the "Sex at St. Pat's" stunt to be "indecent" to the point of being illegal, the same must be so *anytime* someone describes any kind of sexual activity taking place, even while using the most general and basic of terms (a syndicated TV show called *Cheaters* does this all the time). Had the reporter on the program in question sounded like he was reading something out of the raciest issue of *Penthouse Forum* or even a steamy romance novel, then clearly *that* would be meant to titillate the audience and appeal only to the prurient interest.

However, that was not what happened. Instead the reporter basically told what he saw in the church in generic play-by-play style. You could even argue that he was reporting on a legitimate "news" story. While there would be obvious ethical issues related to creating the circumstances that caused the "news" to break out in the first place, nothing illegal, at least from a broadcasting/speech perspective, would appear to have occurred.

Would it have been suddenly "indecent" if another broadcast outlet just happened to be there and also merely described as a news story what was happening inside St. Patrick's Cathedral? I certainly hope not, but it is very difficult to come up with the logical/legal argument for how one report from the scene is illegal and the other is not when (in this hypothetical situation) they are describing the same event in a substantively similar fashion.

The bottom line is that the only *real* reason Infinity Broadcasting got fined for this mess was that it occurred in a famous Catholic church—and yet, *because* it did happen in a famous Catholic church is the very reason that the broadcast should have been given full First Amendment protection. Instead, for many reasons (including fear of the Catholic Church as well as news media ignorance/group think) that element of this issue was never even mentioned in the frighteningly one-sided public discussion of the matter.

I want to make absolutely clear that I totally agree with Opie and Anthony being taken off the air and their actions being condemned by society. My only points here are that their broadcast should not have been deemed "illegal" by the government, and that when this did occur it should have been greeted with a chorus of outrage instead of with petrified/apathetic silence.

These circumstances may be the ultimate example of how we have failed miserably to live up to one of the primary tenets of protecting free speech: if we fail to defend the most repugnant variety of speech, we have failed to preserve any of it.

Of course, despite all the damage Opie and Anthony may have inadvertently done to the cause of securing our right to free speech, things have seemingly worked out for the duo. After staying silent for two years while being paid through the rest of their contracts, Opie and Anthony signed a first-of-its-kind deal with XM Satellite Radio, one of two emerging companies that broadcast to "radios" using satellite signals instead of "over-the-air" radio frequencies.

The use of "public airwaves" by traditional radio and television broadcasts is the flimsy foothold upon which the government has used to creep inside the previously secured door of speech regulation. Because of massive technological innovation since the creation of the FCC and its guidelines, what was once merely a dubious distinction is now downright laughable (of course there was *always* something ridiculous about regulating TV and radio for using the "air," but not doing the same for newspapers even though they utilize the public roadways to deliver their product).

Because cable television does not use the magical "public airwaves" it is largely exempt from FCC regulations, though most "commercial cable" outlets abide by them anyway, just to be safe. However, even though the vast majority of viewers now get their local "over-the-air" TV stations via cable connections, the same antiquated rules still apply.

Absurdly, as the number of unregulated TV channels has exploded and the size of the traditional network audience has been severely splintered, the burden of adhering to now antiquated FCC regulations has only accelerated the demise of "over-the-air" TV stations. How it is that traditional broadcast networks that run commercials and are not allowed to use real-life language or show any nudity can possibly compete long-term in a world with HBO (with no commercials or content restrictions) seems almost impossible to comprehend.

The irony here of course is that the FCC restricts content under the premise that it *preserves* "decent" programming, but in reality it is helping to destroy those who carry it and effectively *reduce* the audience of family-oriented television on the networks. The inability to use many real-life situations has not only cost those networks viewers/revenue to cable, it has also forced traditional TV to rely more much more on violence as a way of remaining "edgy," while still maneuvering around the FCC regulations which absurdly punish the split-second sight of a woman's breast (real or fake) and not that of a person (real or fake) being shot to death. Only the federal government could be so incredibly inept as to not only fail to achieve their stated goals, but to also effectively produce exactly the *opposite* results.

Barring a government subsidy of some sort or an extension of FCC regulation across the board (isn't it amazing how when government screws something up the answer always seems to rely on the government overstepping its authority even *more*?) it would seem that the days of traditional network TV are both numbered and few. In a very real sense, the FCC is inadvertently helping to kill off the very type of broadcasting it is pretending to preserve.

Now, with the advent of satellite radio, an extremely analogous situation is taking form in the medium where broadcasting began. With Opie and Anthony already there via XM Satellite Radio and Howard Stern scheduled to join Sirius Satellite Radio by 2006, billions of dollars are being bet that radio listeners will be willing to pay to hear "shock jocks" and other content on the radio supposedly free from FCC intervention.

In late 2004 there was speculation that the FCC may seek and obtain the power to regulate *all* broadcast outlets. While the argument that the FCC should be *retreating* from its current, increasingly barren, terrain instead of conquering new frontiers is, in my opinion, far stronger, there is at least some logic behind going in that opposite direction instead.

For one thing, satellite radio actually *does* use the "public airwaves" (as if the air through which satellite signals travel is fundamentally different to begin with just because it goes in and out of our atmosphere) because most of their transponders use a local FM frequency to transmit their broadcasts.

Secondly, much like with television, for the FCC to control content only on terrestrial radio would be to create market conditions that could cause an outcome in contradiction to the intent of their recent indecency crackdown. For if unregulated, commercial-free radio becomes dominant, then traditional radio could become unprofitable to the point of extinction. Should that happen, the FCC will have actually fashioned an environment that will end up generating far more "indecency" on the radio than anyone ever conceived of before the recent stricter enforcement of their regulations.

However, it is quite possible that those market conditions may not materialize. One of the intricacies of the "shock jock" phenomenon is that for a broadcast to be "shocking" it needs to be perceived as breaking, or at least pushing, some sort of rule. If there are no rules whatsoever (not to mention, at least at first, very few others listening) then it is difficult to see how Howard Stern and those like him maintain the illusion that they are getting away with anything. As with a class clown in a school where there are suddenly no teachers, chances are that his antics will soon become tired, stale, and boring (perhaps even for the members of Stern's "student body" whose mental capacity is so limited that they get excited about Stern persuading a stripper to take her panties off for the 1,653rd time).

At least for now, it appears as if the satellite radio realm will indeed be largely without any real rules. At the end of 2004 the FCC denied a petition to make those broadcasts subject to the same indecency regulations as terrestrial radio (though two powerful Republican lawmakers later indicated that they would pursue authority to regulate all broadcasting). The commission said they do not "impose regulations regarding indecency on services lacking the *indiscriminate access* to children that characterizes broadcasting." Frankly, while I am personally in favor of any FCC decision that embraces less restriction, this ruling makes no logical sense at all.

Does the FCC think that the buttons on a satellite radio are somehow more difficult for a child to reach than those of a traditional radio? I guess the thinking could be that a child would never buy a satellite radio and the subscription service, but since when have youngsters ever made a habit of buying traditional radios on their own?

Of course that whole argument denies the reality that once an adult has purchased the satellite system any child will have easy access to it. It also is based on the absurd premise that the government can and should limit free expression because our speech rights are somehow outweighed by the naïve notion that the government can possibly prevent children from ever hearing "bad" words. Excuse me, but isn't that what *parents* are for?

Thankfully, some of our leaders are at least paying lip service to this extremely important principle. President Bush told C-SPAN in 2005, "As a free speech advocate, I often told parents who were complaining about content, you're the first line of responsibility;

they put an off button on the TV for a reason. Turn it off . . . Government can, at times, not censor, but call to account programming that gets over the line. The problem, of course, is the definition of 'over the line.'" Even then FCC Chairman Michael Powell recognized this reality when he wrote an editorial in the *New York Times* entitled, "Don't Expect Government to be a V-chip."

The apparent judgment by the FCC not to regulate satellite radio also brings into even greater question the basis for cable TV being largely outside the reach of the government. While the difference between a child's access to satellite and terrestrial radio may be minuscule, the distinction between how most children access cable versus broadcast TV channels has become totally nonexistent.

Again, the point here is not to argue for greater regulation, but rather to illustrate the flawed thinking behind the FCC's feeble attempts to prop up their prior nonsensical and overreaching decisions. Much like what would happen to Barbara Walters and many of her aging guests if her TV specials were stripped of the heavily filtered camera lenses, the faulty foundation underlying most FCC judgments has had its many flaws and cracks exposed by the harsh light of reality. While many vast advances in technology since the FCC's inception have laid bare the faulty reasoning behind much of what the commission does, it remains to be seen if enough of the right people will be appalled enough by what they see to actually do anything about it.

Often, the government's greatest and most insidious impact on restricting free speech in the realm of entertainment comes not in situations where rules have actually been broken, but rather through the chilling effect of fear and uncertainty. Because of the hypersensitivity toward litigation in the corporate culture, as well as the schizophrenic enforcement of the irrational and ambiguous guidelines, the vast majority of censorship in broadcasting comes from within. Self-censorship has become such an epidemic in broadcasting that, much like the smog in Los Angeles, it clouds everything and is so ubiquitous that it rarely even gets noticed or mentioned.

Broadcasters, especially those who work without a script, must develop a very strange and almost mysterious mental "blocking" mechanism. Without any formal training, or even barely a mention of the phenomenon, the brain of a commentator seems to create two separate filters to aid him in the process of word choice.

One is for profanity/indecency, where almost magically the same person who routinely drops the "f-bomb" during commercial breaks never comes close to doing so when the little red light is on. Since the FCC's new war on indecency, this filter has had to be significantly tightened, largely because broadcasting companies, in an effort to kiss up to the FCC, have made it mandatory in most on-air contracts that the company itself has the right to enforce vague indecency provisions at their own discretion. This means that a talk show host could be fired for "violating" an FCC rule even if the FCC never comes to the same conclusion or is even aware that a potential violation has occurred. There is even a movement to hold performers personally (and, according to one congressman, "criminally") liable for any fines incurred as a result of their broadcast—penalties that very easily could reach hundreds of thousands of dollars if some members of Congress get their way. If these developments materialize, the chilling impact they will have on speech should not be underestimated and go far beyond simply the use of "bad" words.

The second on-air filter is for general content, and, especially in talk radio, is a much finer (not to mention usually unreliable) sieve for words or sentences that may cause more trouble than they are worth. Here, a broadcaster must decide in a nanosecond whether a joke or flip comment is "over the line" and worth the risk of the potentially life-altering consequences. One of the reasons that our discussions of race relations and religion in this country is so stunted and broken is that it has become so incredibly dangerous to speak honestly about these subjects that most commentators simply prefer to stay away from them altogether.

While the notion of trying to figure out instantaneously what potential impact a chosen phrase may have while simultaneously making an immediate cost/benefit analysis of one's decision may seem bizarre (if not, over the long haul, nearly impossible) as well as extremely detrimental to the cause of honest and provocative commentary, it is not the most ridiculous form of self-censorship. Incredibly we are now seeing more examples of self-censorship in situations where everyone knows well in advance that what is going to be said/done/seen is within the rules and yet there are still decisions being made to keep perfectly legal content from being broadcast.

SAVING PRIVATE RYAN

"Free speech is the whole thing, the whole ball game. Free speech is life itself."
—Salman Rushdie, British novelist

Perhaps the most prominent example of the aforementioned trend occurred on Veterans Day, 2004, when the ABC television network planned to air Steven Spielberg's epic World War II movie *Saving Private Ryan*. Because of Spielberg's deal with the network, ABC was not allowed to edit the film in any way. This meant that numerous uses of profanity, including the "f-word," would be aired on "broadcast" TV. Of course this would not be the *first* time ABC had done so. On Veterans Day of both 2001 and 2002 the network did so without incident, posting parental advisories at every commercial break.

However, this time around dozens of ABC affiliates (mostly in "Red State" America) suddenly balked at the idea of airing *Saving Private Ryan*. Citing fears of FCC fines for indecency, sixty-six station managers decided to pull the plug on the movie and replace it with alternative programming. This despite pleas from Senator John McCain who issued a statement saying the film "comes nowhere near indecent."

So, what happened between 2002 and 2004? Two seemingly irrelevant incidents were blamed for changing the environment to the point that stations no longer felt safe airing a reality-based movie about one of history's most important days.

The first occurred at the 2003 Golden Globe Awards, which was broadcast live on NBC. While accepting his award Bono, the lead singer in the group U2, exclaimed, "This is really, really *fucking* brilliant!" About 200 complaints were registered with the FCC (the commission does not act unless it receives a formal complaint) and an investigation into the incident was opened.

Several months later the FCC ruled that since Bono had used the "f-word" as an *adjective* (technically it was a modifying adverb) and *not* as a verb, and the context was clearly not sexual in nature, that his use was not a violation of FCC regulations.

This decision stunned many observers (including this one who was astonished that the FCC had actually interpreted their own rules correctly and used a little bit of common sense), though it should not have. Since Bono's use of the word obviously had absolutely nothing to do with sex and was merely a way for him to express just *how* "brilliant" the award was, the original FCC verdict was absolutely correct.

However, that did not stop numerous news outlets and special interest groups from grossly mischaracterizing (either because of ignorance or an agenda) what the FCC had actually done. Organizations like the American Family Association sent out mailings asking its members to send 1,000,000 e-mails to the FCC and Congress to reject the ruling they described as: "The Federal Communications Commission has approved the use of the 'F' word for use on any TV show or radio program, *ANYTIME DAY OR NIGHT!*"

Even though doing so would have been well within the boundaries of the Constitution, this was not even *close* to what the FCC did in the Bono case. Despite that inconvenient reality, this bogus interpretation of the FCC ruling found fertile ground upon which to grow, largely because of an "urban legend" that has taken hold regarding what the rules actually are.

In the early 1970s, legendary comedian George Carlin began doing a hilarious anti-FCC rant referred to as the "Seven Words You Can Never Say on Television" routine. Up until Carlin's bit the FCC's authority to issue indecency fines had never been established legally. Ironically, it was the 1973 airing of Carlin's material on a Pacifica radio station that finally led to a 1978 Supreme Court ruling that dubiously upheld the FCC's authority in this area. Incredibly, there has never been another major legal test of the FCC's power, though in early 2005 there were numerous reports that, in an effort to stem the tide of overzealous FCC enforcement, the broadcast industry was finally planning on bringing one.

Today, thanks largely to the famous Carlin routine, most people understandably think that there actually is a list of words that can never be said on traditional radio or television. While in practice (ironically partially *because* of the Carlin bit) that is *essentially* the case, thankfully, there is no official list of legally "banned" words in the United States of America. At least not just yet.

But that does not mean that the government is not *trying* to ban words (is anyone else disturbed that most people think there *is* a list and seem to have no problem with that?!). After the original FCC Bono ruling there was actually a bill in Congress that would make certain words *illegal* to be aired at *any* time and in *any* context. Soon after that absurd bill was written, and over which there was absolutely no public outrage or well-deserved mocking, Janet Jackson exposed part of her right breast for a split second during the halftime of the Super Bowl and suddenly the anti-indecency crusade became powered by nuclear energy.

With the political climate then having been dramatically altered by the hysteria surrounding the Janet Jackson episode and with lawmakers being bombarded with angry correspondence from often ill-informed and prudish citizens, the FCC inexplicably completely reversed its prior ruling on Bono's benign use of the word *fucking* while basically *apologizing* for their original judgment, which had been both very sound and rather stern.

The dangers of radically changing the interpretation of the law based solely on perceived public sentiment were seen clearly by our Founding Fathers and have been well documented. However, there have been few more clear-cut or impactful examples than this one of it happening in a way that effectively curtailed a Constitutional right in a substantive manner.

So, almost entirely because of this sudden and illogical about-face by the FCC on the Bono case, the law of unintended consequences took hold and numerous TV stations were now absurdly afraid of showing *Saving Private Ryan* on Veterans Day. The decisions to drop the film about the D-Day invasion were made because the "f-word," in the least sexual context one could possibly imagine, was used frequently while often gruesome images of bodies being blown apart were shown on the screen. Considering that thousands of Americans gave their lives on the shores of Normandy in what they thought was a fight for freedom, one wonders if this boneheaded decision caused enough collective spinning in the massive graveyard there to create an earthquake.

Even more absurd than allegedly sexual words being restricted while shots of heads being blown off are not is that the

The DEATH of FREE SPEECH

122

FCC would not give prior permission for the *Saving Private Ryan* broadcast. This despite the fact that it had aired previously without incident and a powerful U.S. senator was lobbying for stations to exhibit some courage and not cave in to their fears of governmental reprisals. In a statement that may have set a new standard in defining irony, an FCC spokesperson told the *Hollywood Reporter* that to comment in advance of a broadcast was wrong because "that would be censorship."

Maybe if the broadcast in question was *live* and *unscripted* this would be a potentially true statement. However, for a *film* that has already aired twice in the past three years to fall under that category is ridiculous thinking even for a government agency. Of course none of this even touches the issue that the movie itself was a tribute to those who died to preserve our freedoms, and fears of reprisal from our *own* government kept much of the nation from being able to view it on Veterans Day.

Just to put the inane cherry on top of the silliness sundae, a month later, the then chairman of the FCC Michael Powell (himself the son of a famous military hero and now former secretary of state) quietly announced that he was recommending that indecency complaints against ABC for airing *Saving Private Ryan* be rejected (which they eventually were). According to the Reuters news agency, "Powell concluded that the agency should not take action against the stations that aired the acclaimed movie because the language was part of accurately portraying the story about the Allied invasion of Normandy during World War II."

No! Really? You don't think, Michael?! Wow. And it only took you several weeks after the third network airing of the movie to come to that startlingly cogent conclusion. Your father must be SO proud!

Showing once again that these decisions have profound and inadvertent negative consequences on important events, network newscasts have taken their cues from these episodes and have inappropriately applied these convoluted "principles" to the way they have covered actual and significant news stories.

Just days after numerous ABC affiliates chose not to air *Saving Private Ryan* because they were afraid to expose their viewers, even with a warning, to the "f-word" in a completely nonsexual context, an NBC news photographer in Iraq caught on tape an

American Marine shooting an injured insurgent/terrorist who was hiding in a Fallujah mosque.

The pictures were disturbing to some because they appeared to show the American soldier killing a helpless man who seemingly posed no threat. However, many of the terrorists had been booby-trapping dead bodies or faking being dead and blowing themselves up in order to take out a few more Americans before qualifying for their seventy-two virgins. Therefore, the context of the circumstances surrounding the shooting was critical to understanding whether the marine had acted properly.

But when NBC aired the tape, for some strange reason they felt compelled to edit out some of the words the marine's comrade said just before the shooting. What the NBC audience was allowed to hear was one Marine telling another about the terrorist in question: "He's faking he's dead, He's faking he's dead."

For many, the fact that the Marine who did the shooting was being warned by a fellow soldier that the terrorist in question was faking being dead (consistent with a tactic being deployed by the enemy to kill our guys) was enough to give the shooter the benefit of the doubt. However, the warning he received was not just that of a rather casual: "hey, that guy over there . . . look at him . . . he is faking he is dead . . . how cute is that?"

In reality, the warning had far more urgency attached to it. What was actually said was, "He's *fucking* faking he's dead! He's faking he's *fucking* dead!" Now considering that profanity on the battlefield is even more common than atheists praying in foxholes, the change in context may not be as dramatic as it would be if the same words were used, say, in a church, but there is no denying that there is a significant difference in the nature of the level of warning.

Regardless of how much the removal of the words altered the meaning of what happened, there is also no question that editing out the "f-word" was important, wrong, and unnecessary. Does anyone really believe that the FCC would have fined NBC for allowing words from a major news story that were completely non-sexual and which were critical to understanding the true nature of the event?

Similarly, CBS "news" magazine show *48 Hours Mystery* did a special on what has become known in the Los Angeles area as the

"Orange County Gang Rape Trial." This was a case in which three teenage boys were accused of essentially using a seemingly passed-out girl as a science experiment, prodding her insides with objects like a Snapple bottle, a lit cigarette and a pool cue, all while they videotaped their obscene acts.

Incredibly, one of the boys was allowed by CBS to describe what happened as nothing more than just "kinky sex." The un-suspecting audience, unaware of the details of the case, undoubt-edly thought that he was referring to three-on-one sex, which, in this day and age of relative teenage sexual promiscuity, may not seem all that outrageous to some. Incredibly, CBS did absolutely nothing to inform its viewers otherwise.

When I interviewed the show's reporter, Bill Lagattuta, about this particular omission within what amounted to a disgraceful in-fomercial for the defense, he comically claimed that, post–Janet Jackson, the network's censors were concerned about a potential indecency complaint if they actually reported what the boys had allegedly done. Apparently we have already reached the point where, thanks to fear of the FCC, a major network news program willingly omits crucial facts about a case they are devoting an en-tire hour to, even when the show airs *after* 10 p.m. and within the FCC's "safe harbor" time period.

I am honestly not sure if Lagattuta was lying in an effort to cover for CBS's horrendous reporting or if the chilling effects of governmental intimidation have really gotten that scary (or per-haps both).

I am certain, however, that if the powers that make such deci-sions really *do* think that the FCC is capable of making such colossal errors in judgment and no one attempts to stop it from overreaching its authority, then we clearly have much with which to be gravely concerned when it comes to our shrinking free speech rights, especially when it comes to what is allowed on a broadcast outlet.

JOHN KERRY & WHOOPI GOLDBERG

The FCC never even got a chance to decide on a somewhat similar situation involving another potentially important news story during the 2004 presidential election.

In one of his first attempts to explain the seemingly inexplicable maze of contradictions that was his stance on the Iraq war, Democratic candidate John Kerry told a print reporter, during what was clearly an "on the record" interview, that he voted for the war because he did not think the President was going "to *fuck* it up as badly as he did."

Even though the White House immediately jumped on Kerry's apparent mistake of using the "f-word" during a formal interview regarding such a serious matter, the remark got very little play in the news media. The fact that the mostly liberal press did not find his use of profanity *nearly* as interesting as when in 2000 then private citizen Dick Cheney *privately* told then governor George Bush that a New York Times reporter was a "major league asshole" was not surprising.

Nor was it as troubling as the reality that not *one* broadcast outlet dared to actually utter the very same word that a major presidential candidate chose to use to describe the current president's handling of perhaps the most important issue in the campaign.

Think about that. In a country founded on the notion that the press should be free to report not only the truth about our leaders, but also, just to make sure they are never intimidated by the government into silence, what they think *could* be true, every single news organization decided it was too dangerous to directly quote a man running for the highest office in the land while talking about an issue as important as his vote on going to war. (In a very troubling and somewhat related development, in 2005 the U.S. Supreme Court incredibly refused to even take up a case where a lower court had ruled that the press can be forced to pay damages for having accurately reported a politician's false charges against a rival, which may end up stripping the media of many of the legal protections upon which this paragraph was at least partially based.)

The absurdity and hypocrisy of this group-think cowardice became even more evident later in the campaign when Kerry constantly attempted to make an issue of Vice President Cheney's much-hyped private comments on the Senate floor where he told Senator Patrick Leahy to "go fuck himself." The gutless, biased, and inconsistent reporting of these events culminated in the insane situation of most of the public being completely unaware of the ridiculousness of Kerry trying to take advantage of the vice president's far less significant use of the "f-word," and the news media essentially unable (or unwilling) to call him on his duplicity at least partially because of fear of retribution from the FCC. The idea that Kerry could actually *benefit* because he used a word so obscene that most of the public was "protected" from hearing it, is, in itself, at least as obscene as the use of the word to begin with.

Similarly, the comments of comedienne/actress Whoopi Goldberg, at what would become an infamous Kerry campaign fundraiser at Radio City Music Hall, were censored to the point that to this day there is still some uncertainty as to exactly what she did say. All we do know for sure is that she attempted to do a comedy routine based on the president's last name being a synonym for one of the more derogatory slang terms used to describe female genitalia.

Kerry made the mind-boggling blunder of referring to Goldberg's rant (as well as the other extremely hate-filled celebrity commentary bashing the president) as representing the "heart and soul of America." Because the Kerry campaign never acceded to the Republicans' request to release the tape of the event (even though they made the unprecedented promise to never use it in a commercial) and the news media never pressured them to do so, we do not really know if Goldberg used the "p-word," "c-word," or some combination of both.

For some reason, despite the obvious political significance of the event, no one ever actually reported what specific words Goldberg used to refer to the president of the United States and which were part of a presentation that was praised by a presidential candidate. Apparently either having access to more information, or simply not needing to know the details, the Slim-Fast diet company immediately fired Goldberg as their spokesperson.

Here are some of the incredibly benign and spineless ways in which what Goldberg said was reported in the *written* press, which is not even subject to any FCC regulations or restrictions:

> Whoopi Goldberg was fired as spokesman for Slim-fast diet products because she dared to poke fun at President Bush during a Kerry fund-raiser at Radio City Music Hall.
>
> (Syndicated Columnist Bill Press)

> At a John Kerry fundraiser July 8, Whoopi Goldberg delivered several crude puns on Bush's name. Complaints led to Goldberg's firing as a Slim-fast spokeswoman and admonishments from both parties.
>
> (Reporter William Keck, *USA Today*)

> Whoopi Goldberg was fired by Slim-Fast for, well, being Whoopi Goldberg. At a star-studded fund-raiser for John Kerry, Goldberg, well-known for her liberal bent, riffed on her genitalia and the President's name.
>
> (Reporter Kristin Dizon,
> *Seattle Post-Intelligencer*)

It is extraordinary that exactly what Goldberg said was so unbelievably and universally censored, even in an age when nearly *EVERYTHING* gets "reported" *somewhere* on the Internet, that no one seems to even know what words she actually used. This reality is a prime example of how laws made by the government can seep into the societal consciousness (and vice versa) to the point that even things that are clearly not against the law become so in a "de facto" manner because of fear and ignorance, which just happen to be two qualities in overabundance when it comes to the news media and politicians.

In *some* areas of life, having society come up with rules that are even more restrictive on behavior than the actual law is desirable and even necessary. Freedom of speech should not usually be considered one of those places.

Beyond the issue of why Goldberg's comments were not publicly reported, there is also the matter of her punishment. It is important to note here that in all of the Speech Punishment cases that we have reviewed to this point (most of which I have argued resulted in unfair penalties), I have never denied the *right* of an employer to fire a public person because of something they have said. If a comment made by a public person renders them no longer able to do their job effectively because society now views them unfavorably, then their employer should be able to terminate that person (within the bounds of their contract) if they think they can no longer be of benefit to the company.

This is why I wholeheartedly supported the firing of Al Campanis from the Los Angeles Dodgers. There was no doubt that, as someone who was in an extremely public management position with the responsibility of hiring and firing others, he could no longer be sufficiently trusted or respected after his blatantly racist statements on *Nightline*.

Most of the objectionable examples of Speech Punishment that have been raised in these pages have dealt with situations in which the employers, usually egged on by the news media, have made decisions which were not based on the "victims" saying anything that *should* have diminished their standing in the community or even really *did* weaken their ability to do their job. This was especially true in those situations where their occupation was largely *based* on them giving their opinions.

In this context, I think it was perfectly appropriate for the Slim-Fast Company to fire Whoopi Goldberg as their spokesperson. There is *no* doubt that, after referring to the president in such an insulting manner at a public event, having their company associated so closely with Goldberg was going to significantly hurt Slim-Fast's image in the minds of a large portion of the weight-loss-system-buying public. In contrast, there was no evidence, for instance, that Fuzzy Zoeller's comments about Tiger Woods eliminated or even affected his ability to help sell golf clubs for Kmart.

Not only was there no uncertainty that her strangely reported comments *did* do massive damage to her ability to sell diet products (or anything else) to a huge segment of the overweight population, but there also was very little ambiguity about whether it was *legitimate* for the "Red State" part of the electorate to view her in that diminished way. After all, one could make a very strong argument that for an entertainer to use their power in a manner that is in *any* way politically partisan is to essentially make themselves ineligible for the *privilege* of being a commercial endorser.

A public person certainly has the right to use his or her notoriety to try to influence the political process, but if an entertainer wants to use whatever real or perceived capital they have with the public to sway our votes, they do so at the risk of falling out of favor with a segment of the population. Those are just the rules and, in comparison with most of the tenets of Speech Punishment, they actually make a lot of sense.

So Goldberg's firing would have been potentially warranted if she had simply spoken in an *inoffensive* manner at the Kerry fundraiser (though for reasons of political correctness that never would have happened), but for her to do so in such a blatantly inappropriate and offensive way when speaking about the president makes the case against her a slam dunk.

Of course, that does not mean that others have not said similar things just as theoretically punishable and gotten away with barely a slap on the wrist. In late 1998, in the midst of the impeachment of Bill Clinton, fading movie star Alec Baldwin went on national TV (where, unlike the case of Goldberg, his comments were actually seen by millions of people) and essentially urged the audience to kill House Judiciary Chairman Henry Hyde. On NBC's *Late Night with Conan O'Brien*, an incensed Baldwin unleashed the following diatribe:

> I am thinking to myself, in other countries they are laughing at us twenty-four hours a day and I'm thinking to myself, if we were in other countries, we would all right now, all of us together, [Baldwin starts to shout] all of us together would go down to Washington and we would stone Henry Hyde to death! We would stone him to death! [studio crowd cheers] Wait! Shut up! Shut up! No shut up! I'm not finished. We would stone Henry Hyde to death and we would go to their homes and we'd kill their wives and their children. We would kill their families. [Baldwin stands up, yelling] What is happening in this country? What is happening? UGHHH!

Probably because most of the news media agreed at least with the spirit of his tirade, Baldwin's bizarre outburst received remarkably little attention and there was almost no formal backlash against him. While his career has continued to slide and his marriage to actress Kim Basinger has since ended, Baldwin still manages to make it into the occasional significant movie role and guest stints on *Saturday Night Live*. Even more inexplicably he is still routinely paid handsomely to voice commercials for high-profile products (it has always seemed strange to me that Hollywood and Madison Avenue make a giant distinction between endorsing a product on camera and doing so via only one's voice).

Clearly, if what Goldberg said deserved her banishment from the lavish and comfy world of conventional commercial endorsements, by essentially urging violence against a congressman and his family, so did Baldwin. But as we have already documented in these pages, the rules of Speech Punishment, much like last-minute airline fares, are hardly ever guided by rationality and almost never result in justice.

The "rules" that led to Whoopi Goldberg's firing as an endorser, while typically poorly enforced, also work in reverse. One of the most underappreciated elements of the modern media is that the tail of commercial considerations is wagging the dog of programming content, especially in the area of politically oriented commentary. Everyone knows (or should by now) that, to varying degrees, ratings drive what kind of news we get on all varieties of media outlets. What is not as well known is that it is not really *ratings* that ultimately drive the news/commentary process, but rather *revenue* that determines what shows get and stay on the air.

Most of the public fails to realize that the more controversial the nature of the content, the greater gap there tends to be between the ratings and the revenue generated by a particular program. If a show has a huge audience but its content is such that advertisers are afraid to be associated with it for fear of the host saying something that will offend potential customers, then the ability to sell advertising at the normal rate for that size of an audience tends to be greatly curtailed. For many broadcasters, this creates a situation much worse than being judged simply on ratings.

While there are numerous problems inherent in having a broadcast's value determined only by how many people were exposed to it, at least that manner is in some way rational and "democratic." But having a program's success dependent mostly on whether advertisers will actually pay to be heard or seen on that show provides an entirely new layer of insanity that is far more likely to send a broadcaster to the nuthouse and has far more damaging repercussions on our public dialogue.

The real stupidity of this situation is that because of the unique connection made between the host and the listener, opinion-based programming (at least on radio) should actually be seen as a fantastic buy for advertisers. Quite simply, the type of person who is a fan of a highly opinionated and inevitably controversial host/program is going to be *FAR* more loyal to the advertisers that are associated with that broadcast entity than someone who is a consumer of a much blander and less memorable show. Especially in this increasingly fragmented media world, the unique connection between host and listener cannot be underestimated from a marketing perspective.

Unfortunately for people make a living by giving their opinions on commercial outlets, those who buy and sell the advertising on most stations are creatures of habit with little imagination or appetite for risk. When I was in Louisville at WHAS-AM, at one point I had 15.1 percent of the radio audience during my time slot (a ridiculously large number that would be impossible to achieve at 99 percent of stations in the country) and yet largely because I was creating so much "heat" I was not offered one reasonable "commercial endorsement" during my first year there. Since I am not a big fan of such commercials, this did not bother me much. However, the lack of personal endorsements made it FAR easier for my bosses to fire me when the proverbial crap finally hit the fan. My situation, though unusual because of its dramatic nature, is fairly common in an industry where ruffling feathers with one's words is often not at all what it is cracked up to be.

The self-proclaimed "King of All Media," Howard Stern, is the exception that proves this rule.

HOWARD STERN

"The right to be heard does not automatically include the right to be taken seriously."

—Hubert H. Humphrey, former vice-president
and presidential candidate

Despite his reliance on highly sexual and potentially offensive material, Howard Stern is still able to produce enormous revenue for his company. Though he was dropped by six Clear Channel stations in 2004 over fears of the crackdown on indecency and some of his affiliates in the "Red States" have had some trouble translating large audiences into cash, Stern makes his main employer, Infinity Broadcasting, huge profits. Stern's show is such a cash cow for Infinity that they have been willing to endure millions of dollars in FCC fines and have allowed him to stay on the air even after he essentially turned his program into an infomercial for satellite radio after announcing he is moving there in 2006.

However, the financial success of Stern's radio show is based on a fairly small group of extremely out of the "mainstream" advertisers who have capitalized on the incredible allegiance Stern's fans have toward anything that supports his show. You will never hear a commercial for Ivory Soap or Wonder Bread on his program, but because a Stern endorsement for the local strip club or breast implant doctor is a sure bet to produce dramatic results and "augmented" sales for advertisers, the show is still one of the most profitable in radio.

Because television relies almost exclusively, at least at the national level, on "mainstream" advertisers, the capability for that medium to absorb and embrace controversial content is dramatically diminished in comparison to that of radio. In recent years, TV networks have become far more hesitant to offend viewers with the commercials themselves and are increasingly refusing to even air any ad content that could be considered remotely controversial.

At least four commercials were disallowed from the 2005 Super Bowl telecast for various reasons, including one that made fun of censorship itself! After the previous year's Janet Jackson incident, even the relatively fearless Fox Network was afraid of airing ads that were remotely edgy (though nixing the one that showed Mickey Rooney's bare ass may have actually been a good idea). There is no doubt that for the creators, buyers, and sellers of "mainstream" advertising the current atmosphere is one in which safety is valued far above the speech of both the ads and the programs on which they run. The impact that this phenomenon has on the nature of free speech on broadcast TV talk shows can simply not be overestimated.

Due to their need to be acceptable to traditional advertisers with a national reach, programs like NBC's *Meet the Press*, CBS's *Face the Nation*, and ABC's *This Week* are much like the castrated poodles of the highly competitive dog pound that is the opinion-oriented broadcasting world, and their ratings have suffered because of it. It is no coincidence that cable TV programs allow their hosts and guests much more freedom of speech than do the national broadcast variety. Because cable companies can sell localized ads that can be afforded by companies that are neither national nor mainstream, talk shows on cable news channels with relatively small audiences can survive with commercials mostly for order-by-phone products like the ubiquitous cable ads for those hoping to shed a few extra pounds, remove unsightly body hair, or enhance an undersized penis.

Because of these factors, opinionated commentary on *local* TV is as rare as an unemployed, short, bald, fat man dating a supermodel. Conversely, when a host or guest says something on Fox, CNN, or MSNBC that offends a viewer in Los Angeles, Chicago, or New York there is no place to focus the rage and no one to pressure into bailing from the program. This is because all the ads are either *extremely* local (meaning, played through the local cable outlet, they have no actual connection to the show and probably did not even buy that specific program), or they are run by a tiny national company with no public relations department. Often this variety of advertiser is made up of little more than a P.O. box and a phone number, and could not care less if someone in Iowa is upset with Fox as long as enough other people keep buying their product.

However, because of the way ads are sold, it is almost impossible for a local TV station to air anything remotely controversial because any area business would be far too easily associated with the program and therefore much too vulnerable to viewer protests. If Fox's Bill O'Reilly ticks off 10,000 people nationwide but only a few in each town, those viewers have absolutely no impact, but if a *local* TV station upsets even 100 customers enough for them to complain to a local advertiser, then there is a huge problem.

Consequently, local news programs are far more averse to tackling tough issues (especially those that may impact an advertiser) and the only commentary they air tends to have less bite than the opening question on *Larry King Live* or Oprah's treatment of a big-time celebrity.

Somewhat like Howard Stern's story, my experience in Louisville TV was a temporary exception that proved this rule.

In Louisville I cohosted a fifteen-minute commentary show on the NBC affiliate that aired once a week during the second half of a 7 p.m. newscast. For a number of reasons, the show had to be the only one in the nation of its kind.

First, the station was one of the few with a 7 p.m. local newscast and a place during the week to put the show where it would be noticed. Second, the station was run by a general manager that once prided himself on taking chances and stirring things up on a local level (the existence of such a person in that position is even rarer than the largely imaginary poor guy with the hot girlfriend) who was also fairly conservative politically. Third, I was the host of an extremely successful radio show which provided a cross-promotional tie-in with this TV station that had just signed an expensive agreement to do the weather on my radio station. Fourth, I had an enormous amount of on-air TV experience and we were able to find an excellent liberal cohost named John Yarmuth who was well-known in the community and with whom I shared great chemistry.

If any of these many factors had not been completely in order, the show never would have gotten started. Even with these fairly miraculous circumstances in place, actually making the show a success was no bargain. As it turned out, we did just as well as the news program we were replacing, but those ratings were completely worthless to the station because of the opinionated nature of the show. No local advertiser would possibly take a chance on buying spots on the program when they could easily face boycotts from the local liberal activists (one of whom was a racial provocateur named Rev. Louis Coleman, who had made himself into the Louisville version of Al Sharpton, only fatter and not nearly as smart).

So with no real sponsorship to fall back on, when I was fired from my radio show, the NBC general manager could not justify keeping the TV show, even though he, as well as thousands of viewers, absolutely loved the program. A couple of months after I was fired from the radio gig, the TV show was dropped like the proverbial hot potato and the station went back to running the far safer extended weather and "kicker" stories that they had done previously.

One episode of speech restriction that occurred during the waning days of that TV show illustrated the increasingly pervasive and insidious impact that cooperate conflicts often have on the public getting important information. Before I was fired from the radio station, my top boss told me in a private meeting that he would like me to stop talking negatively about Ben Chandler, the Democratic gubernatorial nominee (an edict the boss would later admit to under oath in a deposition taken in relation to the lawsuit that came out of my subsequent firing). His "thinking" was that he was concerned he would not be able to do business with the state of Kentucky if I was constantly attacking the would-be governor on the air. To say that I was absolutely stunned by this decree would be like saying Ron Goldman was only mildly surprised when he witnessed O. J. Simpson killing his ex-wife and then turning on him. I knew that there was no way that I could remain credible on the air if I abided by his wishes, and after consulting with my direct boss, I decided not to do so.

Before my firing from the radio show the Democratic candidate had agreed to appear on the TV program for what promised to be an extremely contentious live special broadcast. After I no longer had the bully pulpit of the radio show, the candidate suddenly backed out of his promise. By any standard, a major candidate for governor of Kentucky pulling out of a scheduled live prime-time TV interview because he is seemingly afraid of his controversial questioner is a huge news story in a place like Louisville. However, no one reported it. Why? Because virtually every single media outlet had a corporately motivated disincentive to tell the story.

The lone local daily newspaper was an avid supporter of the candidate and absolutely despised me because I had skewered their obvious bias. The other TV stations in town did not want to give publicity to another station. The lone news radio station had just fired me and did not even want to admit I existed. Even the TV station I was still temporarily working for did not want to endanger their relationship with that radio station, and the TV station's GM not only heavily edited my script when I tried to talk about the situation, but required the show to be taped when it was usually live. I was also largely prevented from telling the full story on my personal Web site because of a release I had been forced to sign in order to receive the severance package in my termination agreement with the radio station. Such releases, in which people are essentially blackmailed into giving up their free speech rights, may be the most common and underreported weapon used by corporate America against the truth becoming public.

In the end, the gubernatorial candidate finally did appear on the show at a later date, but I was heavily restricted in what I was allowed to ask him. He ended up losing the race, but was almost immediately elected to Congress, all without the vast majority of the public ever being aware that this issue even existed.

In this difficult corporate environment, how is it that Howard Stern can have a TV show (essentially a rebroadcast of highlights of his radio program) on the E! Entertainment Network? Simply because the explosion of national cable channels has created a situation where relatively tiny but loyal audiences sliced from a huge national pie are enough to sustain the show with the same type of advertisers that support his radio program (unfortunately, despite my "boob"-related downfall in Louisville, selling ads to local breast enhancement doctors for the politically oriented TV show we were doing was just not a viable option).

Also, on cable TV, Stern is exempt (sort of) from FCC indecency regulations. While his TV show does not go nearly as far as many on HBO with regard to showing nudity, he routinely allows things to air that would surely get him heavily fined on a broadcast network.

In fact, the FCC proposed a record $1.2 million fine against Fox TV for a raunchy episode of *Married by America* that, complete with strippers, whipped cream, pixilated nudity and spanking, looked as if it was cut right from Howard Stern's TV show.

Interestingly, it turned out that the FCC received only *THREE* completely separate official protests against that Fox program. Those three complaints would not only cause Fox to be fined, but that ruling would later result in the ridiculous specter of the network using pixilation to cover up the naked butt of a *cartoon character* on an episode of *The Family Guy* which had run without incident five years earlier.

Similarly, but even more exasperatingly, the FCC began an investigation of NBC's coverage of the opening ceremonies of the 2004 Summer Olympic Games because just *NINE* citizens filed indecency complaints. (It is important to note the Olympic broadcast had well over three times the audience of the Fox show.)

What caused such uproar about the Olympic Games? Well, the Opening Ceremonies featured a group of male dancers dressed as anatomically correct ancient Greek art and a topless female dancer wearing little more than body paint. While the performers' lack of costume certainly did raise eyebrows (luckily none of the men playing Greek art also got a rise out of the situation), NBC was careful never to actually show the semi-nude actors during their *taped* broadcast. But despite that inconvenient reality, plus the fact that NBC's Olympic program won the title of "family-friendliest special of 2004" at the Family Television Awards, the FCC instigated an investigation based on *nine* viewers who apparently were offended by something they did not really see.

One of the many dirty little secrets of the FCC system is that broadcasting companies are now being fined millions of dollars and huge programming decisions are being radically altered because of literally only a handful of anti–free speech "morality" zealots with far too much time on their hands.

During the years of both 2000 and 2001 there were fewer than 350 indecency complaints to the FCC. In 2002 the number jumped to 14,000. In 2003 it skyrocketed to 240,000. During just the first ten months of 2004 there were over *one million* official protests.

Before you start to think that these facts obviously disprove the previous premise, keep in mind that just over half of the 2004 complaints were prompted by the Janet Jackson Super Bowl "wardrobe malfunction." A survey of the other 500,000 protests found that 99.8 percent of them came from the very same conservative Christian activist group, the Parents Television Council (PTC).

Luckily, at least some of the PTC's more ridiculous complaints have been rejected. In January of 2005, the FCC turned down their requests to fine the hit show *Friends* because there was discussion of fertility treatment at a medical office, the *Gilmore Girls* over two situations where characters *talked* about someone being nude, and the legendary cartoon *The Simpsons* for having students carry picket signs that asked, "What would Jesus *glue*?" Depressingly, only three of the five commissioners (two of whom had already stated their intention to leave the FCC) voted against all of the proposed sanctions described here, while two, including that nutty Democrat Michael Copps, did not. Once again, the situations in which clearly allowable speech is *almost* punished by the government provide the most striking proof of how scary the climate really has become.

The vast majority of these mostly silly complaints were not really even filed by actual individuals, but rather as a result of the PTC sending out e-mails to their mailing list and getting their followers to fill out ready-made forms from their Web site. In all likelihood, most of those claiming to be offended by these "indecent" broadcasts probably never even saw or listened to the program in question.

While the miracle of the Internet has been one of the few areas in which freedom of speech has actually expanded in recent years, with regard to the sudden exponential increase in FCC complaints the Web has been used extremely effectively as a weapon to dramatically inflate the perceived influence of a stunningly small number of people in their war to rid the airwaves of programming they simply do not like and probably do not even consume.

In the case of Howard Stern, there is actually a wacky lawyer from Florida with *far* too much time on his hands who fervently believes (with some evidence) that his obsessive recording of Stern's show, combined with his fanatical quest to have Stern knocked off the air, caused Stern to be removed from six Clear Channel stations in early 2004. While the reality of the circumstances is more complex than that, it is not too much of a stretch to say that just one highly motivated nut job (and I know from personal experience that this guy definitely qualifies) can actually exert enough pressure on the FCC so that a huge corporation decides that the potential governmental fines no longer make airing an extremely popular program economically justifiable.

It is important to point out that the amount of money that broadcasting companies were fined by the FCC also exploded *exponentially* in 2004. Prior to that year, FCC fines were extremely rare and, in all likelihood, had little or no negative economic influence on programming. In fact, a strong argument can be made that the fines that Howard Stern incurred (up until 2004) were actually a *positive* net effect on his show's bottom line because of the massive amount of free attention and publicity they created during a time period when his show was just starting to get syndicated.

While Stern had always pretended to be outraged by the nitpicking of his FCC "boogieman," up until 2004 he used his status as the poster boy for indecency masterfully while simultaneously creating for himself the image of the crusader for justice against a mean, faceless "big brother." However, in 2004, after that boogieman suddenly turned out to be real and grew some rather sharp teeth, it was apparent that this was no longer just a game. Stern quickly realized that due to the increase in the frequency and dollar amounts of the FCC fines that his show was on the verge of becoming economically unviable. One 2005 bill passed by the House and sent to the Senate would raise the limit on potential fines to $500,000 *per incident, per station* and would effectively be a death sentence for any program like Stern's.

If this bill passes, according to *Rolling Stone* magazine, "For the price of Janet Jackson's 'wardrobe malfunction' during the Super Bowl, you could cause the wrongful death of an elderly patient in a nursing home and still have enough money left to create dangerous mishaps at two nuclear reactors." Vermont's "Independent" congressman, Rep. Bernie Sanders, rightfully castigated the vote, saying, "Free expression and First Amendment rights are the real target of this legislation. This is not what America is about." If such a plan ever does become law it would simply send broadcasting back to the days of *Leave It to Beaver*, if not end it as we know it.

Realizing the environment had radically been altered, Stern got serious and mounted a counteroffensive. His first target was none other than one of America's most beloved figures: Oprah Winfrey.

Seemingly deciding that if you can't beat them then you might as well join them, Stern engineered his own series of FCC indecency complaints against Oprah. Outwardly akin to Saddam Hussein trying to get the United Nations to impose sanctions on the United States (but without the benefit of the oil-for-food kickbacks), Stern's attack on Winfrey actually did have some merit. Winfrey had recently aired a program on teen sex in which a guest had been allowed to use graphic sexual language that was almost identical to that for which Stern had been fined by the FCC.

Stern was trying to make the valid point that hypocrisy and inconsistency run rampant in the FCC's decision-making process. He was also attempting to illustrate the equally important (if true) notion that a person's *popularity* may have a profound impact on who gets to break the rules and who does not. Stern claimed that the double standard evidenced by the disparate manner in which he and Oprah were treated by the FCC was a clear indication that he was picked on because he was perceived as a "bad boy," while she was seen as the "golden child" of the broadcast world.

While there is no doubt that those perceptions do exist (and if the law were being enforced on the basis of who was more or less likeable, that would be a grave injustice), there is little evidence through which to validate Stern's claims. While surely the government, like any other human entity, is more than prone to treating people differently based on their likability, the reality is that the FCC mandate to enforce indecency standards has always supposed to have been based on the context of the words and not just the utterances themselves.

The intent of Oprah's program was unquestionably to *educate* parents about what kind of sexual activity their kids may be engaging in (though there is also little doubt that some of the subject matter was chosen for shock/ratings value as well). Meanwhile, the objective of the Stern show was simply to titillate the audience.

In a weird way the rules have been set up so that if you want to hear the words in question and get some *enjoyment* out of listening to them, then the broadcast is probably "indecent," while if you do *not* like hearing the very same words then the show is probably perfectly safe. Similarly, exposing Janet Jackson's rather fine nipple on TV is illegal, while showing the breast of an old lady during a medical operation is not, though that did not stop NBC's *ER* from absurdly editing such a scene in the weeks after the 2004 Super Bowl.

While fining Stern but not Oprah is perfectly justifiable by following the FCC guidelines, once again the absurdity of the system was exposed because the commission had just ruled in the Bono case that, for all intents and purposes, context does *NOT* count any more. Here, as in many areas of Speech Punishment, the arbiters of right and wrong are trying to have it both ways while discarding any legal or logical foundation for their actions in the process. While he may not have been technically right, Stern's attack on Oprah certainly did expose the FCC commissioners as hypocrites.

Unconvinced, or at least undeterred, by the context argument, Stern decided to take aim at an even higher authority than Oprah (if there even *is* such a thing). Convinced that he was the target of a political witch hunt designed to help a reelection campaign, Stern unleashed his wrath on President Bush. Seemingly motivated by equal parts paranoia, hubris, and a desire for publicity/credibility, Stern transformed his program into a virtual nonstop Bush-bashing session.

Certain that the president had taken time out of his busy schedule to personally order the FCC to go after him in order to score political points with Christian conservatives, Stern switched from being a post-9/11 Bush supporter to openly campaigning for his defeat. He even called into a San Francisco radio talk show where then FCC Chairman Powell was a guest and accused him of being an unqualified puppet who got his job through his father (though he was actually appointed to the commission by Bill Clinton).

While Stern did not seem to have much impact on Powell, at one point in the 2004 campaign several liberal columnists, armed with some very dubious poll numbers, went so far as to pontificate that the Howard Stern voter could actually turn the election against the president. As it turned out, Stern's relentless attacks on President Bush had little or no impact on the final outcome (perhaps the Stern voters thought the election was being held on a Wednesday) and the president was somehow reelected despite the objections of a radio DJ whose studio boasts a "spanking machine" that it uses on the show's more daring female guests.

While Howard Stern's FCC issues did not seem to have a major influence on how we chose our most recent president, there is no question that several other free speech matters did have a profound effect on the process.

CHAPTER FIVE: CAMPAIGN 2004 . . . AMERICA DODGES A BULLET

> *"The greatest threat to freedom is the absence of criticism."*
>
> —Wole Soyinka, Nigerian political activist

If there is one area of life that our Founding Fathers believed should be given complete and total insulation from governmental intervention and restriction on speech, it was undoubtedly the political arena. Obviously when it came to deciding our elections, the framers of the Constitution knew well the dangers inherent in allowing the government to control or disarm, in any way, the very weaponry of political campaigns: words and ideas. This was one of the reasons why they were so remarkably unambiguous when beginning the First Amendment with the unequivocal words, "Congress shall make *no* law. . . ."

However, if the 2004 election cycle is any indication, it is, without a doubt, in this very realm that governmental constraints on speech are in danger of having their most dramatic impact. While in the end, the results of the 2004 election may not have been decided by this reality, it is difficult to imagine that those who created this country would be anything other than horrified by the numerous impediments to free speech during the campaign. Just because the essence of their original Constitution remains mostly intact (at least for now), does not mean that we should not all be gravely concerned that elements of it have been left in such tatters

by what happened in 2004 that its ability to survive another similar battering may be questionable at best.

While the influence of attempts to constrict campaign speech
can be seen within countless aspects of the presidential race, it
may be most instructive to fully examine just one element of
2004's battle for the White House.

On a warm summer night in his hometown of Boston, Senator
John Kerry took to the stage to accept the Democratic presidential
nomination by dramatically saluting the audience and proudly declaring, "I'm John Kerry, and I'm reporting for duty!"

The gesture was intended to introduce Kerry as a Vietnam
War hero to a huge audience of American TV viewers, many of
whom had little or no knowledge of his personal history and may
have been prone to see the liberal senator as weak on defense issues. While the stunt came off as an insecure act of contrived
overkill, its real lasting damage to Kerry would come in the form
of opening the pages of a book that the senator, literally, did not
want the electorate to fully read. His campaign would spend
much of the remaining months leading up to November desperately trying to make sure that voters had as little chance as possible to know the *full* story of John Kerry's Vietnam experience.

While *much* has been said about whether John Kerry's military record *should* have been an issue in the campaign and
whether those who attempted to educate the American people
about it had a political agenda or ties to the Republican Party, the
vast majority of voters were, for better or worse, abjectly ignorant
of the facts of Kerry's military service. No matter how one views
Kerry's war record, it is impossible to argue, especially after he did
everything possible to make it the centerpiece of the Democratic
convention, that his actions before, during, and after going to
Vietnam were at least extremely relevant in assessing his fitness
to be commander in chief.

In the not-so-distant past, the news media would have fully
examined the many issues surrounding Kerry's Vietnam experience, informing the vast majority of the public who would then
make their own decision with regard to whether those facts
should impact their vote.

However, in the last generation the so-called "mainstream"
news media (TV networks and major newspapers) have allowed a

distinct pro-Democratic/anti-Republican bias to permeate virtually every aspect of the media's political coverage. This has created a situation in which it is *far* more likely for news stories that may be interpreted as "bad" for Democrats to mysteriously fall through the ever-widening cracks of the media's coverage, or, at the very least, be muted to the point that only the most fervent of news consumers, most of whom are not politically pliable to begin with, are ever made aware of them.

Add to this development the enormous fragmentation of media outlets as well as the exponential increase in non-news entertainment choices, and the result is that it has never been easier for massive portions of the American electorate to remain blissfully ignorant about any given news story. We now live in a world where, thanks to the Internet, nearly everything gets *reported* somewhere, but it is that which gets *repeated* over and over that reaches the largely busy/apathetic "independents" who usually decide elections.

In short, if the news media does not go out of their way to jam a story down our throats most of us will never even know it happened. When it came to John Kerry's Vietnam experience it was obvious that most of the news media was completely unwilling to do any of the heavy lifting essential to making our political system work in a remotely fair and efficient manner.

So with the old "mainstream" news outlets unwilling to fully inform the public about a subject around which Kerry based his party's convention, the "dirty work" (as some in the campaign would disparagingly refer to it) of telling the complete story was left to normal citizens willing to endure great risk and personal hardship to tell their version of the truth.

The Swift Boat Veterans for Truth was a group of Vietnam vets who had served "with" John Kerry and were outraged that the Massachusetts senator was portraying himself as a one-dimensional war hero. They strongly believed that Kerry's record showed that he unquestionably lied about his service over the years on numerous occasions, greatly exaggerated his heroism, and perhaps even engaged in treasonous acts while protesting the Vietnam war.

While their specific charges are too numerous to completely outline here, many of them were very serious, compelling, and seemingly highly credible. Among the most severe and relevant allegations levied by the "Swift Vets" were that at least two of the three Purple Hearts Kerry needed to end his super-quick four-month Vietnam tour were awarded under highly suspicious circumstances. For instance, Kerry had written in his war journal that he and his shipmates had never been under enemy fire, *after* he had already put in for his first Purple Heart, which resulted from a wound that required almost no medical attention. There was also ample evidence to suggest that his third Purple Heart (the one he would use to get himself out of Vietnam) was awarded for a self-inflicted injury that may have occurred when Kerry was goofing around with a hand grenade in a pile of rice.

The Swift Vets also claimed Kerry perjured himself and destroyed troop and POW morale when testifying before the Senate in 1971 about alleged war crimes by U.S. soldiers, offenses for which he had no evidence. They pointed out that ironically the only soldier they knew who had engaged in such illegal activity may have been John Kerry himself. Though Kerry had admitted having committed "atrocities" in the past, he has never been forced to be specific as to what he meant by that. Though the Swift Vets produced several stories of Kerry having killed innocent civilians (including shooting a nearly naked teenage boy in the back), those accounts were among the most difficult to verify and seemed to be largely mitigated by the "fog of war" phenomenon.

Kerry's former mates also detailed how the future senator may have engaged in a treasonous act when he met with leaders of the North Vietnamese enemy in Paris while the war was still being waged. They also produced strong evidence that Kerry had wrongly accused the United States of an illegal act when in 1986 on the floor of the U.S. Senate he claimed to have been in Cambodia during Christmas of 1968. Kerry was supposedly so sure that he was in Cambodia, which would have been against the law for a U.S. soldier at the time, that he twice insisted in his speech that the experience was *"SEARED"* in his memory. Later, when evidence surfaced that Kerry's Cambodia story just did not hold water (including the fact that he implied he was there under orders from President Nixon, who was not yet even president), he quietly had it removed from his authorized biography, *Tour of Duty*.

The Swift Vets also raised the persuasive specter that Kerry was hiding *further* indiscretions and limiting their ability to prove their current allegations by refusing to sign "Form 180" so that his entire military record would be open to the public. Kerry understood that with most of the news media blocking for him on his shaky war record all he needed to do was make sure there was enough confusion among voters for him to get the benefit of the doubt. Without access to all of the available documentation, Kerry's willing accomplices in the media were perfectly willing to ignore the story. He also gambled, correctly, that deep down the media did not *want* to find what was likely in those records, and therefore the mainstream press had no incentive to pressure him into doing what would seem to be mandatory for a man running for president largely on his (at least partially hidden) military record.

While the purpose of this chapter is not to fully adjudicate the claims of Kerry's critics, as someone who has researched them extensively and who, like the rest of America, has been given no alternative explanations from the Kerry camp, I strongly believe that most of what the Swift Vets asserted during their campaign was based at least partially in fact. While I have some doubts about a few of their innumerable charges, I know for *sure* that, while reasonable people could easily differ over the political significance of the answers, there was *no* doubt as to the legitimacy of the essential questions that the group raised. In a telling testament to the dysfunctional nature of the process, these are questions that, for reasons that will become obvious, barely ever got asked and, at least until the election was long over, *never* got answered.

Not long after the balloons and confetti had been swept up from the floor of the Democratic convention, the Swift Vets aired their powerful first TV commercial aimed at spreading their truths about John Kerry. The ad was fueled by only a couple of hundred thousand dollars that had been scraped together after a well attended but pathetically reported news conference announcing the group's formation months earlier. However, getting the money to produce and air the ad was only the first of many hurdles for the Swift Vets.

If Senator John McCain, the champion of the extremely popular (at least among the news media) campaign finance reform movement, had had his way, the ad would never have been seen on a traditional TV outlet. The ad was only "allowed" to air on the few small stations on which it was purchased because the Swift Vets had been designated as a tax-exempt political organization known as a "527" group (named for that section of the Internal Revenue Code). Senator McCain and others see these 527 groups as taking advantage of a loophole in the Campaign Finance Reform Law that President Bush signed early in his first term, even after pledging during the 2000 campaign not to validate any proposal that had six of the anti-speech provisions that were indeed in the version that passed.

The true absurdity of Bush signing that bill into law was that, according to numerous reports and a cursory reading of the tea leaves involved, he did so based on the notion that the U.S. Supreme Court would reject much if not all of its contents on the grounds that restricting political speech was a violation of the First Amendment. Bush apparently figured that, while the free speech battle might be worth fighting, he did not need to spend valuable political capital torpedoing a "popular" bill when he could rely on the courts and the Federal Election Commission (similar to the FCC for political campaigns) to do his heavy lifting for him.

While the courts largely spit the bit and failed to protect our right to be heard without restriction in a political campaign, the FEC ruled that 527 groups like the Swift Vets could still raise "soft" money without limitations on dollar amounts. Members of Congress would actually sue the FEC for having the audacity to allow American citizens to form groups separate from political parties and ask other like-minded citizens to donate money to help them voice their opinions about an issue or a candidate.

Damn! Voters getting together for the purpose of expressing their political opinions? Now *THAT* is the kind of outrageous threat to democracy that I want my congressman to stamp out!

During the 2004 campaign, these 527s would be vilified from virtually every perspective. They were derisively referred to as "outside groups" (*outside* of what exactly?), "shadowy" (even though all who give to them are in the public record), purveyors of smutty "attack ads" (since when is pointing out someone's record inappropriate?), who according to McCain were "openly flouting the law." Even the supposedly conservative Republican administration said 527s should be "shut down" and "outlawed," even filing an FEC complaint asking the government to do just that.

Let's make it clear what 527s really are. They are a group of people who register themselves as a political committee so that they can then collect unlimited money from people whose names are then made public. The organization may then use that money to produce, buy, and air political ads as long as they don't directly tell anyone to vote for or against a particular candidate. And yet, despite the benign circumstances surrounding the existence of 527s and the fact that their freedom of speech is already *FAR* more restricted than the Constitution would seem to permit, they are being roundly castigated as a corrupting influence on our politics and plans are being devised (by *conservatives* no less) to facilitate their demise. If you have not realized yet why this book needed to written, you probably never will.

Without the ability to use unregulated "soft" money through unlimited individual contributions, the Swift Vets never would have gotten their boat out of dock and the nation would have had even less upon which to evaluate John Kerry than they eventually had. Most of the Swift Vets original, rather meager, funding came from one wealthy Texas businessman, who, get this, was a *REPUBLICAN*!!!

Can you believe it? Bob Perry, who lived in *Texas* and was rich enough to spend over $200,000 to help a group of highly decorated Vietnam vets get their decidedly credible story out about a Democratic presidential candidate, was registered as a *Republican*. He had even given that party a lot of money! Truly stunning!!!

Even more shocking was the revelation that, as an affluent Texas Republican who was willing and able to give big political donations, he had become friendly with, get this, the president's top political advisor Karl Rove!!! Get out of town!

While such disclosures should have caused even less surprise than Hollywood finally admitting that it makes so many dumb movies because most of their ticket-buyers are stupid, judging by the coverage in the "mainstream" news media you would have thought that the Swift Vets had been discovered to have been lip-synching on *Saturday Night Live*.

After the chilling first ads hit the airwaves in presidential battleground states, and the authors of the Swift Vets comprehen-

sive and well-documented book *Unfit for Command* began making almost daily appearances on Fox News Channel and talk
radio, the mainstream press finally decided that it had to acknowledge the story. However, they did so by focusing on the only aspects of it they found remotely compelling; what happened to
campaign finance reform, and who was *behind* the effort to tell
the other side of Kerry's war story?

In one of their few news reports devoted to Kerry's Swift Boat
problems, NBC's Tom Brokaw made it clear that the allegations
were not the *real issue*, but rather that this private group was even
being allowed to *make* such charges in the first place. Brokaw in-
troduced the story by opining, "A harsh political attack ad attacking Senator John Kerry's Vietnam War record is putting the
spotlight back on the independent organizations which are 527s.
They're raising money and running ads separate from the campaigns and the parties themselves. And as NBC's Andrea Mitchell
tells us tonight, the campaign finance law supposed to fix the system left this very big loophole."

In her report, Mitchell failed to detail any of the groups actual
allegations against Kerry and did not even play any of the audio
from the ad in question (even though NBC news had previously
run, unedited, the *trailer* for Michael Moore's far less credible attack on President Bush called *Fahrenheit 9/11*). Mitchell exposed
her prejudice against the Swift Vets ad by going on the *Imus in
the Morning* radio/TV show and declaring the ad as having
"grossly distorting the record, according to anybody who knows
anything about Kerry's record."

Mitchell failed to give any evidence for that bold and rather
unusual assertion from a "reporter." Nor did she say specifically
who she was referring to that she trusted to know the "real" story
of Kerry's record, but it is safe to say she was talking about Kerry,
his campaign staff, and Kerry's handpicked, ardently liberal biographer. Of course none of *them* were saying very much at all
about the whole thing, at least not publicly.

Unable to point to any legitimate explanations provided by
Kerry himself or even his campaign, instead of trying to find the
truth, the mainstream press became virtually obsessed with con-
necting the efforts of the Swift Vets to the Bush campaign, which,
if proven to have been coordinated by them, would make the ads

illegal. With their collective panties in a nearly unprecedented bunch, the "old media" resorted to tactics that defied logic and bordered on the hilarious.

The formerly prestigious *New York Times* made fools of themselves by displaying a bizarre flow chart that claimed to connect the Swift Vets to the Bush campaign through a convoluted web of mostly feeble associations reminiscent of the cult game/book *Six Degrees of Kevin Bacon*. The graphic, looking like something straight from the Far-Left Web site Moveon.org, essentially told its readers that the group could not be trusted because a registered Republican had given them most of their start-up money and because a Republican senator was "close friends" with their spokeswoman who was in turn married to someone who was a law partner with one of the leaders of the over-200-member Swift Boat Veterans for Truth.

For the sake of argument, let us stipulate that the members of the Swift Vets were not perfect. When you have well over 200 members providing recollections of events from thirty years ago, it is inevitable there are going to be at least a few pieces of the puzzle that just do not fit. Several of them seemed to have either changed parts of their story, had apparent conflicts of interest, or told tales that were not completely verifiable. Let us even concede that maybe *some* of them *were* conservative Republicans and that those who funded them were *indeed* "partisans" who wanted to see George Bush beat John Kerry.

While obviously it is always important to know someone's potential agenda or motive when evaluating their credibility, since when did that become the *SOLE* criteria upon which to judge their veracity? Unless the extraordinarily high threshold of illegal collusion is proven (no one ever came close in this case) why should the merits of a story be judged *ONLY* on the biography of those who tell it?

By this faulty and dangerous "logic," any account that does not come from someone who has a personal *dis*incentive to tell it must automatically be presumed to be telling a lie. Taking this theory to its ultimate absurd conclusion, the Nazi Holocaust would have been presumed to be a complete fabrication unless people who were *not* Jewish, or were not *friends* with a Jewish person, provided all of the verification.

Was this a new rule that the media was creating? Are we only to ever believe someone in circumstances when they have *NO* incentive to tell their story? Does this mean that only allegations that come from the same side of the political spectrum as the accused will ever again be taken seriously? While it has always been true that a person's self-interest went to the *weight* of their charges, this was the first time that just the unproven accusation of a potential conflict of interest went to the *admissibility* of an account into the public domain.

Can you imagine the coverage of the Nazi Holocaust under these media "rules"? The German anchorman may have sounded something like this:

> The Jewish group that has been attacking German leader Adolph Hitler for alleged and unsubstantiated acts of racially motivated mistreatment is under fire itself tonight. It was revealed today that the group calling itself Auschwitz Survivors for Truth has been funded by a wealthy Russian Jew who in the past has made negative public statements against the Führer and who may have been registered as a member of the Communist Party. As Franz Reichenbauer reports, while the members of the group could not be found for comment, the German people are now wondering how this discredited organization was ever allowed to be heard from in the first place. . . .

When it came to the peculiar nature of the Swift Vet coverage, rather than an official alteration of the unofficial media "rule book," this was really just a case of a *VERY* selective and biased misreading of current "regulations" and not an interpretation that would likely be repeated if the charges were focused on a conservative. As we would learn just a few weeks later during the Dan Rather "Memogate" scandal, when those making the allegations against President Bush were *far* more closely connected to Democrats and *much* less credible, CBS literally rushed them into the most prestigious primetime slot they could find, with catastrophic consequences.

At least as maddening as the non–Fox/talk radio media's fixation with who was *behind* the anti-Kerry ads, was the ludicrous notion that they could tell *this* small part of the story without even *mentioning* exactly what the Swift Vets were actually alleging in the first place. Later, when their book hit the number-one slot on the *New York Times* bestseller list, and it was obvious that the Swift Vets had gained significant traction despite their best efforts, the "old media" took yet another astonishing step in their effort to plug the gaping hole in the side of Kerry's sinking boat.

Led by the New York and L.A. *Times*, numerous "respected" outlets used the extraordinary measure of actually declaring an unequivocal victor in a matter that was still very much up for public debate. The very same newspapers who, despite *overwhelming* proof, never had the guts to refer to O. J. Simpson as a murderer or Bill Clinton as a perjurer, were suddenly defying journalistic convention by stating as *fact* assertions for which there was almost *no* evidence.

In their news pages the very subjective words *unsubstantiated* or *largely discredited* were almost always attached to the allegations, the details of which were either *still* magically absent from the accounts. At best, any mention of the actual allegations would usually be focused on the most inconsequential and unproven assertions. For the vast majority of people who only got their news through "old" sources, if they were even aware of the charges made by the Swift Vets (an August poll by the extremely liberal Annenberg Public Policy Center indicated that 41 percent of the public admitted never having heard of them), they probably thought, much like they were fooled into thinking Bill Clinton was impeached for having sex with an intern, that the whole thing was just a petty fight over how many medals John Kerry should have won.

The *New York Times* went so far as to finally run a scathing review of the book *Unfit for Command* (weeks after it had finally fallen from the top of the paper's bestseller list) that was full of lies and distortions and which was written by a member of the Kerry campaign press pool! In her review, the writer, Susannah Meadows, despite not telling her readers much of what the book said, claimed that the tome is "totally unconvincing."

On what did she base this remarkable conclusion? She said that one of the co-authors (John O'Neil, who has been an adversary of Kerry's since his own Vietnam days) is "so curdled with hatred for Kerry" that "you can't trust what he says." So, going back to the Holocaust analogy, I guess if someone screws you enough to the point that you really despise them, your story is deemed to be automatically and inherently untrustworthy? How is *that* for a dangerous and unsubstantiated precedent?!

The most ridiculous example of the "old media" bending over backwards to try to rid the Swift Vets from the campaign dialogue came from the editorial pages of the *Los Angeles Times*. Here their readers were treated to the remarkably declarative headline: THESE CHARGES ARE FALSE . . . Considering the incredibly scant coverage of those allegations by their own news pages, one could not have blamed the average L.A. *Times* reader after seeing that headline for asking themselves, "*What* charges??!!"

After once again completely avoiding the actual issues raised about Kerry's potential fitness to be Commander in Chief of the Armed Forces, the *Times* editorial board comically concluded, "Not limited by the conventions of our colleagues in the newsroom, we can say it outright: These charges against John Kerry are false. Or at least, there is no good evidence that they are true. George Bush, if he were a man of principle, would say the same thing."

Oh my! Where to begin? First of all, their newsroom already *had*, though more subtlety, made it clear what they thought of the allegations. Secondly, George Bush already *had* said that he thought Kerry's service was *more* admirable than his. Thirdly, if you were going to jump out on a limb and declare that dozens of allegations were dead wrong, don't you think you would be certain enough that you did not then have to mute the statement by adding, "or at least, there is no good evidence that they are *true*"?

Or, if you are so uncertain, how about an investigation by the paper into what the truth really is? Of course, had that ever fully occurred, anything short of a video of John Kerry shooting himself in the foot and screaming, "Yipeee! My third Purple Heart! Now I can get the hell out of here, claim to be a hero, protest the war, and run for Congress as a famous anti-war activist!" would have likely been insufficient for these arbiters of truth that had long ago made up their minds, probably without even ever having heard the facts. Personally, I am utterly convinced that the vast majority of the news media never even bothered to pick up a copy of *Unfit for Command*. Conservative columnist Michelle Malkin reported that after she was castigated on and then thrown off *Hardball with*

Chris Matthews that the host simply did not understand what she was saying about the accusations against Kerry because he had obviously not read the book. When she tried to alert the show's producers to what she was specifically referring to, they had to borrow her copy of the book because they did not even have one of their own.

Members of the liberal media did not need to have a copy of *Unfit for Command*. Their minds were already made up and there was no sense in wasting time by potentially confusing themselves with the aspect of a story that they had no interest in reporting.

The point of all of this is not to further beat the nearly dead horse of proving the overwhelmingly obvious liberal bias of most of the news media. Instead, it is to illustrate the ever increasing importance of citizens being able, when necessary, to go around the old avenues of communication to the public. After what happened to the Swift Vets there is little doubt that the traditional outlets of information can no longer be trusted to provide the people with the free and fair flow of relevant information. This is why the "extra-media" impediments that the Swift Vets also faced while trying to tell their story are of more importance than ever and exactly why we should be moving toward fewer governmental restrictions of speech rather than the dangerous direction we are currently heading.

Instead of facing the issue by answering reasonable questions, the Kerry campaign filed an official complaint with the FEC claiming that the Swift Vets ads should be banned because they were organized by the Bush campaign. If this were true, it would be a violation of the campaign finance laws because the 527 groups could raise money through unlimited donations, while the Bush campaign could not. A couple of weeks after the ads were first aired, the Kerry campaign released a statement announcing it had "filed a legal complaint against Swift Boat Veterans for Truth before the Federal Election Commission for violating the law with inaccurate ads that are illegally coordinated with the Bush-Cheney presidential campaign."

However, there simply was no evidence of such a connection, no matter how hard they tried to find one. To anyone who had bothered to read their book, it was obvious that the Swift Vets could not care less about George Bush. Their gripe was solely with John Kerry claiming to be a war hero and telling lies about his service in his biography *Tour of Duty*. Their mission was clearly not to elect George Bush, but rather to make sure the American people knew about what they saw as the real John Kerry before they made him commander in chief.

Were they also motivated by revenge against Kerry for accusing them of war crimes in Vietnam? Absolutely. Does that make them liars? Hardly. Does it indicate that they were somehow illegally connected to the Bush campaign? Not a chance.

As it turned out, the FEC never found any reason to stop the ads, but it was still shocking that a presidential candidate would even seriously *consider* asking the *government* to *censor* a group of honored veterans from being allowed to tell their relevant and far from repudiated story. Even *more* mind-blowing was the reality that Kerry could do so without ever actually addressing the charges and seemingly not suffer *any* political repercussions for a cowardly act that was so clearly in conflict with the spirit of the Constitution.

Think about that one. A presidential candidate gets legitimate questions raised about his military service from veterans who served with or alongside him, he never bothers to even try to respond to the charges, he then runs to the government to try to shut the group up, it turns out he has no real grounds for doing so, and yet none of that even becomes an issue in the campaign??! In a country where free speech was still taken seriously, John Kerry's FEC complaint would have dealt a deathblow to his candidacy. Instead, his campaign saw it as simply a tactic to try to stop the bleeding by giving the impression that they were fighting back without actually responding directly to the charges. Amazing.

If possible, perhaps even more astonishing were the Kerry campaign's attempts to sink the Swift Vets before they could even drop anchor by intimidating bookstores that carried *Unfit for Command*. Kerry campaign spokesperson Chad Clanton called for the book to be withdrawn, telling the ultra-left Web site Salon.com, "No publisher should want to be selling books with proven falsehoods in them, especially falsehoods that are meant to smear the military service of an American veteran. If I were them, I'd be ducking under my desk wondering what to do. This is a serious problem."

It is one thing for a presidential candidate to question if a TV ad should be allowed by the government to run. After all, even if the law is clearly unconstitutional and does not apply to the circumstances in the case at hand, at least there *is*, however misguided, a law that regulates such matters. However, there is no such law with regard to the printed word.

For some reason, for better or worse, the written word has always been considered "sacred" and almost completely immune from any form of government censorship. This is why, in most cases, newspapers and books at not subject to FCC or FEC rules. It is also why someone like ultraconservative author/commentator Ann Coulter can get away with statements that ordinarily would not be allowed in the public discourse (after all, there is nothing really to fire her from, and since she is sexy and well-known, Fox News Channel will have her on frequently enough to fuel big book sales for her conservative publisher).

Why there is such a dramatic distinction between the constitutional protection provided words that are written rather than spoken is truly a mystery to me (though why it is that nearly every newspaper was in favor of campaign finance reform that would *not* impact *them* is not). But instead of arguing that the printed word should be subjected to more restriction, once again the inconsistency and hypocrisy inherent within the system exposes exactly why the rules controlling free speech, especially in the political arena, should be curtailed rather than extended.

But despite the disturbing and unprecedented nature of their bookstore ploy, the Kerry campaign was forced to pay no consequences for their unwarranted attempts to stifle free speech. Thankfully, the publisher and bookstores did not back down and the title became one of the most purchased of the year. However, without Fox News Channel, talk radio, and the Internet to pump up publicity for the book, it is easy to imagine that, if the financial payoff had not been so strong, *Unfit for Command* would have been pulled from the bookshelves at the prospect of offending the man who could be the next president of the United States. Thankfully we did not find that out, but we easily could have. Such is the precarious and fragile state of free speech in modern America.

Of course, if the news media had been remotely doing their job or if John Kerry truly had nothing to hide, the Swift Vets story should have, or at least could have, been over in a couple of days. But for some strange reason, John Kerry never formally addressed any of the many issues raised by the Swift Vets. In fact, at least one Democratic "spinner," Susan Estrich, would complain after the election that when she requested "talking points" on how to respond to questions about Kerry's Vietnam record, she was dumbfounded to find out there were none to be had.

Instead, Kerry seemed more than content to bank on the hope that he would never be forced to answer any tough inquiries from his friends in the news media. For over a month after the first Swift Vets ad, Kerry did not hold a press conference and limited his media exposure to only the most frivolous and harmless of programs. This led to at least two rather laughable and illuminative moments.

The first occurred when Kerry, while on the phone with radio/TV host Don Imus of *Imus in the Morning*, Kerry said of *Unfit for Command*, "Look, it's a pack of lies. It's an absolute pack of lies. It's been proven to be a pack of lies, and I have no interest in reading it." Imus, who was an outspoken supporter of Kerry throughout most of the campaign, never bothered to ask Kerry how it was he knew the book was a "pack of lies" if, probably just like Imus himself, he had never even read it.

The second episode said at least as much about the broken nature of our national dialogue as it did about Kerry's pathetic response to his Vietnam problem. If there was just one question that Kerry absolutely should have been forced to answer before ever thinking about being elected president, it was, "Senator, where were you on Christmas Eve of 1968?"

Although it may sound silly, such a question should have revealed much about the man who would be president. Having stated several times in the past, in both print and on the floor of the U.S. Senate, that he was certain he was illegally in Cambodia at that time, Kerry would have to either admit that he lied in an effort to elevate himself at the cost of U.S. credibility, or come up with a way to explain a growing mountain of evidence that convinced even his very liberal biographer that the story was not plausible. Incredibly, Kerry was never even forced to make that choice until after the campaign was over.

Kerry finally came out of his Vietnam-induced hibernation from direct contact with the TV media on, of all places, *The Daily Show with Jon Stewart* on the Comedy Central channel. While such appearances on entertainment shows used to be considered beneath a presidential candidate, they have quickly gone from being acceptable as a frivolous break from the campaign grind to suddenly being considered a legitimate way to communicate about "serious" issues. In a sense, the cotton-candy variety of interview has not only become a suitable part of the newsmaker's diet, it now often substitutes for the entire main course as well.

Kerry's appearance with Stewart is the quintessential example of how this sad phenomenon has enabled politicians—even those seeking our nation's highest office—to avoid answering the simplest of questions while still gaining access to a large audience of voters. Here is a verbatim exchange from that "interview" in which the candidate is asked, for the only time during the campaign, what should have been the no-brainer Cambodia question:

Jon Stewart: Now how—how are you holding up? This has been a—it's been a rough couple weeks. I've been following—I watch a lot of the cable news shows. So I understand that apparently you were never in Vietnam. (laughter)

John Kerry: That's what I understand, too. But I—I'm trying to find out what happened.

Stewart: Now is it—

Kerry: That part of my life. I don't know.

Stewart: Exactly. It's nice, though. I know—thirty-five years ago I have friends that have come forward and say—you did have cooties. You know, that sort of thing. (laughter) Is it—do you—do you—is it hard not to take it personally?

(overtalk)

Kerry: —too. It's about—

Stewart: Oh, with you, as well?

Kerry: Yeah.

Stewart: Is it a difficult thing not to take personally when—when they come out and—and your word, it's—it's in the public files. So—

Kerry: You know what it is, Jon? It—it—it's disappointing because I think most Americans would like to have a much more intelligent conversation about where the country's going. And—(applause) yeah, I think that—you know, and—and, yeah, it's a little bit disappointing. But believe it or not, I've been through worse.

(laughter)

Stewart: Right. I—I can imagine. When—when—these guys—were you surprised at all that—

Kerry: No.

Stewart: —they—that they—that they—

(overtalk)

Kerry: Sure I'm surprised. But surprised in a sense. But now that I begin to see the web and the network, I'm not surprised. I think—you know, it's politics. And for whatever reasons, the—the—and I think Americans will discover it as we go forward in the next four or five weeks, George Bush doesn't wanna talk about the real issues. I mean, what's he gonna do? Come out and say we lost 1.8 million jobs? Four million Americans lost their healthcare. We're going backwards on the environment. We—angered everybody in the world.

Stewart: Sir, I'm sorry. Were you or were you not in Cambodia on Christmas Eve?! (laughter) They said—you said five miles. They said three. (laughter) (applause) No, I—(unintelligible). I think that's a very interesting—

(Silence as Kerry and Stewart slowly move within a few inches of each other's face)

Kerry: (unintelligible) Look at that profile.

Stewart: No, believe me, I know.

Wow. Now *THAT* was some hard-hitting questioning.

If you could not discern a coherent answer out of that exchange (or even much of a question for that matter) you are not alone. Amazingly, Kerry's only response to the Cambodia issue was *total* silence followed by a bizarre move in which he appeared for a moment as if he might actually kiss Stewart. What made this pathetic non-answer even more revealing was that Kerry was presented with a golden opportunity to counter the query once and for all before an impotent questioner who was openly supportive of his candidacy and who clearly lacked the knowledge or the desire to follow up after Kerry chose which way he was going to lie.

Instead of coming up with *something* remotely reasonable so that he could at least claim if ever asked again in the future that he had already answered the question, he literally said *nothing* and desperately hoped for some sort of physical "comedy" to form a bridge to the next kiss-up inquiry. Since his Cambodia question was intended more as a way to mock what he saw as the media's (just Fox News Channel I am sure) fascination with the Cambodia issue, Stewart was more than happy to oblige him.

Ironically, the only one who would ever face any pointed questioning about the embarrassing "interview" was Stewart himself. In a much ballyhooed appearance on CNN's *Crossfire* in which the media darling got spanked and yet would be declared the "victor" when the show was canceled a few months later, Stewart was confronted about the softball nature of his questions. A more than testy Stewart retorted that it was not his job to ask the tough questions because his show was a *fake* news program and asking difficult questions was the responsibility of a "real" newscast.

While Stewart was 100 percent accurate in his damnation of the news media's dereliction of their duty (of course, it is interesting to note that Stewart did not have the guts to make a similar point during any of his appearances on Larry King's program, which is by far the worst example of an interview show bending over for its guests in order to maintain access to celebrities), he seems to fail to realize that it is because of shows like his that the "real" news programs—if there still *are* any—no longer ever get the *chance* to ask John Kerry where he was on Christmas of 1968. Because Stewart let Kerry off the hook and because no one bothered to pick up on Kerry's clearly petrified response, the candidate was somehow able to get through an entire presidential campaign without ever even having to *try* to answer that question. Incredibly, it was not until late January of 2005, when NBC's Tim Russert finally grilled Kerry on the issue and he finally, lamely, admitted that he had gotten events mixed up and what had been "seared" in his memory had not actually happened.

By the middle of September, Vietnam's role in the presidential campaign had taken a dramatic turn. Instead of John Kerry's experience, it was George Bush's that dominated the headlines. Dan Rather had reported on *60 Minutes Wednesday* that he had uncovered documents that seemed to prove that Bush had received preferential treatment in getting into the National Guard and that he also may have disobeyed a direct order while failing to fulfill his obligations.

Even if true, the story was dubious at best because the president had already *been* commander in chief for almost four years and two wars, and because, unlike Kerry, was not telling voters to support him based on his military service. However, those points would be quickly lost amid the wreckage that would be created by the Internet-driven revelation that the documents were obviously fake. Despite the fact that the documents turned out to be as authentic as the average Hollywood lunch invitation or a Seattle winter tan, Rather pathetically refused to ever fully acknowledge such or apologize to those whom he accused of having a "partisan" agenda when they had the gall to question Rather's clearly biased work.

The scandal not only exposed Rather and CBS News as the poorly veiled partisans conservatives always knew them to be, but it also further revealed the hypocrisy of most of the news media in their handling of the Swift Vets. While the Swift Vets were presumed to be lying for some sort of political agenda unless they provided absolute evidence that was impossible to provide, Dan Rather's report and those behind it were given every possible benefit of the doubt.

Even as it became overwhelmingly clear that the documents were forged, that those behind the story were blatant Bush-haters, and that the CBS producer on the piece had actually requested that Kerry aide Joe Lockhart call the source of the Kinko-faxed documents, most of the news media was still very wary of condemning CBS or coming to any hasty conclusions. Even *after* Rather's lame apology, the *Los Angeles Times* somehow still referred to the CBS report as "controversial" and the contacting of Lockhart as an "apparent ethical lapse" that created a "potential conflict of interest—giving the appearance that the network had assisted a candidate in the presidential race." This was roughly the journalistic equivalent to calling the 9/11 attacks "controversial" and an "apparent ethical lapse."

It was finally announced just *after* the election that Rather's retirement date as anchor of the *CBS Evening News* would be moved up about a year. This announcement was supposedly unrelated to the "Memogate" scandal, but most people instinctively understood that the two events were about as unconnected as a wealthy man losing his fortune and then getting dumped by his young mistress. Any doubt about this reality was removed when the investigative panel finally released its detailed, though belated and impotent, report which made it impossible for even the most ardent Rather/CBS apologist to maintain their innocence (though Rather himself would absurdly claim to David Letterman, in the only semi-real interview he would give on the subject, that the documents could still be real, he had been exonerated on the issue of bias, and that no one "ever lied" during the affair).

As outrageous as the "Memogate" scandal and the news media's handling of it were, the free speech issue that came out of it was almost as shameful.

California Republican Congressman Christopher Cox actually wrote a letter to the House Subcommittee on Telecommunications demanding that the chairman initiate an investigation into CBS's flawed report. Incredibly, a supposedly *conservative* member of Congress sought the *government* to investigate how a news story was reported, and he felt so strongly about it that he actually *wanted* the public to know about his harebrained idea.

Thankfully, Rep. Joe Barton, the Republican chairman to whom the letter was addressed, recognized the inherent danger of using the government investigate the veracity of a news report and dismissed the probe, saying, "A news organization's responsibility is to facts and truth, but the oversight of network news generally is a matter best sorted out by the viewing public and the news media."

Once again, when it comes to protecting the First Amendment, even when the right side wins, it is scary how many battles must be fought in ways that would have been unthinkable not long ago—and often against foes that should be allies.

While the CBS fiasco turned the campaign spotlight away from the Swift Vets, it would eventually return to issues related to both John Kerry's Vietnam record and, indirectly, freedom of speech.

Sinclair Broadcast Group (one of the many media companies to have employed and fired the author of this book) announced in early October that it was going to air an independently produced documentary called *Stolen Honor: Wounds That Never Heal.* The film about John Kerry's anti–Vietnam war protests was slated to air on each of Sinclair's sixty-two television stations throughout the country just a few days before the election. Sinclair also said that, even though no law required them to do so, they were offering John Kerry valuable free airtime to respond to the film.

In a country in which free speech was still fully protected, what would have happened next is that Kerry would choose whether to participate, viewers would decide whether to watch, the news media would report on the film's factual accuracy, and voters would determine if the information they gleaned from the film was worthy of impacting their vote. But apparently we no longer live in that sort of nation because that scenario is not even close to what transpired next.

Instead, the Democratic Party and their friends in the news media, having just extracted their panties from the bunch that was created by their reaction to the Swift Vets controversy, began whining again, reaching an entirely new level of childishness.

Immediately the Democratic National Committee filed a complaint with the Federal Election Commission alleging that the airing of the film would violate campaign finance laws as an "illegal in-kind contribution to the Bush-Cheney campaign." Even as grotesquely anti-speech as those laws are, this assertion was patently absurd. By that scary standard of campaign "contribution," what positive or negative media coverage of a candidate would *not* qualify as a "contribution" to one candidate or the other and therefore be subject to governmental censorship? Heck, the vast majority of network newscasts prior to the election looked as if they could have been infomercials for the Kerry campaign, or were at least opposed to the president's reelection.

While lines always have to be drawn somewhere, there are VERY good reasons why our Founders made the First Amendment as clear as possible when they wrote, "Congress shall make no law. . . ." They knew well that when it came to certain rights like free speech there could be no ambiguity about where that line is and that it should be intractable. Because of the inherently subjective nature of speech, it is of paramount importance that no one, especially not the *government*, ever be able to determine that certain types of speech are too detrimental to the process to protect.

When it comes to free speech, "Oh, don't worry, we are just draw-
ing a line, it's for your own good" just doesn't cut it.

However, neither these principles nor logic stopped the Kerry
campaign from mounting a full-scale attack on Sinclair and free
speech. Chad Clanton, a spokesman for the Kerry forces, went on
Fox News Channel of all places and directly threatened Sinclair.
"We've got thousands of people now very mad, jackballed up,
calling these stations, protesting, threatening boycotts of their
sponsors," said Clanton. He then went on to chillingly add, "I
think they're going to regret doing this, and they better hope we
don't win."

While a presidential campaign attempting to intimidate a
media organization from airing a film that was mostly a compila-
tion of actual clips from the candidate's past should be considered
ill-advised because of the backlash it should inspire, there is obviously nothing fundamentally wrong with using consumer boycotts
to send a message to a broadcaster. However, appearing to openly
threaten that broadcaster with governmental retribution if one
gets elected goes so far beyond the pale and flies so directly in the
face of everything this country used to stand for that it should
have resulted in Clanton's immediate firing and become a major
issue in the campaign. In yet another sign of our meek willingness
to defend free speech (not to mention the anti-conservative collusion of most of the news media) neither even came close to happening.

In fact, Clanton survived with enough gall to later release this
statement: "Sinclair Broadcasting has a history of putting their
own partisan politics ahead of honest journalism. We do hope they
will reconsider their decision to help their friend, George W. Bush,
by imposing false, negative attacks upon their viewers. It's not the
American way for local television stations to promote their own
political agenda."

I guess that Clanton was correct about local television stations
promoting a political agenda. I suppose that realm is supposed to
be reserved for the decidedly liberal *national* networks.

The outrages hardly stopped there. Realizing that, since there
was absolutely zero evidence of a connection between *Stolen
Honor*, Sinclair, and the Bush campaign, there was no way that the
FEC could get involved, eighteen Democrats in the U.S. Senate

signed a letter urging the Federal Communication Commission to investigate Sinclair's plan to air the film. Eighty-five Democrats in the House (including Nancy Pelosi, whose daughter's documentary about the Kerry primary campaign was airing on HBO at the time) signed a similar letter to the FCC.

Thankfully, at least for now, the last line of defense was still able to fend off the assault on this particular front. FCC Chairman Michael Powell told reporters, "Don't look to us to block the airing of a program. I don't know of any precedent in which the commission could do that. I think that would be an absolute disservice to the First Amendment and I think it would be unconstitutional if we attempted to do so."

However, proving once again that some of the best evidence that our free speech rights are in peril comes from situations in which liberty has actually triumphed, or at least survived, came a statement from one of the FCC's other commissioners. Wacky Democrat Michael Copps said of the Sinclair plan, "This is an abuse of the public trust. And it is proof positive of media consolidation run amok when one owner can use the public airwaves to blanket the country with its political ideology—whether liberal or conservative. Some will undoubtedly question if this is appropriate stewardship of the public airwaves."

Oh really, Mr. Copps? Liberal or conservative? Where were you when CBS ran a story using forged documents to smear a sitting president using its well over 100 stations with a much larger reach than Sinclair ever dreamed of? Just as the government was right not to get involved with "Memogate," it also had no right to get its grimy hands anywhere near the Sinclair situation.

To add the seemingly ubiquitous free speech irony to constitutional insult, Copps finished his proclamation with this warning: "Sinclair and the FCC are taking us down a dangerous road."

While Copps was referring to the consolidation of big media companies, he should have realized that the far more precarious path is the one leading to governmental control over political speech by people like him who appear to have never read the Constitution.

With their pleas to the FEC and the FCC proving fruitless but, sadly, not at all politically dangerous, the Kerry campaign decided to go directly to the source. In a letter to the president of Sinclair broadcast group, a lawyer from the Kerry camp hilariously argued that the film should not air because of complaints from, get this, Democrat officials and liberal commentators. The lawyer also cited a "Fairness Doctrine" that had not been in the law for many years. The letter then asked for "equal time" for Kerry supporters, which Sinclair was under no legal obligation to provide, but which had already been offered and was, essentially, turned down by his own client!

Whether such ludicrous arguments had an impact is uncertain, but eventually the Kerry team got what they wanted. The tide seemed to turn after Sinclair endured even more criticism for the ill-advised firing of its Washington bureau chief after he called the planned program "blatant political propaganda." After having confidently and defiantly stood by their guns for weeks, in the face of relentless pressure from Democrats, the biased news media, and a dropping stock price, Sinclair's resolve suddenly melted like that of Michael Moore faced with his favorite dessert on an empty stomach.

Sinclair decided that instead of airing *Stolen Honor* on all its stations, that they would broadcast a watered-down, self-produced, one-hour special entitled *A POW Story: Politics, Pressure and the Media* on only about two-thirds of their outlets. The program was a diluted hodgepodge of different elements, including just five minutes from *Stolen Honor*. The show gave about as much airtime to a pro-Kerry film called *Going Upriver: The Long War of John Kerry*. The special even gave time to the topic of President Bush's military service and, appropriately, the free speech issues that were created by the entire episode.

Inadvertently revealing just how much the threat of governmental intervention had facilitated Sinclair's concessions, the program ended with a pathetic plea for viewers who found the show "balanced" to please let the Federal Communications Commission know how they felt. This element of the equation became even more evident after the election when a coalition of liberal political groups launched a nationwide protest of Sinclair. One of the groups, ironically named "Free Press," went to the FCC to challenge Sinclair's license renewals for six stations on the supposed (but ridiculous) basis that their *aborted* plan to air a documentary about John Kerry proved that they were not operating, as required, in the "public interest."

The loss of a license is the "death penalty" for a broadcaster. Even though it hardly ever happens, especially for airing politically oriented material, just the mention of such a possibility is often enough to cause gutless media managers to squeal like castrated rats. In the case of Sinclair, it is obvious they got frightened and, unfortunately, with the scary state of free speech protection right now, it is difficult to blame them too much.

It is important to point out that the FCC has many more weapons of intimidation in its arsenal than just license renewal and fines. Like most government bureaucracies, there is discretion to either make the day-to-day processes and intricacies of broadcasting either easier or more difficult for an owner. The FCC, much like the Mafia, denies that they have a way of making life miserable for those outlets whose behavior it is unhappy with; nevertheless, things seem to get done with much more efficiency for those with whom it is pleased.

Howard Stern publicly claimed that his bosses cited this reality as one of the reasons they wanted him to tone down his act. Quite simply, they told him the FCC was making the day-to-day operations of their business a pain in the ass (or, as the FCC might prefer, *buttocks*). Since the vast majority of broadcast executives care *much* more about the bottom line and making things run smoothly than they ever could about protecting free speech rights, their appetite for fighting the FCC is almost nonexistent. Consequently, free speech principles often go undefended in an effort to just get along. This creates circumstances whereby the FCC is able to produce an environment where companies self-censor to make sure they stay well within the law.

In a sense, broadcasting entities are now like highway drivers who are so afraid they will be pulled over for going the speed limit that they drive (partially because the speed limits are erratic and sometimes not even posted and also because there is a strong argument that there should be no speed limits at all) 15 miles per hour under it. It is quite obvious that, despite being uniquely suited to navigate such an obstacle course properly, this is what happened in the case of Sinclair and their plans to air *Stolen Honor*. When Sinclair caved in to the pressure and chose not to air the program instead of forcing the government to make the outrageous decision necessary to have stopped them from showing the film, they set a damaging precedent and allowed an important piece of our free speech rights to die without even a proper burial.

So on November 2, 2004, the vast majority of Americans went to the polls blissfully believing that John Kerry was a war hero. Despite a well-funded group of over 200 decorated veterans with a best-selling book, and a large media company with sixty-two TV stations trying to inform the public, most of America voted without ever hearing the *other* story of John Kerry's Vietnam experience. Amazingly, Kerry was not only able to keep most of the public in the dark about a vital part of his past, but he was also somehow allowed to slide through the entire campaign without being forced to answer even *one* legitimate question about it.

Even though President Bush was reelected with a surprisingly large margin of victory, it is extremely significant to note that over 56 million Americans, far more than had voted for any candidate in our history, cast their ballots for a man who may very well have been a complete phony, a war criminal, a perjurer, and a traitor. Even more startling than that, thanks in large part to restrictions on our free speech and the broken state of our national dialogue, most voters did not even know that those issues were on the table.

As with many of the examples we have scrutinized in this book, disaster was averted, though barely. Regardless how one feels about President Bush (I personally am not nearly the fan that I used to be) a strong case can be made that, in narrowly avoiding a John Kerry presidency, America dodged a bullet.

But real life is not like an old-time Western-style movie where the hero can survive being shot at forever without eventually getting hit between the eyes. The law of averages dictates that, with our free speech force field no longer impenetrable and getting weaker by the day, the near misses will start hitting their targets while creating real and lasting damage. If the events of the 2004 election are any indication, that day is coming sooner rather than later.

Stolen Honor was hardly the only documentary to play a part in the drama that was the 2004 presidential election. Michael Moore's *Fahrenheit 9/11* set a new standard for publicity/money generated by a movie allegedly based on facts. Provided a platform and launching pad by the Hollywood "elite" and the more than sympathetic news media that none of the anti-Kerry forces enjoyed, Moore's hatchet job on the president's handling of 9/11 and the Iraq war set all sorts of attendance records for a "documentary" and won numerous awards for filmmaking.

Whether Moore's film had any real impact on the 2004 election is highly debatable. It was seen by only a small percentage of the electorate and mostly by those who were already voting against the president. The rage created by Moore's lies may have actually produced a larger backlash than the force of its initial attack. Regardless of whether Moore's film helped or hurt Republicans in 2004, there is little doubt that his movie helped expose them as hypocritical traitors to the cause of free speech.

This became obvious when a pro-Republican front group called Citizens United filed a complaint with the Federal Election Commission alleging that advertisements for *Fahrenheit 9/11*, because they were being paid for by Miramax and not by individual and limited contributions, were a violation of campaign finance laws, which prohibit corporate-sponsored ads targeting a presidential candidate within thirty days of his party's nominating convention.

Even as stupid (though undoubtedly well-intended) as this part of the law is, it is simply asinine to claim that running an advertisement for a movie that is critical of the president is somehow *illegal*. Once again, we have a situation where people are trying to draw a line, for an obvious political purpose, which makes no sense and would create total chaos if ever enacted. If an ad for Michael Moore's *movie*, in which absolutely no mention is made as to whom voters should vote for or against, is deemed illegal, then one could easily argue that all ads for products that are remotely political should also be banned in an election cycle. For instance, ads for both *The Manchurian Candidate* as well as *Team America*, which came out just before the 2004 election and had subtle but strong messages directly related to the presidential race, would also have to be considered illegal.

Of course, such a ruling would be absurd, but once we start sliding down that slippery slope we have about as much chance holding on to where we are as Michael Moore riding downhill on a greased luge.

As much as I despise Michael Moore personally, I absolutely defend his right to advertise his movie. If I did not, I would be a worse charlatan than even he is—something the Republicans are apparently fast becoming.

Their complaint was unanimously rejected by the FEC, but unfortunately it was done so on technical grounds. Based on other FEC rulings, it is certainly theoretically possible that Moore could have lost the Republican attempt to enforce the insane campaign finance provisions in an inappropriate fashion.

Of course, when the rules infringe on a *conservative* group's ability to share their speech, the Republican Party tends to take a *very* different view of those laws. Such was the situation in 2004 when Wisconsin Right to Life sought to run radio and television ads that dared to mention Senator Russell Feingold, a pro-choice Democrat who was running for reelection.

The ads were banned because interest groups cannot run corporate-funded (those where contributions are unlimited) ads that even use a candidate's name within thirty days of a primary or sixty days of a general election. In complete defiance of the "Congress shall make no law" provision of the First Amendment, and in a move belying the absolutely absurd notion that this current U.S. Supreme Court is "conservative," the high court upheld such blatant restrictions on free speech in its *McConnell v. Federal Election Commission* (named for Republican Senator leader Mitch McConnell of Kentucky, who was suing against a law his own party had voted for and whose president had signed) ruling of 2003.

However, this was first time that an actual case, rather than just a broad theoretical principle, had been brought to the court since that outrageous decision, and it contained a couple of important elements. The most significant was that the ad not only failed to advocate the election or defeat of any particular candidate, but it was not even an ad whose purpose had anything directly to do with an election. Instead, the intent of the ads, at least as they were written, was to "lobby" Senator Feingold and his fellow Democratic Senator Herb Kohl on the issue of filibustering President Bush's judicial nominees, which Democrats in the Senate had been holding up, largely on fears of allowing pro-life judges to take higher positions.

Had the ads only targeted Kohl, they probably would have been declared legal (I am sure our Founding Fathers would be *so* proud), but because Feingold, who just happened to co-author the law in question, was running for reelection, the ads were found to constitute "electioneering" rather than "lobbying." The powers that be came to this conclusion despite the fact that the proposed ads did not ask anyone to vote against Feingold or even acknowledge that he was running for office. All the ads were trying to do, at least on their face, was to get citizens to ask their senators to stop filibustering judicial candidates.

The most distressing aspect of the judicial decisions that resulted in Wisconsin Right to Life not being allowed to air their views was the subjective political criteria that was used to reject them. One of the U.S. district court judges who ruled against the ads actually cited the fact that Wisconsin Right to Life had already publicly endorsed Feingold's Republican opponent and therefore anything they said about him was clearly intended as a backdoor attempt to influence the election (as if *that* would be such a horrible thing).

While such information may be of great significance in determining the *intent* of the ads, they should have had zero bearing on their *legality*. Once judges become mind readers our entire justice system is doomed to break down. This is why we are supposed to evaluate the legality of an act based on *what* was done and not *why* it was done. Instead, this ruling seemed to ludicrously suggest that if Wisconsin Right to Life had not used their free speech rights in other areas, that they would *not* have had those formerly sacred rights restricted in another.

In effect, since both of Wisconsin's U.S. senators were Democrats, according to this judgment, any group who had publicly endorsed Republicans was deemed to have somehow forfeited their right to speak out against their representatives, on *any* matter, unless they adhere to extremely restrictive fundraising restrictions.

Adding further to this insanity were the comments of the FEC's lawyer on the case. David Kolker argued that even if the Wisconsin Right to Life ads were in fact "grass-roots" lobbying, the Supreme Court had already ruled that even those types of ads can be restricted. Kolker theorized that the Supreme Court sustained those bans "despite the fact that some genuine issues could be caught up in the definition."

What??! So our courts are now officially working under the assumption that free speech is to be *restricted* unless *proven* otherwise and under the presumption that even some ads that are not supposed to be legally restricted will be effectively deemed illegal??! And we are OK with that? This is roughly the equivalent of our legal system saying, "We know a certain number of completely innocent people are going to be wrongly put to death, but hey, what can we do?" Once again, this is why, when it comes to free speech, it is simply impossible to thread the needle without the Constitution getting pricked in the process.

In this case there was no white knight to ride in and save the day for free speech. An appeal to the U.S. Supreme court for an injunction was rejected by Chief Justice William Rehnquist. In his two-page order, Rehnquist declared that Wisconsin Right to Life had not provided enough evidence that the campaign-finance law violated free speech rights in order to substantiate the Supreme Court's intervention. No one ever got the chance to ask the allegedly conservative Justice Rehnquist: if being barred by the government from expressing your opinion about your elected official's political decision does *not* qualify as enough evidence to prove a violation of free speech rights, what exactly would?

Republicans claiming to be conservatives once again showed themselves to be far more concerned with political expediency than with constitutional principles when talk show hosts on my own radio station in Los Angeles embarked on a unique quest to send a message about illegal immigration.

John Kobylt and Ken Chiampou, who make up the extremely popular duo on KFI-AM's *John and Ken Show* (on which I fill in when they are on vacation), decided that, with the state of California essentially already ceded to John Kerry, they would focus on the congressional elections in order to make a point about what was by far the most underreported issue in federal elections. In the past, John and Ken had virtually single-handedly raised awareness in southern California about the negative implications of allowing the flow of illegal immigration to run unimpeded.

With both political parties completely dodging the issue for fear of offending anyone, John and Ken decided to focus their attention on the local Republicans who were facing reelection. Their thinking was that, since Democrats are *completely* beholden to the interests of illegal immigrants and because the KFI audience tends to skew Republican, they could knock off an incumbent by flipping Republican votes to the Democratic challenger. The goal was not to get anyone in particular elected, but rather to defeat an incumbent in such a way that it would be obvious why he was beaten. The theory was that shockwaves would then be sent through Republican ranks everywhere and then the party would be forced to take notice, now more fearful of the consequences of *not* facing the issue than of ignoring it.

Such were the seeds of what John and Ken would grow to call "Political Human Sacrifice." Patterned loosely on CBS's hit reality show *Survivor*, five local Republican incumbent congressional representatives were chosen as "finalists" and were invited on the program for a special grilling on their 50,000-watt spit. The only congressman to refuse the invitation was the powerful David Dreier from the Pasadena area, who was understandably afraid to have his dreadful record on illegal immigration uncovered in front of one of the nation's largest talk radio audiences. Not surprisingly, Dreier was chosen as the "winner" of "Political Human Sacrifice" and targeted by John and Ken for political destruction.

For about the next month the *John and Ken Show* devoted much, though hardly all, of their four-hour daily broadcast to educating their audience about Congressman Dreier's weak stances on issues related to illegal immigration. They also provided ample airtime to Dreier's Democratic opponent, an unknown lesbian socialist named Cynthia Matthews. On a couple of occasions John and Ken took their show into Dreier's district to rally their listeners to their cause. Congressman Dreier was provided a blanket opportunity to respond to the charges, but he never had the guts to take advantage of the offer (though, oddly, he did pay for special advertising that aired on the *John and Ken Show*).

Then just over two weeks before the election, the National Republican Congressional Committee shocked nearly everyone involved when they suddenly filed a complaint to the Federal Election Commission against the *John and Ken Show* and KFI radio. Here are some excerpts from the filing in which the Republicans attempted to claim that *felonies* had been committed because talk show hosts had expressed an opinion about who should win a local congressional race:

Conducting corporate radio shows and political rallies that expressly advocate for the election or defeat of a
clearly identifiable federal candidate does not fall within
the First Amendment "press exception." This express
advocacy removes the station from such protection and
places it squarely within the governing jurisdiction of the
Federal Election Commission.

For over three months the *John and Ken Show* and
KFI AM 640 have made illegal in-kind corporate contributions to the Matthews' campaign and they have also
failed to report these corporate expenditures on behalf of
the campaign. This behavior is in clear violation of federal law.

The illegal coordination test has been satisfied in this
case. First, the radio station is paying for the public communications that advocates the defeat of Congressman
Dreier and the election of Matthews. Second, federal
candidate Cynthia Matthews has appeared on the show
numerous times and has had material involvement and
substantial discussions with the *John and Ken Show* and
KFI AM 640 regarding public communications. This satisfies the conduct standard. Third, radio broadcasts have
been aired within 120 days of the general election, refer
to federal candidate Cynthia Matthews and Congressman Dreier, and are directed toward the voters in her
district. This satisfies the content standard part of the
test. This behavior is illegal and must be appropriately
punished.

Willfully and knowingly using the corporate radio
station to benefit Matthews' campaign and the radio station's willingness to participate in this activity for over
three months seems to meet this criminal threshold. Such
actions are considered felonies and if found knowing
and willful should be prosecuted to the fullest extent of
the law.

Does any of that sound like something that has any business coming out of one of the major political parties in the *United States of America*? Maybe it could come from Saudi Arabia, Ukraine, or Syria, but certainly not America. But, then again, it often seems as if California is not really part of America anymore.

The problems with the Republican Party filing were numerous. First of all, much of what you just read is not accurate. Among other things, the time period during which Dreier was directly targeted was nowhere near three months and to suggest that the Matthews campaign was in "substantial discussions" with KFI is just plain laughable. John and Ken hardly knew anything about Matthews when they chose Dreier as their "sacrifice." She was not the point—he was. And while she did get free *air*time (not *ad* time) and attended the rallies that KFI hosted, she was simply a guest and Dreier would have been provided probably even *more* time on the program than she was had he possessed the fortitude to show up.

But far more egregious than the erroneousness of some of the Republican complaints was the blatantly hypocritical and unconstitutional nature of their argument. The only theoretically semi-legitimate point the Republican Party attempted to make was that since KFI is run by a corporation (the same Clear Channel Communications that the news media goes out of its way to label as "conservative") which was paying for "rallies" to be held in Dreier's district, that this was somehow akin to an illegal contribution to the Matthews campaign.

However, if this interpretation of events and the law was ever adopted by the FEC it would create a domino effect of serious problems with no apparent solutions. For instance, if it is suddenly illegal for a radio station to pay the meager costs of a "remote broadcast" that may *look* like a political rally in which an opinion is given about a candidate for office (and over which his opponent had absolutely *zero* control), then what is the possible difference between barring *that* behavior and preventing the corporation in question from paying any of the *other* numerous and vital costs of normal broadcast, including the salary of the commentator? There simply isn't any. There is just no way to make a reasonable distinction.

This is yet another one of those aforementioned slippery slopes where finding a safe/logical place to stop is impossible. For all intents and purposes, if we start down that incline then expressing a political opinion on *ANY* broadcasting outlet (other than maybe on homemade ham radio) would be completely outlawed within the restricted pre-election time periods. By extension you could then make the argument that opinions expressed in corporately owned newspapers and magazines would also be considered illegal. There is almost no end to the lunacy that would ensue should this clearly misguided reading of the law be established in reality.

Of course, the true madness of the Republican effort to get the government to criminally punish broadcasters for expressing opinions they do not like under the guise of preventing "corporate donations" was exposed by that party's deafening silence when it came to far more transparent threats to this element of the campaign finance laws.

At the exact same time that the Republican Party was filing grievances with the FEC against KFI, they were more than happy to benefit, for instance, from radio/TV host Sean Hannity's corporate-funded tour of presidential swing states. There is no doubt that the amount of "corporate" money that was spent on travel and logistical expenses for Hannity's quest to help get George Bush reelected dwarfed that which was spent on KFI's "Fire Dreier" campaign. Almost as significant was the fact that while John and Ken had numerous goals and intentions for their campaign that may have trumped the actual defeat of Congressman Dreier, Hannity's crusade was unquestionably primarily motivated by a desire to influence the outcome of a federal election.

Another dangerous element of the Republican effort to censor KFI was their effort to forward the lamebrain notion that simply interviewing a candidate is somehow analogous to a financial contribution to their campaign. This would be just plain nutty in circumstances where a broadcast outlet was forced to give "equal time" to all the candidates in a race (as used to be the case), but in a situation like the one where Dreier continually ducked interview requests it rises to a level of insanity that can only be compared to the proverbial child who kills his parents and then whines about being an orphan.

Hopefully, even the Republican Party fully understood the absurdity of what they were seemingly attempting to do. It is probable that their *real* motivation in filing the FEC complaint was simply to intimidate KFI/Clear Channel into aborting the entire "Fire Dreier" effort. As we have already documented, it is hardly unusual for media owners and managers to be easily scared into backing down when faced with the specter of having to deal with legal issues, especially when the government gets involved. It would have certainly been logical if the Republican forces had figured that KFI, advised by lawyers who have absolutely no incentive to take any chances whatsoever, would simply collapse like a weak folding chair after a lunch meeting of Michael Moore, Al Sharpton, Kirstie Alley, and Aretha Franklin.

Even as legally misguided as it was, such a gambit may have worked with most corporate-owned media outlets. Thankfully, for many reasons, KFI is rather unique in the broadcasting world. Because the station has become so successful based largely on its take-no-prisoners attitude and embracement of politically incorrect topics that others fear to touch, those that run the show at KFI fully understood that this was not a situation from which they could afford to back down. To their credit, the KFI managers were unaffected by the legal threat and they allowed the *John and Ken Show* to go forward with their "Fire Dreier" broadcasts as planned.

As it turned out, Dreier was still able to win reelection, but with by far the smallest margin of his twenty-four-year congressional career. John and Ken's "Political Human Sacrifice" could have easily worked completely, but Dreier's district was just drawn too safe, and the Democratic Party (in what appeared to be a deal to protect the Pro-Mexico Congressional Democrat that John and Ken were also targeting) refused to support his opponent. Thanks to her own weaknesses as a candidate, Matthews was understandably not considered a viable alternative by many voters who would have otherwise considered sending a message by defeating Dreier. Of course, the victory or defeat of David Dreier is largely irrelevant to the cause of free speech, which he and his Republican buddies proved once again is under relentless and ferocious assault by foes that should be friends.

The FEC has not formally ruled on the Republican's complaint against KFI, but, in a somewhat similar situation the *FCC* did rule against a group of radio and TV stations that attempted to donate airtime to Republican county committees in California. Pappas Telecasting had donated $325,000 in airtime to thirteen GOP county committees, but after Democrats filed a complaint the FCC ruled that the airtime did indeed constitute an illegal contribution because the same amount of free ads were not also offered to Democrat campaigns.

While the idea of a governmental agency restricting the expression of free speech is abhorrent to my sensibilities, at least from a legal perspective this decision actually made some sense. But there were some extremely important distinctions between the Pappas case and what happened with KFI. Pappas was trying to donate actual *ad* time over whose content it would have no control, while KFI had simply invited the Democratic candidate on a *show* as a *guest*. Also, Pappas made the silly mistake of not formally offering the same deal to Democrat committees, while Dreier was repeatedly asked on KFI as a guest.

In this one isolated case, it appears that the FCC acted properly, though it would have been really interesting had the airtime Pappas had been donating been valued *less* than the largest allowable corporate donation to a local political party. As with so much in the largely brand-new and unlitigated realm of speech regulation, this is an issue that appears to not yet have been fully resolved.

The 2004 campaign unquestionably revealed that the government's role in restricting free speech has never been nearly this pervasive. It also showed anyone who bothered to pay attention that this overreach of authority is in the process of expanding exponentially and is cause for great concern. Unfortunately, elections are not the only area of life where the government is sticking its foot in doors that we have never explored before and which were never intended to be opened in the first place.

CHAPTER SIX: THE LAW LOWERS THE WALL

"Congress shall make no law respecting an establishment of religion, or prohibiting the free exercise thereof; or abridging the freedom of speech or of the press. . . ."
—First Amendment to the
United States Constitution

While purely political speech is certainly under inappropriate and unconstitutional assault from the forces of government, politics is hardly the only area of life where the government is abusing its power when it comes to curbing our right to freedom of expression. There are numerous aspects of "normal" life in which "speech rights" are now being routinely regulated by the government and where the law, which used to be the ultimate protector of such rights, has now become one of their greatest threats.

Often, our freedom of expression is being controlled and even punished with the vast majority of the populace unaware that it is happening. Even when the public does happen to stumble upon this reality, they are usually not even conscious that speech rights are at issue.

By far the most glaring example of this phenomenon, as well as one of the greatest long-term threats to our speech rights, is the concept of so-called "hate crime" legislation. While the vast majority of news media has robotically accepted and even trumpeted the idea of punishing people for hate crimes, and most of the public has not a clue about why that might be remotely dangerous or even unwise, a very persuasive argument can be made that doing

so may be by far the most blatant current violation of our constitutional rights in this area.

Congress first enacted a federal hate crime prevention law in
1968, covering violent crimes motivated by a person's race, religion, or national origin. Subsequent legislation in the early 1990s
expanded data collection and reporting and enhanced sentencing
for bias-motivated crimes. In recent years, while most efforts to
further institutionalize and expand hate crimes protection on the
federal level have been fended off in both the Congress and the
U.S. Supreme Court, the vast majority of states have also adopted
legislation that puts this bizarre notion into law, often going way
beyond what Congress has already done.

For those who may be unaware (the press coverage of "hate
crimes" is so pathetic and biased, no one could blame you), if
someone is convicted of a "hate crime" they are given a harsher
punishment for that offense than if they had just broken the law
for no apparent reason. In other words, because of hate crime legislation, if someone beats another person up while robbing them
the punishment is *less* than if they assaulted them because they
"hated" them or at least *might* have hated them.

For any thinking person there are several huge problems with
this idea. The first is the obvious issue of trying to determine what
exactly motivates anyone to do *anything* and how in the world
you can establish *legally* what was in a person's mind when they
decided to commit a crime. Even if we could all agree that it even
mattered (for the purposes of punishment) why someone did
something wrong, how we got to the point of being comfortable
with *guessing* what someone was thinking in order to come to
such an important conclusion should be a source of great mystery
to anyone who cares about how we form our judicial system.
Being reduced to mind reading to determine punishment is just
plain silly. Why don't we just appoint the Amazing Kreskin and
Johnny Carson's old Carnac the Magnificent character to state
supreme courts?

Of course, since we do not yet appear to have reliable mind-
reading technology, we are instead using an even more ridiculous
method of determining if a crime was committed because of
"hate." State legislatures have arbitrarily decided for us, before a
crime is even committed, whether the victim of a crime is eligible

for extra protection from hate crime statutes. How did they do this? Did they interview each citizen individually and determine which were worthy of invoking hate and which were not? Do they have the ability of Santa Claus to create a flawless "good" or "naughty" list? Obviously not.

Instead, most states have determined that only if you are a member of a particular *group* of people that *they* believe might make you more vulnerable to being "hated" by a prospective criminal can you then receive this extra protection under the law. How did they discern which of these groups are hated enough to qualify? As you might expect, that determination was conducted almost entirely on a subjective, political, and nonsensical basis. Depending on which state you live in, committing crimes against virtually any minority group, be it racial, ethnic, religious, or sexual orientation, will cost you extra punishment. In California, for instance, for all practical purposes just about the only person a "hate crime" could *not* be committed against would be a straight, healthy, American, white male who does not believe in any particular organized religion (a group which just happens to include the author of this book).

This is not an exaggeration. In California, thanks to legislation signed by Governor Schwarzenegger in 2004, a "hate crime" is now defined as "a criminal act committed, in whole or in part, because the victim is perceived to have one or more of the following actual or perceived characteristics: disability, gender, nationality, race or ethnicity, religion, sexual orientation, or association with a person or group with one or more of these actual or perceived characteristics."

This may be the most ridiculous definition in our law today. What this means is that if a crime is committed against someone who is, for instance, either gay, or *seems* gay, or someone who *associates* with a gay person, then the person who committed the offense is eligible for greater punishment than if they had done the deed to a heterosexual person who has no gay friends (in fact or in appearance). The mind simply boggles at all of the possible utterly absurd unintended consequences that could come out of this law.

But wait, there is even more silliness to come. The law also defines "intimidation" in a way that could easily be interpreted by ultraliberal judges to mean that it would be illegal to even *protest* against a person or group that could fall under hate crime protection. Another juicy tidbit included in the California law is that, get this, if an illegal immigrant is a witness to a "hate crime" they are protected from being turned over to federal immigration authorities. And some people wonder how California got its reputation for lunacy?

This law, while extreme, illustrates the multiple layers of irrationality to this entire notion of hate crimes. On the one hand there is a presumption that because a crime is committed against someone who is gay, or *seems* gay, or *hangs out* with someone who *seems* gay that their connection to homosexuality had to be the reason they were victimized.

This idea has already led to at least one rather comical situation when some nut job fired shots at the home of former Vegas legends Siegfried and Roy. The authorities immediately declared the attack a "hate crime" even though there was absolutely no evidence that the shots were fired because the duo is gay, nor do we even know in fact that they *are* gay. While it is certainly not a stretch to say they do *seem* gay, the authorities put themselves in the peculiar position of interpreting someone's sexuality in an effort to designate the nature of the crime. Later, when it became obvious that the guy who fired the shots was just mentally unstable, the hate crime label was quickly dropped from the investigation. Shoot at the house of Siegfried and Roy because they seem gay? Outrageous!!! Fire at their home because you went nuts? That is not such big a deal.

While all the groups that fall under hate crime protection are dubious (if only because treating groups of citizens differently under the law would seem to be a blatant violation of the Constitution's equal protection clause in the Fourteenth Amendment), the fact that most states are now including sexual orientation and religion is most egregious. I have *nothing* against homosexuals or people who believe in certain religions. As far as I am concerned people can believe anything they want and act however they want as long as no one else gets harmed. However, the idea that someone should be able to *choose* to be part of a group that gets *extra* protection under the law is both preposterous and repugnant.

While I agree with those who say that most homosexuals do not *choose* to be gay, it is certainly theoretically possible to choose to at least *act* gay and it is certainly a choice to *seem* gay or associate with gay people. Despite these obvious facts, a desire to protect homosexuals from real, perceived, or simply made-up social dangers has been the major driving force behind the recent expansion of hate crime legislation.

Interestingly, the event which triggered the most media coverage for this cause was the 1998 brutal beating death of Matthew Shepard in Wyoming. As it turns out, according to a 2004 ABC News investigation, the murder likely was *not*, as the news media presumed, motivated by Shepard's sexuality, but rather by a desire to rob him for drug money. Does this scenario make the killing any less horrible? Of course not. But the state of Wyoming has been relentlessly ridiculed in the press ever since Shepard's murder for not adopting some sort of hate crime legislation, as if that would have saved Matthew Shepard even if his sexuality *had been* the impetus behind his senseless slaughter.

The Matthew Shepard situation was not the only one to reveal that hate crime laws are really nothing more than a politically correct weapon of the Left to gain favor with minorities, as well as a threat to the essence of our Constitution. During the 2000 presidential campaign the NAACP shamelessly ran perhaps the most obscene political TV ad in American history when they had the daughter of James Byrd, a black man who had been brutally dragged to his death in Texas, claim that George Bush's failure to enact hate crime legislation was akin to killing her father "all over again." This despite the remarkable fact that, using only the current laws in Texas, all of the primary perpetrators of the despicable act had already been given the *death* penalty by that time! Last time I checked, even the state can only kill you one time!

At least when it comes to race there is a real and horrible history of actual violence against people who were targeted because they were black. This unambiguous and heinous record, combined with the reality that one can obviously not choose their race (with the possible exception of Michael Jackson), make giving extra legal protection to blacks at least understandable. However, allowing religious groups to fall under such a shield is even more illogical than doing so for sexual orientation because one's religion is clearly one's own choice even more so than one's sexuality, except perhaps for those who decide to become transsexuals.

Since organized religion has been the cause of far more killings than any other source in the history of man, it is obviously possible that people in this country are occasionally targeted for crimes because of their religion. However, the very nature of such creeds makes it impossible to craft a law that makes any sense whatsoever. Quite simply, it is unfeasible to even define what qualifies as a religion; and even if we *could*, how would we determine which ones should qualify for the extra protection?

In January of 2005 two teenagers were charged in New York with hate crimes for attacking a twenty-year-old man with a metal club and an ice scraper. The assault resulted in the man getting twelve stitches. This was clearly a serious crime, but because the man called himself a "satanist" and dressed in black clothing with a blue-tinted bouffant hairdo, the boys were charged with second-degree assault as a hate crime and faced up to fifteen years in prison.

Obviously nobody is defending the crime or suggesting that it is OK to physically attack someone because of their belief that Satan is worthy of worship. However, it should also be at least equally apparent that giving someone extra protection under the law because they worship the *devil* is so silly that the whole idea seems stolen from a late-night TV comedy sketch. If we allow "satanists" to be a protected group, then where can the madness possibly end? As one of the defense lawyers in the case said of the victim, "The kid is gothic with blue hair: He falls into the category of kid. At worst this is a simple dispute between kids, not an attack on a minority. What's next? Someone being accused of attacking a preppie or a nerd?"

For someone like myself who has belonged to both of those groups, it may be appealing to add "preppies" or "nerds" to the list of protected classifications, but the reality is that this not-so-far-fetched proposal illustrates the inherent ludicrousness of the entire hate crimes concept.

Obviously no one is in favor of committing hate crimes. But dividing our nation into groups of allegedly aggrieved "minority" legal classifications for the purposes of allowing some liberals to feel better about themselves is not going to prevent crime and it certainly is not going to stop human beings from occasionally hating one another. While there is no evidence that hate crime laws actually reduce crimes against protected groups (partially because crimes that may not be real hate crimes are often reported as such in order to bolster bids for federal funding), the amount of potential damage that they could wreak on our nation is substantial.

For instance, has anyone ever considered that there may be some negative repercussions for so demonizing "hate"? This may sound asinine at first, but largely only because the vilification of the word by the forces of the Left has been so incredibly effective. While hate is very *often* "bad," this should not *always* be presumed to be the case. Take the hate fueled by the attacks on Pearl Harbor. Yes, it may have caused national embarrassment with the Japanese internment camps, but did that hate not also help us maintain our vigilance during the ensuing war and give us the resolve to defeat Nazism and make much of the world safe for democracy?

Can anyone deny that the media's decision to largely stop showing the images of the September 11th attacks for fear of promoting hatred has helped diminish the nation's tenacity in fighting the "War on Terror"? While indirectly teaching Americans that "hate" is *never* good may not be the most devastating aspect of the "hate crime" concept, it is certainly the most overlooked.

The most dangerous element of the hate crime hysteria is that it has opened the door to the government becoming the "thought police." Now that the government is allowed to punish people because of what they *assume* someone was *thinking* or *believing* while they committed a crime, it is difficult to see where, in the long run, the government's ability to punish perceived thoughts/beliefs could possibly end. As in so many areas of free speech/expression, there is just no place to draw the line and, as we have already seen with the steady expansion of the protected groups, once the snowball starts down the mountain it only gets bigger and tougher to stop. In a nation of laws where treating everyone as equally as possible should be the goal, citizens should be punished for what they *did*, not *why* they did it, what they were allegedly *thinking* when they did it, what their political *beliefs* are, or because of the political power of the group to which their victim supposedly belongs.

If you think I am overestimating the free speech element of this equation or the impending long-term threats of it, consider what is already happening here and around the world as laws that supposedly deter "hate crimes" are already morphing into ways to punish "hate speech."

In 1999, Matthew Hale, a graduate of the Southern Illinois University law school, was denied the right to practice law by the Illinois State Bar even though he had passed the state bar exam. At that time, Hale had been convicted of no crimes and there was no legal reason to bar him from being a lawyer. However, Hale was an avowed "white supremacist" and the leader of a well-known "hate group." Incredibly, based on only his controversial and unpopular beliefs, Hale was prevented by the government from pursuing a profession for which he was legally qualified. (It should be noted that Hale was later convicted of threatening to kill a federal judge and his group was suspected in the 2005 killings of that judge's husband and mother before finally being exonerated.)

In 2001, a fifteen-year-old boy from San Jose, California, was expelled from high school and served 100 days in juvenile hall after passing around a poem in school in which he stated, "For I can be the next kid to bring guns to school . . . For I am Dark, Destructive and Dangerous." In 2004, saying, "the poem plainly does not constitute a threat," even the California Supreme Court was smart enough to unanimously overturn the conviction.

Similarly, also in 2001, an Ohio man named Brian Dalton was convicted of charges of child pornography for depictions of *fictitious* acts about which he fantasized in his personal *diary*. The conviction marked the first time that an American had been sentenced to prison over the content of his private diary. In short, he was convicted and sentenced to eleven years in prison not for what he *did*, but for what he *thought*. In 2003 a state appeals court overturned the conviction on the grounds that he did not have effective counsel because his attorney failed to raise the First Amendment defense.

Once again in 2001, a Houston, Texas, man was arrested and convicted for disorderly conduct after he gave "the finger" to the driver of a car whose slowing of the fast lane he did not approve of. Robert Lee Coggin was forced to spend over $15,000 in legal fees before the Third Court of Appeals in Austin finally ruled in his favor that flipping someone the bird is not inherently illegal.

The year 2001 also saw a white man in Florida lose his membership to a *public* golf club because he jokingly (he says) asked a black groundskeeper who was watching a tournament on television, "How is that nigger Tiger Woods doing?" After groveling at a meeting of the Palm Beach Golf Commission, the man was finally able get his membership back.

In 2003, the quarterback of the Middletown (New Jersey) High School South's football team got into legal trouble for a racial statement he made on a student-produced cable show. During an interview after his team had defeated a mostly black team, Dan Johnson crossed his arms on his chest and said, "BONES." Apparently, BONES was known in the school as an acronym for Beat On Niggers Every Saturday. After the video aired, offended students apparently contacted police and told them what the acronym meant. The authorities actually had to conduct an investigation to determine that stating the word *BONES* did not constitute a "bias crime," and finally, as it should have, left the punishment up to the school and the team.

In 2004, the Louisiana Supreme Court suspended a judge for six months, without pay, for a costume he wore to a Halloween party. Judge Timothy Ellender, whose wife accompanied him to the private party dressed as a policewoman, wore blackface makeup, handcuffs, and a jail jumpsuit. Even though the state Supreme Court justices acknowledged that Judge Ellender did not mean to insult blacks, they had no problem punishing him for his attempted comic expression at a private party by costing him $50,000 in salary and forcing him to take a sociology course to get "a greater understanding of racial sensitivity."

Again in 2004, a professor at Rhode Island College was forced to go before school officials to adjudicate whether she violated campus policy by failing to punish someone for engaging in offensive speech. Lisa Church, the coordinator of the college's preschool program, was not even present when three mothers of children in the school got embroiled in a heated conversation about welfare and race. Passions apparently got so enflamed that one of the mothers (who happened to be black) felt the need to complain to Church that she was insulted by what had been said.

When Church did not punish the other two women, the offended mother took her case to the college Affirmative Action Office, claiming discrimination and intimidation by Church. The fact that Church was being castigated by school officials and called in front of a disciplinary board for *not* punishing free speech got enough negative attention that the college eventually determined that the matter required no "further formal action."

Also in 2004, the *Tucson Citizen* newspaper was sued for printing a *letter* to the editor that some considered "hate speech" and which seemingly "distressed" some local residents. The letter was about the situation in Iraq and urged a rather radical solution for our problems with insurgent terrorists there. Dr. Emory Metz Wright wrote, "We can stop the murders of American soldiers in Iraq by those who seek revenge or regain their power. Whenever there is an assassination or another atrocity we should proceed to the closest mosque and execute the first five Muslims we encounter."

The letter allegedly caused some Tucson Muslims to irrationally keep their children home from religious schools and resulted in protests from readers. The paper apologized for their decision to print the letter and added that Dr. Wright had written a follow-up letter explaining that he intended that his idea to kill Muslims only be carried out in military actions and combat zones.

As of early 2005, the Arizona Supreme Court was deciding whether the newspaper could in fact be sued for printing a letter that, no matter how inflammatory, expressed an *opinion* about a legitimate public matter in a way that threatened no one in particular. If the court does allow the suit, among other things it will officially mean that our judicial system takes *writing* about killing unnamed Muslims far more seriously than most of the Muslim world seems to judge the actual killing of Americans, which, ironically, is what provoked the letter in the first place.

Also in 2005, Brian Bruch, the football coach at Lakewood High School in Florida was suspended for ten days without pay, fired from his job as coach, required to take two "diversity training courses," and forced to transfer to another high school. All of this punishment was inflicted on the popular twenty-three-year teaching veteran because he told a black player on his team to get his "black ass" back into the huddle. Despite an apology as well as an outpouring of calls and letters from St. Petersburg's black community who said he had sacrificed to help black students over the years, the school board voted 4–3 to fire Bruch. They also sought to institute a total ban on "profanity" from all school employees, an attempt that caused a problem when one of the board members used the forbidden word *ass* in quoting the coach. No disciplinary action was taken against the official and the remark was allowed to be repeated in the broadcast of the meeting.

In early 2005 four Philadelphia Christians (known to many as the "Philly Four") were still facing a total of forty-seven years in prison and fines up to $90,000 each for doing little more than publicly reading the Bible via a bullhorn in the fall of 2004 to a group of pro-gay activists. Among the charges they faced for their peaceful and videotaped verbal altercation with those attending a gay rights parade were "inciting a riot" and "ethnic intimidation." They were charged with such offenses and were forced to spend up to twenty-one hours in prison. This despite the fact that their words were limited mostly to biblical passages, no riot came close to occurring, and even the most ardent gay rights advocate would have a very difficult time arguing that homosexuality is an "ethnicity."

Despite the famously Far-Left judges in the Philadelphia jurisdiction, in February of 2005 the charges against the Philly Four were dropped, with the jurist ruling that, get this, peaceful expressive activities like those of the Christian demonstrators are fully protected by the First Amendment! The judge also stated that prosecutors were unable to make even a minimal showing of any criminal conduct. Despite this scolding, prosecutors said they were considering an appeal, while the group representing those arrested planned a federal lawsuit over the violation of their First Amendment rights.

Finally, in January of 2005 two *third grade* boys from a *special education class* in Ocala, Florida, were taken from school in handcuffs by police because they drew a "violent" stick figure of a third boy in their class apparently being stabbed and hanged. According to the father of one of the arrested boys, their pencil and crayon drawings of the threesome were simply the result of a normal falling-out among kids. Even though there was no known history of violence among them, the police said that the third boy may have felt endangered by the writings and the nine- and ten-year-old boys were charged with the felony of "threatening another person."

As horrible as most of the all-too-real and recent examples we just listed may have been, the idea that the government/legal system even *contemplated* punishing those who committed them should be far more horrifying. Just because none of these situations has yet to result in an absolute sinking of our free speech ship, each one makes it clear that we are taking on lots of water at a far too rapid pace.

While here in America we are still usually able to barely keep above sea level in this area, in some supposedly more sophisticated parts of the Western World they are already drowning.

In France, for instance, for years it has been an illegal and jail-able offense to engage in public racist or anti-Semitic insults. In late 2004, following almost the *exact* same pattern of American hate crime legislation, sexist and anti-gay slurs were added to the list of unlawful acts. The law defined the latter violations as: "defamation or incitement to discrimination, hatred, or violence on the grounds of a person's sex or sexual orientation." Such an act is now punishable by sentences of up to a year in jail and a very heavy fine. Meanwhile, voicing an anti-gay remark "of a more general nature tending to denigrate homosexuals as a whole" in public is also an imprisonable offense. In case your blood was beginning to run cold with fear and disgust, you should be pleased to know that in France making *private* sexist or homophobic taunts between individuals is only vulnerable to a rather small fine.

The profound and chilling impact of these laws should be obvious to all. The *Guardian* newspaper reported that the laws "could mean that devout Christians who denounce homosexuality as 'deviant' would be prosecuted; comedians can no longer make mother-in-law jokes; producers and distributors of the camp comedy film *La Cage Aux Folles* could end up in the dock; and parts of the Old Testament might be banned." Other than that, there did not seem to be much wrong with the whole idea.

Lest you think that somehow the enforcement of these insane provisions is more narrow than the letter of the law or that this is just an isolated spot of lunacy, consider the case of Far Right (why is it that Far Right is somehow synonymous with "racist" or "crazy"?) political leader Jean-Marie Le Pen. In early 2005, the Paris prosecutor's office announced an inquiry to determine if Le Pen broke the law when he described the Nazi occupation of France in World War II as "not especially inhumane." The investigation was to resolve whether Le Pen's comments to a magazine constituted "denial of crimes against humanity" or "apology for war crimes," both of which, believe it or not, are *criminal* offenses in France.

Le Pen's comments, while potentially historically inaccurate, were incredibly benign. It was obvious that his political opponents were simply using the nutty law to try to punish and diminish him. In America, free speech advocates would consider this kind of activity by the government the "Doomsday Scenario" and yet here it is already happening in France, the country our most recent Democratic presidential nominee seems to want us to emulate most!

It is not just the French who are capable of restricting and punishing opinion in a way that seems more consistent with an anti–Free Speech horror movie. In 2004 the Supreme Court of Belgium officially branded the nation's largest political party as "racist," effectively shutting it down in the process. The "Far-Right" (there we go again), "anti-immigrant" Vlaams Blok was found guilty of "permanent incitement to segregation and racism." This is apparently considered a serious crime in Belgium and the court ruling cost the party its public funding.

The party had been both controversial and popular for advocating that the Dutch-speaking region of Flanders secede from Belgium largely because of unease over an invasion of nonwhite immigrants. While there are still, thankfully, many differences between America and Europe, it is certainly not difficult to imagine a frighteningly similar scenario occurring in the southwest portions of the United States where illegal immigration is destroying both the economy and the culture. Of course, that would require one of our political parties standing up against illegal immigration which, even before the banning of the Vlaams Blok, was highly unlikely.

Perhaps the most dramatic contemporary example of blatant governmental censorship in the Western World comes from

Venezuela. In 2005, the National Assembly there passed new regulations on Venezuelan media that restrict the broadcasting of scenes of violence or vulgarity, including images or words that "cause anguish." Not only that, the legislation even could prevent any information or commentary that might defame public officials or harm national security. Even news clips depicting unrest or confrontation (whether live or edited, domestic or foreign) are being barred from the airwaves until after 11 p.m.

Under the new law, an eleven-member board will decide infractions and punish them with fines, *prison time*, and revocation of licenses. The Venezuelan government justified these Draconian measures by claiming that they were acting in the best interest of family-friendly programming. I could joke that this sounds an awful lot like our own FCC, but frankly it really does. Let us hope that the commissioners were too busy investigating cartoon characters to notice this scary development just to our south.

One of the many reasons why it is so very important for the law to hold a hard and fast line against allowing any erosion of our free speech rights is that an increasingly uninformed and apathetic public can no longer be counted on to rise up in defense of those rights. Even those who should be well educated in these matters and who have an extreme self-interest in protecting free speech are coming up increasingly flaccid in this fight.

In January of 2005, during a discussion on Fox News Channel of some New York radio DJs rightfully getting into trouble for playing an inane and highly offensive song parody that made fun of victims of the Asian tsunami, highly rated TV and radio talk show host Bill O'Reilly exposed his abject ignorance when it came to what the law says about punishing speech. During an interview with a free-expression advocate who had to politely correct O'Reilly on several factual matters, the most popular host in cable TV talk actually revealed that he thought "hate speech" was illegal. When informed by his bemused guest that that, no, the Constitution protects all kinds of speech, O'Reilly went on to strongly imply that the government should do more to crack down on all sorts of "offensive" expression. O'Reilly then spent the next several weeks endlessly campaigning for the firing of Ward Churchill, the University of Colorado professor who wrote that crazy stuff about the victims of 9/11, at one point actually accusing him of treason.

What is truly amazing about this is that O'Reilly is a smart guy and a pro that makes millions of dollars because he is (mostly) protected from being legally punished for giving his opinions!! His position is also particularly hypocritical because he just happens to be a man who, if the FCC actually enforced indecency over the phone lines (which technically they can do), would have been vulnerable to retribution for his now infamous sex calls to a female Fox producer. If even Bill O'Reilly is not willing and able to fight this battle, how can anyone expect the average citizen to give a damn?

O'Reilly is hardly the only influential person who is ignorant of the law regarding speech rights. In January of 2005 a Denver police officer threatened to arrest Shasta Bates for displaying a bumper sticker critical of the president that read, "Fuck Bush." Apparently a Bush supporter was offended by the message and got in an argument with the woman and then flagged down Sgt. Michael Karasek and urged him to do something about the "situation." The officer then accosted Bates and told her that he was giving her a warning and that the next time he saw her truck that she would be arrested if she had not removed the sticker.

According to Bates the officer told her, "You need to take off those stickers because it's profanity and it's against the law to have profanity on your truck." According to a reporter who just happened to be there, Officer Karasek then wrote down Bates's license-plate number and told her: "You take those bumper stickers off or I will come and find you and I will arrest you."

The only problem here of course is that there is no law, or even a local ordinance, against "profane" bumper stickers, nor should there ever be one (regardless of which officeholder people are being urged to have sex with). Who knows why the officer erroneously thought there was one, but it certainly seems reasonable to presume that his ignorance of the law may have been at least somewhat influenced by public cases of Speech Punishment in general and "profanity" in particular. Perhaps this is a classic case of how misperceptions caused by the onslaught of politically correct culture have almost literally seeped into the law and affected how it is enforced.

Denver police launched an investigation into the incident, but at the time of this writing Officer Karasek still had a job. Even if he were to get fired, his job prospects would still appear to be quite good. After all, it would seem that, given the current political climate, he may be a prime candidate to replace Michael Powell as the chairman of the FCC.

As if that story is not enough to prove the point, numerous studies and surveys indicate that both the knowledge most Americans possess about, and the value they place on, their right to speak their mind has been generally decreasing in recent years. As you might expect, support for free speech took a nose dive after the events of September 11, 2001. Though there have been some signs of resuscitation since then, the rebound has been, at best, anemic. Regardless of the direction that support for free speech rights is heading, such backing is undoubtedly far feebler than it should be.

For instance, according to the annual poll on the state of free speech taken by the First Amendment Center, in 2002 an incredible 49 percent of the general public agreed that the First Amendment goes *too far* in the rights it guarantees (by 2004 that number had shrunk back down to 30 percent). In 2004, 42 percent said that the press has *too much* freedom to do what it wants (down from a previous high of 53 percent), while only 12 percent said they have too little freedom. In 2003, 28 percent of the public *disagreed* that newspapers should be allowed to publish freely without *government approval* of a story, while less than half the public strongly agreed with that statement. In 2001, 35 percent approved of government regulation of press stories *prior* to publication. In 2004, 49 percent said that, in general, the press has *too much* freedom to publish, while only 34 percent thought that there was too much censorship. Unbelievably, 45 percent of the same survey respondents said that the government should be able to regulate sexual content on late-night cable television, which is one power that even the government does not currently think it should have!

The 2004 poll also revealed that a remarkable 44 percent of respondents *disagreed* that people should be allowed to say things in public that might be offensive to religious groups. Meanwhile, a ridiculous 63 percent of the public *disagrees* that Americans should be *allowed* to say things in public that *might* be offensive to racial groups. The 2003 survey revealed that an amazing 22 percent of Americans *strongly disagreed* that individuals should be allowed to protest in public against America's involvement in war during a period of active military combat.

While there was some hope in the latest survey that at least a portion of the public is catching on to what is clearly the diminishment of our freedom of expression (28 percent said we have too little freedom to speak freely while 11 percent claimed we have too much), it is all too obvious that for huge portions of America, free speech rights are not only not in peril, they are not even remotely appreciated.

How did this happen? Well, simple logic would allow one to conclude that younger Americans are tending to value their free speech rights less than, say, the World War II and Vietnam generations. There is certainly plenty of anecdotal evidence to explain how younger Americans are not being imbued with the same reverence for our speech rights and the willingness to protect them as previous generations seem to have been given. Quite simply, our news media and educational systems have been indirectly teaching children for quite a while now that free speech rights can and often should be curtailed.

According to a massive 2004 survey of students and teachers conducted by the University of Connecticut, these suppositions have plenty of foundation in fact. The poll of over 112,000 high school students found that 36 percent believe that newspapers should get "government approval" of stories before publishing, while only a meager 51 percent said they should be able to publish freely. According to the survey, a depressing 75 percent of students mistakenly believe that it is illegal to deface the American flag as a political statement. Finally, while 97 percent of teachers said they supported people being *allowed* to express "unpopular" views (what's up with the *other* 3 percent?!), only a shocking 83 percent of the students thought that Americans should be allowed to voice unpopular opinions! Hodding Carter III, president of the foundation that sponsored the study, said of its findings, "These results are not only disturbing; they are dangerous. Ignorance about the basics of this free society is a danger to our nation's future."

While we have already documented some of the many ways in which the news media has "instructed" the public (of all ages) that it should not tolerate certain types of expression and should not be outraged by many forms of censorship, it is important that we not let schools and teachers off the hook for their blatant complicity in this effort. While it is no secret that for far too long most public school systems have enthusiastically embraced and furthered the cause of political correctness, over the past few years there have been a seemingly endless supply of examples of having kids in public school having either been prevented from expressing themselves or punished for having done so.

In fact, many schools are finding the First Amendment to be such a source of aggravation that they are simply dropping their newspapers altogether. The *Los Angeles Times* reported in January of 2005 that, "Partly because principals would rather avoid tensions that come with journalism programs, and because of budget cuts and increased focus on core curriculum, journalism courses are being scaled back. Between 1998 and 2003, the number of high school journalism classes in California declined by 15 percent."

Clearly, a value and appreciation for free speech is not being taught in our schools as much as it should be, and through examples of Speech Punishment, students are essentially being told that their speech rights do not mean very much. However, since the vast majority of cases in which students have been reprimanded for their expression can be clouded by issues related to school discipline, dress codes, and just keeping order in the classroom—clearly one of the most pressing problems facing public school teachers today—they rarely make for good individual examples of pure speech restriction. After all, even the most ardent advocate of free speech must concede (as the Supreme Court has) that children may not always have the same speech rights as adults.

So while on an individual basis, these circumstances do not usually rise to the level of violating freedom of expression, there can be absolutely no doubt that the hostile environment for free speech that has been created in most public schools has produced a terrain where fertile ground for growing an appreciation of free speech among our children may be difficult to cultivate. In short, our schools undoubtedly create an atmosphere that greatly diminishes the value of free speech, so it should not surprise us when our children grow up reflecting that reality.

While in most cases our public school system has an excuse because of the age of its students and the demands of keeping order in the classroom, the same can certainly not be said for our colleges and universities. The realm of higher education has, until recently, been considered a place where *any* thought or expression, no matter how wacky, was fiercely protected under the realm of "academic freedom." The thinking was that it was of paramount importance to guard against any violation of this sacred concept because we must feel free to throw out a thousand absurd ideas in the hope that the next off-the-wall inspiration may be the one that cures cancer or ends war.

I wholeheartedly endorse that vision of academia. However, if that place ever really existed, we certainly know now that it no longer does, especially if the idea being posited happens to conflict with liberal doctrine or politically correct thought. For instance, in 2005, LeMoyne College, a Jesuit school in New York, expelled a student named Scott McConnell from its Masters of Education program for writing a paper, for which he originally received a grade of A-, in which he vigorously advocated the use of corporal punishment in public schools.

The chances of a student getting kicked out of liberal academia for promoting the ultraliberal notion that we should *never* discipline a student in *any* manner (a proposal that is far loonier than corporal punishment), would be less than those of Michael Jackson becoming the spokesperson for the Big Brothers organization. During this very same time period in which McConnell was being expelled from college, the University of Colorado professor who said that those who died on 9/11 were not innocent victims was holding on to his job. When it comes to free speech (or lack thereof) among our academic "elite," the double standards along ideological lines are simply staggering.

One of the most egregious recent examples of this reality was an inane controversy surrounding Lawrence Summers, the president of Harvard University, who suggested that innate differences between men and women may be one of the reasons why men tend to dominate the fields of math and science. In January of 2005, while speaking at an economic conference that dealt in part with the state of women in the workplace, Summers, who was asked to be "provocative," outlined the relative dearth of women in the fields of math and science and laid out several possible explanations for this phenomenon.

He included the possibility that women who have children are unable to commit to the eighty-hour work weeks sometimes required to excel in those fields, and he mentioned the glass ceiling of direct and indirect gender discrimination. He also raised the issue of whether women had a lower interest level in those fields partially because society had told them that could not succeed there. Finally, he said that it may also be possible that innate differences between the way that men and women think are the cause for the disparity in math/science achievement.

When he was finally forced to release a transcript of his comments, it turned out they were even more measured and benign than originally reported. Summers' actual key quote was, "In the special case of science and engineering, there are issues of intrinsic aptitude, and particularly of the variability of aptitude, and that those considerations are reinforced by what are in fact lesser factors involving socialization and continuing discrimination. I would like nothing better than to be proved wrong. . . ."

Despite the incredibly careful nature of the remarks, a few women in attendance were so offended by the idea that the president of Harvard would suggest that maybe the minds of men and women are different that they simply walked out on the speech (perhaps in doing so, proving that women may indeed be more emotional than men). Partially because there was no video or audio of the speech and partly because it happened during the week of the president's inaugural, the story took several days to fully ascend to the top of the media food chain and then simmered there for several weeks before eventually resulting in a *Time* magazine cover article devoted to exploring the issues related to the differences in the male and female minds.

Several (though hardly all) of the women in attendance expressed their outrage and then so did many Harvard professors who signed a letter condemning the president for daring to suggest what seems to be an obvious reality to the vast majority of open-minded people. Eventually there would be small protests on Harvard's campus calling for Summers to be fired. The National Organization for Women (NOW) actually came out and demanded

Summers' resignation. (NOW's deafening silence during the Clinton impeachment scandal revealed them to be little more than whores to the Democratic Party, and should have caused them to be stripped of all their credibility—but *please* not their clothes!)

The fact that NOW could be taken even remotely seriously as they called for the resignation of a university president (who at one point happened to have been part of the Clinton administration) whose only "crime" was positing some extremely reasonable and rather measured *theories* in an attempt to *fix* a problem for women, when they did not come close to doing the same for the president of the *country* who was a serial user and abuser of women, is about as solid evidence as you will find that our national dialogue truly is broken.

More to the point of the actual content of Summers' statement, it seems almost impossible to make a reasonable assessment that his comments were remotely inappropriate or even incorrect. Does anyone honestly believe that the brains of the *typical* man and the *normal* woman function in exactly the same way with identical strengths and weaknesses? To most people who bother to pay the least bit of honest attention to the way the genders interact, the question is not *if* they are *different*, but rather if they are really even part of the same *species*. While there always important exceptions to these "rules," and it may be impossible to completely quantify or discern how much is as a result of nature as opposed to nurture, it appears rather obvious that women are generally stronger in some mental areas like intuition, creative expression, and multi-tasking, while men appear to have inherent advantages when it comes to things like problem solving, logic, and strategy.

Why is it that men completely dominate activities like chess while women control numerous other creative endeavors? Why is it that homosexuals often seem to possess the mental strengths/ skills in many of the very same areas as their *opposite* sex? Simple coincidence or even differences in nurturing just cannot explain such significant disparities of achievement between the genders in certain endeavors.

This is not to say that nature controls or can explain everything, however. While conventional wisdom dictates that women are far more verbal than men, men still almost completely dominate three professions, talk radio, rap music, and stand-up comedy, which would seem work against that premise (of course, this may represent more of a testament to female taste than an indictment of their relative verbal abilities).

The bottom line here is that no one, and certainly not Summers, is even *suggesting* that women are not as *smart* as men. Rather, the point is that *maybe* our types of intelligence are *different*. It has always baffled me how we as a society do not seem to be able to handle this rather simple distinction. Just because you say that two groups of people are *different*, that does not mean they are not *equal*. Would anyone have argued with Summers if he had said that innate differences may be why women do not do as well as men in weightlifting or why women have a higher tolerance for physical pain than men do? Obviously not. So we have already established (as if a quick trip to one of our uncontroversially segregated public restrooms would not have already done so) that the genders are fundamentally physically different and that it is "OK" to say that. But if we are *physically* dissimilar, then why could we not also be mentally different, and why would it be even slightly inappropriate to say so or even just theorize about that possibility? Even if Summers was "wrong," what could be so horrible about just asking this extremely relevant and legitimate question?

The answer, as is so often the case with speech issues, is simply fear and insecurity. We are so afraid of what we might find out about our own weaknesses and frailties that we often stick our heads in the sand rather than risk learning the truth, and then we seek to "punish" anyone who forces us to take stock of uncomfortable realities. While the reason that some women get upset at the suggestion that they may not have the same mental strengths or weaknesses as men is certainly understandable, that does not make it rational or a legitimate foundation on which to base a punishment, especially in the academic realm where freedom of thought and expression (at least of liberal ideas) is supposedly sacred.

This intellectual cowardice has great costs to our society far beyond even the bounds of its impact on freedom of speech. Does anyone else wonder why it is that more has not been done in the medical profession to ease the suffering that most women experience during their menstrual cycle? One could make a very powerful case that no other medical "condition" comes close to creating a greater negative influence on our society, and yet remarkably little research has seemingly been done in this area of medicine. While I am sure there are many reasons for the strange lack of emphasis on this far-reaching problem, may I suggest the possibility that the extreme hypersensitivity that most women have regarding this issue may have something to do with it?

Is it not more than possible that medical researchers, when faced with a multitude of possible ailments to fight, may shy away from *that* one because it is just more trouble than it is worth? The overly harsh reaction to Summers' comments are certainly not going to make it any easier for a future researcher to say, "Hey, guess what?! I found out how the female mind is different and why it reacts the way that it does during the menstrual cycle! It's because the female mind lacks . . ." without the fear of hearing gunshots at close range before finishing their thoughts.

This chilling effect on medical thought and action may be even more profound when it comes to issues related to race. Why is it that more has not been done to cure sickle cell anemia? Could it be because researchers are afraid to conclude that African Americans are physically different from other races, and that is why they are more vulnerable to the disease? If so, it would be difficult to blame them. At the end of 2004, one drug maker reluctantly announced that it had created the first drug approved by the FDA for use by African Americans for certain types of heart ailments. Some in the black community actually had the audacity to cry racism over the creation of a drug that was intended to help *save* the lives of black people!

Similarly, when it comes to seeking answers to the profoundly important mystery of why black kids do not do nearly as well in school, on average, as white or Asian children, the silence is deafening. The spinelessness is simply staggering and is also a direct result of the apprehension of being perceived as politically incorrect or, even worse, racist. Clearly, these types of speech restriction are not just fodder for academic discussion and fuel for fearing future implications. They most certainly have profound real-life repercussions, usually to the detriment of the very people who most need help.

As for Summers, he ended up apologizing for his remarks and being forced to grovel and placate in order to save his job. In a sacrifice to the gods of political correctness, he created two task forces on women and at least one senior position to support gender diversity. What made the shoddy treatment of Summers particularly infuriating is that it occurred during the exact same period as the Ward Churchill uproar at the University of Colorado, where Churchill's far more offensive writings created much less outrage among the academic elite than what Summers said in a setting where he was asked to stir things up.

Summers barely survived at least in part because what he said was not on tape. Without a tape, television and radio quickly tired of the story, and there was not enough fuel to stoke the illegitimate fire. All of which proves once again that, especially when it comes to Speech Punishment, it is far better to have circumstances on your side than just the truth.

In 2003 and 2004, issues of free expression and academic freedom were also at the forefront of another significant controversy involving a high-profile university. During that time period, thanks to a bizarre series of circumstances, the University of Louisville faced questions about what kind of speech was allowable or preventable on a college campus. It all began with a boneheaded maneuver in which a credit card company sponsored a clearly racist T-shirt that was designed to get students to sign up with them. In an effort to make amends, the company donated money to the university to sponsor any speaker of the university's black community's choosing. They chose a black female rapper named Sister Souljah.

Sister Souljah became infamous in 1992 for saying, after the Rodney King riots in Los Angeles, "If black people kill black people every day, why not have a week and kill white people?" Even Bill Clinton distanced himself from her in a way that was so effective that, in political circles, when a candidate rejects the far extreme of their party it is still referred to as a "Sister Souljah moment."

Sister Souljah spoke without incident until the radio talk show host who took my place at WHAS-AM in Louisville decided she would try to make a name for herself in the market by attempting to organize a protest after the fact. Her idea was that since Sister

Souljah was so clearly a racist the University of Louisville should be forced to also allow white racists the same chance to express their views on campus (even though no credit card company had made any blunder by offending white people). The talk show host decided it would be a great idea for the local KKK to be a sponsored speaker, and she began to campaign on her show for that to occur.

As it turned out, after a long and contrived battle, the university rejected the KKK's radio-aided demand for $11,000, the same amount that Souljah was paid to speak. The KKK was offered the chance to speak for free, but no one showed up to represent them. Later, two KKK members were banned from campus for supposedly breaking rules regarding the posting of "insensitive and offensive" fliers. The whole episode was much ado about very little and the controversy's most significant aspect may be that it could soon lead to the severing of the longtime relationship between the talk host's radio station and the university's sports teams (but since, unlike her predecessor, she has apparently not talked negatively on the air about any ex-lovers who were local public figures, it appears she will keep her job).

More noteworthy, however, was one of the ways in which the University of Louisville tried to fight having the KKK on its campus. One of the professors at the university, Ede Warner, wanted the school to ban the KKK from campus and then get a court to rule that they are a "terrorist group" and therefore vulnerable to expanded governmental restriction and oversight under the Patriot Act. The Associated Press reported that Warner's actions had "stirred [a] debate among faculty and administrators that has taken place on campuses around the country: how far the university can go to keep some groups off campus and how best to deal with unpopular ideas in the academic setting."

What? How best to *deal* with *unpopular* ideas in the academic setting? How about listening, debating, and, if necessary, debunking? Why, in academia of all places, do we need to be officially labeling groups whose views we do not like in such a way that some of their constitutional rights may be taken away before they have even committed a crime?

While the "terrorist group" branding as articulated in the much castigated but little understood Patriot Act is indeed extremely dangerous if misused, contrary to perception on the Far Left, there is little if any direct evidence that this has come close to happening. Passed by Congress in the wake of 9/11, the Patriot Act has become a favorite whipping post for those who want to blame the Bush Administration for anything they can possibly find. As an obvious advocate of free speech if I saw any indication that the Patriot Act was actually being abused (other than attempts to do so by leftist college professors trying to keep the KKK off their campus), I would be the first to scream bloody murder. However, though I constantly ask those who insist that the Patriot Act is a grave threat to our civil liberties, "Where is the beef?" I have yet to receive an even marginally satisfactory response.

Any doubts that the Left is crying wolf (at least so far) on the Patriot Act should have been removed after Michael Moore's remarkably impotent attack upon it in his disgraceful pseudo-documentary *Fahrenheit 9/11*. For all of his lies, Moore is an expert at finding "facts" which appear to back up what he wants his viewer to believe, and he is also a master at manipulating that information for maximum impact. And yet, even with his prodigious skills of distortion, all Moore could come up with on the Patriot Act was one old man being awakened from a nap by investigators who wanted to ask him about some comments he made at a health club that were supportive of Osama bin Laden. (Interestingly, there is no evidence that Democratic Senator Patty Murray was ever questioned by anyone about her favorable statements to schoolchildren regarding bin Laden.)

That was it. That was all he had. When it came to attacking the Patriot Act, Moore came up microscopically small. Moore would have had a much better case if he had used the U of L example (which also never went anywhere), but he seems far more comfortable coming to the aid of a bin Laden backer than the KKK.

Frankly, if waking an old guy from a nap is all Michael Moore can find when you know that he badly wanted to dig up something much better, then I feel pretty comfortable about the way the Patriot Act is currently being administered. This is not to say that we shouldn't keep an extremely watchful eye on the government so that they keep it that way. That ought to be self-evident. However, in order to maintain credibility, it is just as important that our howls over speech restriction be limited to those situations in which it is clearly warranted. With that in mind, false claims of speech restriction should be viewed with almost as much contempt as the actual limitation of expression itself.

The Patriot Act is hardly the only example of a situation where some have attempted to improperly wrap themselves in free speech protection in an effort to claim they have been wronged or to get away with a wrong.

One of my very favorite phony free speech gripes comes yet again from the realm of academia. The University of Mississippi's football team is nicknamed the "Rebels." It is an unambiguous and unapologetic tribute to the soldiers who fought for the Confederacy (i.e., "the South") in the Civil War. For many years, as part of their celebration of their rebel heritage (though some would claim because of more nefarious reasons) the fans at their football games had a tradition of waving little Confederate battle flags at the game. Whenever the team made a big play the cheering section was a sea of "stars and bars," with thousands of small battle flags painting the stadium red and blue.

As the Confederate flag became more and more vilified in the politically correct press and slowly became synonymous with racism, the university suddenly had a gigantic public relations problem on its hands. When it became obvious that recruiting top black athletes to the school was becoming impossible because of the powerful image that the tiny flags portrayed, the University of Mississippi finally acted. However, instead of doing what most leftist ivory-tower academic types from the "Blue States" would have almost certainly done, the school did something as absolutely brilliant as it was startlingly simple.

In 1997, rather than forbidding the Confederate *flag* from their football games, the school decided it would be best to just ban fans from bringing *sticks* into the stadium. Under the guise that thousands of jubilant and packed-together fans waving sticks was a threat to public safety, the ban said nothing about the flags themselves and was in no way a violation of anyone's speech rights.

The real beauty of this solution was that the spectators essentially enforced the ban themselves. Since any fans who would protest the decision by still bringing stick-less flags to the games would have to hold them up with both hands (and therefore make a nuisance of themselves in doing so), the university bet that by letting human nature take its course the flags would quickly disappear. Sure enough, like puddles being dried up after an early afternoon Mississippi summer thunderstorm, the presence of the flags largely evaporated almost immediately.

This is not to say that the university's action did not create discontent. One well-intentioned but overmatched Rebel fan who was asked to leave the stadium in 1999 because of his Rebel flag on a stick actually took his "free speech" case all the way to the Supreme Court. The court correctly declined to hear his appeal of previous rulings that the ban on sticks was not a violation of the First Amendment.

While there is absolutely no doubt that the intent of the stickless rule was to create an atmosphere in which speech that the school did not like would no longer be expressed, and a legitimate argument could be made that there was nothing inherently wrong with the type of speech the school wanted to get rid of, this was a very rare situation where speech was suppressed by a state institution in a manner that was not a direct threat to the Constitution.

An even more inventive, though far less legitimate, claim of free speech infringement came in the form of a last-ditch effort to save a man from the death penalty. In 2005, just days before three-time murderer Donald Beardslee was scheduled to be the first person in three years to be put to death by the state of California, his attorney actually argued that death by lethal injection would violate his First Amendment right to free speech.

That's right. Death by lethal injection would be a violation of Beardslee's free speech rights. How so? The "argument" was that the combination of the sedative and a paralyzing agent that are part of the lethal injection process would mask whether he is experiencing excruciating pain and would prohibit Beardslee from crying out as he was dying. His lawyer expressed concern to the court that the public witnesses would be prevented from seeing his client contort in pain and viewing "movement that might be unpleasant and unsightly."

The point seemed to be that seeing his client clearly suffer would make an important political statement about the nature of the death penalty. Of course, what he really seemed to be claiming was that lethal injection was such a *humane* way to die that it hid from the public how hideous it supposedly really is.

While anything that comes out of the mouth of a criminal defense attorney, especially one desperately trying to save the ass of slime like Beardslee, should be viewed as inherently suspect, this feeble attempt may have set the bar to a new height of absurdity. While claiming that a multiple murderer is having his constitutional rights violated because he cannot express his thoughts as he is being put to death may be creative, even the ultraliberal, vehemently anti–death penalty, Ninth U.S. Circuit Court of Appeals was hip enough to the scam to unanimously reject this incredibly lame line of reasoning. Beardslee was indeed put to death and, while the world was left to wonder how much pain was involved (let's hope plenty), we did not have to fear that a piece of the First Amendment went with him.

California was the sight of at least two other recent legal situations where the First Amendment was invoked in strange and inappropriate ways. The first dealt with a San Bernardino man who claimed that television's Discovery Channel had violated his First Amendment "privacy" rights by, get this, airing a documentary in which his criminal record was revealed.

The Discovery Channel show was about a twelve-year-old San Diego murder in which Steven Gates had been convicted of being an accessory after the fact. Since that conviction Gates had served his time and gotten his life back on track. A court had awarded him a certificate of rehabilitation. He thought he had put his past behind him and none of his neighbors seemed to be aware of his record. When the Discovery Channel program suddenly changed that, he sued them for invading his privacy (a dubious "right" not actually found in the Constitution).

Was Gates disputing the facts presented in the television show? No. He just did not want anyone to know the unfortunate truth about his past and felt as if he had been damaged by the Discovery Channel program. Oddly, there was actually some legal precedent for such a questionable claim. However, this time the California Supreme Court unanimously overturned the inhibition from media outlets disclosing dated but truthful information regarding non-public figures.

While it was certainly unlucky and perhaps unfortunate that Gates's life was disrupted by the fluke that the Discovery Channel happened to take an interest in his case, *his* claim that his First Amendment rights were violated was ridiculous. Obviously, the idea of punishing a media organization for telling the unquestionable *truth* is a far graver and more blatant violation of constitutional protections. In yet another indication of how weak our free speech rights have become in *real* life, even in this case, where the court ruled to finally fortify them, the truth lost because the Discovery Channel took the documentary off the air as soon as Gates's absurd lawsuit was filed.

Even Gates himself appeared to be a bigger loser because of this ill-conceived lawsuit. Far more people in his local area found out about his criminal past from the news coverage of his court battle than ever could have from a show on a national channel watched by a tiny sliver of the television audience. In fact, had he just shut up about it, I personally never would have even heard about his criminal past and, in all likelihood, neither would you.

Then there is the case of former San Diego police officer "John Roe" who was fired from his job after he ignored warnings from his bosses that he stop selling a video of himself via the Internet. The video in question was not just any ordinary piece of tape. Roe had videotaped himself stripping off a police uniform and then masturbating. Roe claimed that he was fired because of his off-duty "expression of free speech" and that this represented a violation of his constitutional rights.

Believe it or not, the case got all the way to the U.S. Supreme Court before Roe's suit was unanimously rejected. The Supreme Court has held in a number of cases that government entities may impose some limits on the "speech" of their employees, even if that would be unconstitutional in the private sector. For the court to do so, it must generally find that the employee's speech in question must not touch on a matter of "public concern." In this situation there seemed to be very little doubt that whatever "speech" Officer Roe was expressing while jerking off on camera failed to meet that test (of course, had there been pictures of political figures involved, perhaps it would have been a closer call). There are certainly no direct references to masturbation in the Federalist Papers, and it seems pretty definitive that when the Founding Fathers were debating the intent of the First Amendment that they were not at all concerned about protecting the right of a police officer to play with himself, essentially, in public.

Stripping as a legal profession in general has always been a tricky area of free speech law. Seemingly every region in the United States has handled the Supreme Court's edict that adult businesses must be allowed, but that they can be stringently regulated in very different ways. The issue of how much regulation of the exotic dancing industry is appropriate or legal has created controversy all over the country in recent years, but especially in the so-called "Bible Belt."

For instance, in 2004, Kenton County, Kentucky, passed a remarkable ordinance that prohibited dancers from even setting foot in areas of the club open to customers. When club owners vehemently objected to what may be the most restrictive of such laws in the country, the County Attorney actually bragged, "If they didn't put up a fight, I would have worried that we didn't make the ordinance strong enough."

As a libertarian I have no problem with adults paying or getting paid for virtually any activity they want as long as no one else gets hurt. I am even in favor of the government legalizing, regulating, and taxing prostitution (which many strip clubs essentially promote). Therefore, it offends me that the government would even consider outlawing consenting adults getting close enough to even talk to one another, especially in a place that is not open to the general public. However, such an objection is based far more on my beliefs about the intended role of government in this country and has very little, if anything, to do with my obvious desire to see free speech rights protected.

While such overly vigilant restriction of strip club interaction may *very* well be a violation of the First Amendment's guarantee of the right to peaceably assemble, it is not, as it is so often mischaracterized by the stripping industry and the news media, a "free speech" issue. A woman should be allowed to get paid for rubbing her barely clothed ass in another adult's crotch, and the two of them should be permitted to say whatever they want to each other while it is happening (interestingly, a Nevada judge, striking a blow for strip clubs in Las Vegas, ruled in 2005 that a prohibition on "fondling" and "caressing" in strip clubs is "unconstitutionally vague"). However, elevating the prevention of such activity to the lofty level of a violation of "free speech" is simply a bastardization of the very same Constitution that those who do so claim to be protecting.

Issues of freedom of speech/assembly have also recently been wrapped together with the always dicey topic of illegal immigration in the California city of Redondo Beach. In 1987 the city passed an ordinance against soliciting jobs on the city's streets. While the regulation was not unusual (at least fifty other cities in California have similar ones), in 2004 the law was used as part of an undercover sting operation to arrest about 150 day laborers who were clearly violating the intent of the provision.

Ordinarily none of this would be particularly noteworthy; however, in *this* case those who were arrested also happened to be illegal immigrants. Now you might think that since those who were arrested for violating the law were not even U.S. citizens there would be *less* commotion/outrage over the episode because, after all, those who were detained were obviously breaking a much more serious and well-defined law every single day by simply being in the country. But such simple wisdom is the exception rather than the rule in Southern California where somehow the interests of noncitizen lawbreakers are often placed well ahead of those who pay taxes so that the children of the aforementioned lawbreakers can slow down the public schools by forcing the teachers to spend valuable time teaching them how to speak English.

Sure enough, the local liberal news media raised a ruckus over the arrests and the National Day Laborer Organizing Network (NDLON) sued the city to stop them from enforcing the law against soliciting jobs on the city's streets. In doing so the lawyer for the NDLON claimed, "The ordinance is an unconstitutional violation of free speech."

Amazingly, an extremely liberal judge, who obviously did not care at all about protecting free speech rights but instead preferred to use them as a legal weapon to protect illegal immigrants, ruled that the city must stop arresting people who violate that law until the constitutionality of the ordinance could be fully adjudicated. Considering the pace of the court system, such a ruling effectively knocked down the law for at least the foreseeable future.

If the judge had done so because there was a legitimate free speech issue that needed to be clarified, I would have applauded such a ruling, even if those who benefited happened to be illegal immigrants (part of the problem here of course is that no one knows, or should presume, that a person is an illegal alien, regardless of his appearance or language, until *after* his citizenship status has been checked out).

However, that does not appear to be even close to what happened here. The judge's ultraliberal past aside, the Redondo Beach law just simply does not unconstitutionally restrict free speech. It does not even appear to stop people from assembling on the sidewalk. It was only intended to prevent a safety hazard and a traffic problem by keeping people from going out into the street and stopping trucks to ask the drivers if they would like to hire some relatively cheap labor for the day.

Curbing such behavior is no more a violation of free speech rights than saying that the police can arrest you if you try to speak against the president while blocking the Inaugural Parade. Just because you are talking while engaging in some sort of illegal activity does not necessarily mean that this act is protected by the First Amendment. If it did, the prosecution of laws against both drug sales and prostitution, for instance, would be almost impossible. Forgetting for a moment that I am not in favor of most of those laws to begin with, such a reading of the Constitution would be simply ludicrous.

This is not to say that there are not a growing number of situations where, in the name of cracking down on hazardous behavior, real free speech rights are being dangerously stifled. The 2004 presidential campaign provided numerous situations, including some that were contrived in order to purposely test free speech rights, where, under the guise of protecting the president, rules for protesting were so incredibly restrictive that a sympathetic court easily could have found them to be unconstitutional.

Of course, in the vast majority of those cases, the campaign just desires an incident-free event, the protesters just want their face on TV for five seconds, and if anyone ever actually goes to court the case is usually thrown out and everyone goes home happy. Where to draw that line between safety and speech is one of the most difficult calls in this entire realm and, consistent with virtually every other aspect of free expression, it is being drawn increasingly in the wrong direction.

On the "bright" side, the Redondo Beach episode shows that at least one judge is taking *someone's* "free speech" rights seriously, even if it seems to be the bogus speech rights of people who are not even legally protected by the Constitution. Maybe someday actual U.S. citizens will once again enjoy the same kind of protection from our judicial system against governmental restriction of real speech as these illegal immigrants did for their contrived variety of expression.

CHAPTER SEVEN: "A CONTINENT, BUT NOT A COUNTRY"

> *"Sometimes our differences run so deep, it seems we share a continent, but not a country."*
> —President George W. Bush,
> 2001 Inaugural Address

> *"There is no justice without freedom."*
> —President George W. Bush,
> 2005 Inaugural Address

In neither of those quotes from his two inaugural addresses was President Bush referring directly to issues of free speech, but he easily could have been—in fact, he probably should have. In his first inaugural address, Bush was referencing the cultural divisions that had seemingly been created or exacerbated during the previous decade and which resulted in the remarkably balkanized "Red/Blue" results of the 2000 election, which would be virtually duplicated in 2004. In his second inaugural, Bush was touting his plan to bring freedom, and therefore the potential of justice, to the rest of world, even as he presided over the loss of liberty here at home.

Why has America become so fractured over the past few election cycles? Well, it is not a coincidence that this era of diminished unity coincided with the two most subtly divisive forces to hit

America in the modern age: Bill Clinton and media fragmentation. Bill Clinton's impact on and development of the "politics of division" (a tactic he still continually decries, which is kind of like Alexander Graham Bell citing the telephone as the scourge of humanity) is fodder for a completely separate work. However, since this book is about the impact of and on free speech in our country, a few thoughts on the latter cause of division are more than in order.

First, it is important to understand that the divisions that currently exist among Americans are not new. Obviously, since the United States of America once survived, barely, a Civil War, there have been times when the differences of opinion, in some ways, were much more dramatic than they currently are. However, just because they have been more spectacularly displayed in the past, that does not mean the relatively stealthy nature of our current divisions should not be taken just as seriously and do not pose a threat to our existence as a "united" nation.

It is also imperative that we recognize that the now much-talked-about political divide between "Red" and "Blue" states goes far beyond political geography, and that location is somewhat more of an effect rather than a cause of these stark differences in the way Americans tend to see the world. More and more each day, we are being divided and segregated (often by force of our own actions) into tiny demographic groups with little in common with those outside of our small faction. One's age, race, gender, religion, and economic status act more than ever as a tall paneled fence that separates us from the rest of the neighborhood community.

The sum of what Americans now truly share in common has been whittled down to frighteningly little. Other than the major holidays, maybe the Super Bowl, a presidential election, or a gigantic news story like an attack on our homeland, it is difficult to come up with events that qualify as countrywide communal experiences in this day and age. Heck, millions of people who live in this country cannot even speak English and rarely suffer any real inconvenience for lacking the ability to communicate with the vast majority of the rest of the nation. Sadly, the totality of information that is agreed upon and shared by nearly every single American is probably not much more than the date and time.

While diversity of experience and differences of opinion are part of what made this country great, it seems that we have surpassed the point of diminishing marginal returns in this area when it comes to our withering national unity.

As with most cultural phenomena of this magnitude, there are many explanations for how and why this has occurred; however, there is no doubt that the fundamental change in the way most Americans get their information is among the most significant and certainly the most underappreciated reason. Up until the late 1980s, the average person had access to only a handful of television channels, one or two newspapers, a couple of magazines, a few movies at the local theater, and at most two radio stations that serviced whatever major format they preferred. Now, thanks to the explosion of television channels, magazines, movie accessibility, satellite radio outlets, and Internet Web sites over the past fifteen years, a person can almost literally customize their media experience to conform to their own worldview. Anything that they do not like or agree with can now be easily edited, bypassed, or completely ignored, while almost any belief, no matter how nonsensical, can find a place where it is nurtured and where ignorance is enabled. (For instance, if you wanted to believe that Terri Schiavo was really "alive" and "responding," plenty of "conservative" media outlets were more than willing to help you out.)

While this revolution in media has created an enormous amount of enjoyment for millions of people (personally, my life has been greatly enriched by the addition of the Golf Channel, ESPN's Classic Sports channel, as well as the seemingly endless varieties of HBO), it has also injected our nation with a cancer of self-segregation, which may very well create the conditions that lead to our ultimate demise.

Prior to the late 1980s, Americans in the modern age shared a huge number of communal experiences, mostly because we had little choice in the matter. The limited number of media outlets created a landscape where the national agenda and dialogue were well defined and most Americans paid at least some attention, if only because there was nothing better to do. Among other things, this meant that whenever the president held a press conference it was a big deal because there was virtually nothing else on television or radio. By default, anytime the president did or said something remotely important a huge percentage of the populace saw or heard it firsthand, and even if you missed what happened, you could catch it on the rebound because it would inevitably be a source of conversation among family and friends.

Today, such events rarely get carried live by the four major broadcast networks, and even when they are most people have over 100 other, usually far more entertaining, channels to choose from that are not carrying the president. This means that even the president's State of the Union speech, supposedly the one time all year when he can tell the nation where we are and where we are headed, is hardly an "Address to the Nation" at all. In 2005, for instance, the *combined* TV ratings on the broadcast networks for President Bush's State of the Union speech was *beaten* by the simultaneous showing of Fox network's hit reality show *American Idol*. There is also little doubt that the following day more Americans were talking at the proverbial water cooler about *Idol* than about the president's dramatic speech.

While the impact of media fragmentation on the office of the presidency alone is rather staggering and simply cannot be overestimated, it is hardly the only consequence. Americans are now able to remain blissfully ignorant about important happenings, often while under the illusion that they are actually paying attention to what is going on. In one particularly amazing example, comedienne/commentator Joy Behar of *The View* virtually bragged just after the *Columbia* space shuttle disaster in 2003 that she had watched television all weekend long and never even heard about the tragedy until a day and a half after it occurred. While this astounding story may say as much about Behar's lack of friends as it does about the impact of fragmentation, it is also undoubtedly commonplace in far more mundane circumstances every single day.

I am often amazed when interviewing public figures at how often they are completely unaware of important things that have been said about them or that have occurred in the media that they really should know about, but thanks largely to fragmentation do not. One of the more astonishing instances occurred when I spoke on the air to former Independent Counsel Ken Starr and played for him numerous clips of Bill Clinton saying some of the nastiest things you could say about someone like Starr who prides himself on acting with the utmost of dignity and professionalism. Starr seemed genuinely surprised (not to mention emotionally impacted) when he heard what a former president had said about him on national TV months before. He appeared to be totally unaware that some of the comments had even been made. Starr was also quite amazed and gratified to learn from his interviewer (about six years late) that Monica Lewinsky had made statements to Barbara Walters that seemed to indicate that some of her impeachment testimony was likely perjurious.

Interestingly, the Clinton impeachment may have been the best/worst example of a situation where media fragmentation had a real effect on the outcome of a major story. When Richard Nixon was under siege over the Watergate investigation, the House Judiciary Committee hearings (the very first stage of possible impeachment proceedings) were shown live on all the major networks and, since most Americans had only a few TV channels, huge numbers of people were forced to watch. This combined with the fact that the evening network newscasts were then seen by over three times the audience of today meant that America was fully engaged from the start of the process and enough momentum was created so that Nixon had no choice but to resign before articles of impeachment even got out of committee.

Contrast that with the case of Clinton where the committee hearings were jettisoned to the cable news channels which routinely interrupted them and where the major networks barely provided any live coverage of the actual impeachment in the House or, unbelievably, the Senate's sham impeachment trial itself. As a consequence, that sent Americans the unmistakable message that what was going on was not very important and that it was OK to tune it all out, which we largely did. Whether America ever could have been persuaded that Bill Clinton should have been thrown out of office is certainly open for debate, but the fact that his bid for survival was greatly helped by media fragmentation is most certainly not.

Similar to the circumstances of my interview with Ken Starr, I myself have been caught in much smaller situations where I was completely unaware that something was being said about me in the public domain. One particular example illustrates not just the reality of the fragmentation phenomenon, but also its corrosive impact on our culture. In 1999 I made a TV appearance on the number-one station in Philadelphia to discuss a series of recent news stories. Joining me on the panel was a rather militant African American writer with whom I disagreed on virtually every point. Finally, after a prolonged verbal battle, we suddenly concluded that neither of us liked notorious boxing promoter/ killer Don King (if two people cannot agree on *that,* what *can* they agree on?). In a spontaneous gesture of goodwill and attempted humor, I raised my hand to give my counterpart a "high-five," and he graciously decided not to leave me hanging and reciprocated the gesture.

At the time, I saw the episode as a light moment to take the tension out of what had been a rather heated discussion, allowing us to end our joint appearance on a "happy" note. I never thought about it again until several months later when I happened to have that writer on my radio show to discuss another matter. I was stunned and saddened to learn then that what I had thought was simply a signal of détente had been interpreted in a totally different manner by many in the black community and that, amazingly enough to me, the incident had become a fairly large "controversy" in some corners.

Apparently, totally unbeknownst to me, the issue of whether the writer should have shared my high-five had been hotly debated on black talk radio and in Philadelphia's black-run newspaper. It seems that many people felt that the writer's action was akin to a "sellout" and that, since I am a white "conservative," I should not have been granted such a peace offering.

When I learned about this I was totally flabbergasted. I was absolutely dumbfounded both that this dispute could be going on without me knowing about it and that blacks and whites could interpret the very same inconsequential event in such dramatically dissimilar ways. There is no doubt in my mind that both of these truths are directly connected. For one of the many reasons that blacks and whites so often see the identical happenings in such radically opposite ways is that their sources of information are so segregated that often neither "side" is even aware of what the other is talking about.

It has been well documented that, in our current "cable era," the media consumption habits of blacks and whites share almost nothing in common. Other than *Monday Night Football*, very few of the top-rated TV shows are on the top-twenty list of viewership for both races. In fact, the almost perennial controversy over whether the "major" networks are hiring enough black actors is completely absurd because the premise discounts the existence of entire networks like UPN, WB, BET, and MTV, among others, which have tended to cater more heavily to the black audience. This self-segregation is even more dramatic in the area of movies, where blacks almost never go to see films they perceive as "white," instead choosing to see those that involve a "black" plot line (Chris Rock even did a humorous bit on the 2005 *Oscar* telecast in which he went to a black theater and could not find anyone who had seen the nominated films).

Because, for whatever reasons, blacks like to watch stories about black people and whites prefer to see shows involving other whites, the TV networks and film studios have simply acted in a Darwinian quest for survival. To call today's media outlets *"broad casters"* is a total misnomer. Broadcasting is almost totally dead. *Narrow*casting is now the key to success in the world of the spoken word. Because of the vagaries of the advertising business (which we have previously discussed), media outlets no longer really care how many people are consuming their product. Instead, they are much more worried about targeting a very specific demographic. So, while the vast majority of cable TV and radio shows have *very* small audiences in terms of a percentage of the overall population, they can be profitable if they are able to attract the very narrow type of audience that their advertisers desire. (When it comes to movies, filmmakers understand that to get someone to the box office to pay $10 to see a film requires a laser-like focus on what kind of person would likely be convinced to do so. Consequently, it is much more profitable for a movie to be of *intense* interest to only a few million people rather than of mild interest to the whole country.)

This means that a TV or radio program that can draw, say, only 5 percent of the overall audience, but which gets 40 percent of, say, the 18–34-year-old white female population to watch/listen, is usually *far* more desirable than a show that attracts 10 percent of the general populace but whose consumers are split across all demographic lines. While this would appear to be counterintuitive and certainly contradictory to a unified country, it is unquestionably the current reality and almost certainly the wave of the future. In fact, in early 2005, Albie Hecht, the head of the Spike TV network, was fired because his channel, designed for men, was attracting *too many* women. Quite simply, radio and television, which once united this country like nothing else before them, are now among the most powerful forces of segregation and separation.

This trend toward narrowcasting has had a profound, though somewhat ambiguous, impact on freedom of speech. In some instances, the fragmentation of media sources has acted as a bit of a shield by allowing certain types of commentators to get away with remarks that could easily, if more of the right/wrong people had heard them, have been deemed to be "speech crimes." Black talk radio and cable TV comedy for instance is often a bastion for hatred and disinformation because almost no one in the "mainstream" media is listening (and would give blacks a pass anyway on PC grounds) and there is more than enough pressure within any given black community to make sure that even if someone really was ever offended that it would be highly unlikely for them to complain too loudly. Whenever I listen to black talk radio or watch a black comic on HBO, what I hear is so alien to me that I usually get the sensation that I am not just in a different country but on another planet, or at least in a parallel universe.

Of course, when it comes to stealth media outlets, nothing compares to those of the Spanish-speaking variety. In Southern California a Spanish speaker can get all the news, talk, and entertainment they want without ever having to learn a word of English. Spanish-speaking talk radio in the area has become a virtual warehouse for the latest information helping illegal immigrants to scam the system and avoid potential legal consequences. Those who are openly helping lawbreakers are doing so via the "public airwaves" of the United States and are getting away with it without any repercussion and without the vast majority of local residents even having any idea they are doing so. (Not that Spanish-speaking stations would care if they were exposed, because their ratings are great. On one particularly incredible Saturday night in late 2004, when a local boy won the Heisman Trophy and the two L.A. pro basketball teams were playing against each other, by *far* the highest rated TV sports program of the evening in Los Angeles was the Mexican League soccer final.)

While being on a station that only intends to service a sliver of the overall population can, in a dysfunctional way, increase one's ability to get away with saying potentially "inappropriate" things, conversely, being on a very popular "mainstream" station can sometimes reduce a host's speech rights simply because more people who might be offended are listening. For instance, had my show in Louisville not been so highly rated and on a station that was as close to a *broad*cast outlet as you can get today, there is a darn good chance no one would have given a damn about the comments that got me fired.

Narrowcasting has also helped lead to the deep political divisions in the country by reinforcing what it is that our citizens want to hear while allowing them to never have to deal with an uncomfortable fact or have their views challenged in any significant way. A conservative can now listen to Rush Limbaugh and Sean Hannity on the radio, watch Fox News Channel on TV, and read only right-wing columnists on the Internet, all while remaining virtually (and blissfully) ignorant of what the "other side" might think. Similarly, liberals can listen to Air America or NPR radio, watch CNN/NBC/ CBS/ABC, read left-wing bloggers, and go to Michael Moore movies without ever hearing a solid argument about why they might be wrong. In an age when more Americans every day are getting *no* meaningful information about what is really going on, it is particularly frustrating when those who do care enough to at least find out are essentially brainwashing themselves to the point that we cannot seem to agree on anything. Getting Americans on the same page has never been more difficult, and often it seems as if we are not even reading out of the same book.

The current debate over partial privatization of social security is an excellent example of this problem. President Bush simply wants to allow people to have some control over a small amount of *their* money that the government is stealing from them. Since the Democratic Party sees this idea as not in their self-interest, they have made it a matter of party dogma to be against it. Hence, those citizens on the Left, hearing mostly what they allow themselves to hear from leftist sources, are almost completely intractable in their knee-jerk reaction against the idea. Meanwhile, since the vast majority of Americans in the political middle are both ignorant about the economic system and fearful of the unknown, the diminished bully pulpit of the presidency in this fragmented media age prevents Bush from being able to convince nearly anyone of the merits of what should be a no-brainer proposal. If a newly reelected president with control of both houses of Congress cannot gain traction on an idea as simple as this, what possible hope is there for meaningful action on the *really* tough issues?

It is not just our political leaders who have been largely rendered impotent by this new media world. Members of the media themselves have seen their power to impact events also greatly diminished. While the positive attributes of such a development have already been documented (e.g., the news media's failed attempt to defeat President Bush's reelection bid), there are also some important negative consequences for this new reality.

In the glory days of CBS's *60 Minutes* (long before the name was soiled by Dan Rather's "Memogate" scandal), the program acted virtually like the morality police. When it took on the bad guys, the evildoers almost always lost and punishments were usually paid. The reason *60 Minutes* could wield such mighty power for good was not just that those who worked on the show were excellent investigative reporters (as the Russell Crowe movie *The Insider* showed, they were hardly perfect), but mostly because of the program's incredibly high ratings. As a Sunday night institution in an age with only a few TV channels from which to choose, *60 Minutes* had a stick so large that giant corporations could be toppled with it if the circumstances warranted. If you were exposed on *60 Minutes* during the 1970s and early '80s, you were simply done. There was just no place to hide.

Today, that is not the case. The stick of *60 Minutes* has now been shrunk to a far more diminutive stature with their power to inflict harm on the bad guys having been reduced to almost nothing. Because of the show's liberal bias, for many conservatives this loss of clout has been welcomed. However, it is important as well as fascinating to recognize that it was not really until *60 Minutes* and other liberal media establishments started to realize just how small their stick had gotten that, like a spoiled child who doesn't get his way, they started to throw a temper tantrum by using what was left of their power in a blatantly partisan manner. I for one wish that shows like *60 Minutes* still had more bite than bark, especially now that the mechanisms exist to be the watchdog's watchdog.

There appears to be a direct correlation between the decline of *60 Minutes* and the corporate scandals of the late 1990s as well as the general decline in morality among the elite (though Bill Clinton should also take some responsibility for that). It is simply human nature to be more likely to take a chance and push the envelope if you are fairly certain you will escape the noose even you get caught.

Perhaps one of the most amazing examples of the lost ability of the mainstream media to enforce justice is the failed attempt to bring down fraudulent "Christian" faith healer Benny Hinn. Hinn, whose disgraceful ministry I have attended, is such a liar and a thief that to call him a snake-oil salesman would be unfair to those sellers of serpent lubricants. Two major TV networks have done exhaustive investigative reports on Hinn, with NBC doing a second hourlong prime-time Sunday night special in 2005. The results were absolutely devastating, and any open-minded person who saw the programs would never again think about giving money to Hinn. However, "miraculously" Hinn has only suffered a small drop in donations and his crusade to scam money from innocent and suffering people has been almost completely unimpeded. Hinn has never even been forced to answer any of the many questions about his giant boondoggle. In fact, he has even gotten away with telling his TV viewers that he did not answer NBC's inquiries because, get this, *God* told him not to!

Because we live in an age where Hinn is able to communicate directly to his followers via a network of small TV stations as well as the Internet, and because no mainstream TV show investigating him has an audience large enough to reach into his largely isolated base, he has been able to withstand what would have been, just a decade or so ago, a knockout blow. Consequently, millions of poor people worldwide are still vulnerable to having their dreams smashed and pockets picked by one of our culture's worst creations. Unfortunately, Hinn is just one of many public figures who get away with doing wrong, safe in the knowledge that the media watchdog has lost its bite.

Media fragmentation has not just made it easier for bad deeds to go unpunished, but has also stolen from us many potentially wonderful developments. The era of homogeny in media, while it certainly had its drawbacks (including a regrettable lack of diversity in both appearance and opinion), also created an environment where some great things could happen. Had it occurred today, The Beatles' now famous emergence on the *Ed Sullivan Show* would not only have failed to launch them into the ultimate career in music history and a revolution that would change the music industry forever, it would barely have even made a blip on the public radar screen. Similarly, Elvis Presley, Michael Jackson, and Madonna, for better or worse, could never had reached anywhere near their levels of notoriety and influence in today's cluttered media world. It does not seem to be a coincidence that the music industry is in crisis during an era in which not one song or performer has broken out to gain true broad appeal and when no one can remember the last time the same song was on the lips of even a quarter of the American populace.

Similarly, the area of life that may have been hit hardest by media fragmentation is that of the sports world. Ironically, thanks to this new media world, exponentially more games are now able to be seen and salaries for professionals have skyrocketed. However, in my view, sports has lost much of its soul and it is only a matter of time before the public completely catches on that the same goose that laid the golden egg of TV has been killed by the side effects.

One of the great things about sports back in the age of limited channels was that all sports fans were pretty much forced to watch what was on, which meant that whatever made "the cut" was automatically deemed to have enormous significance simply because a huge number of people were watching. So even if the contest in question was not for a championship, it was still at least a little bit special simply because it was on TV. Today, nearly *every* pro and major college game is on TV somewhere and the audiences are microscopic in comparison to the '70s and '80s. Now when one buddy asks the other, "Did you see the game last night?" the most likely response is a quizzical, "Which one?" So much for male bonding.

Because sports fans now know that if they miss the game that, if anything interesting happens, they can see it dozens of times on the highlights, they will be more and more likely to simply not watch. Then, over time, they will come to realize that they actually *can* live without spending three or four hours on a sports event and their connection to the sport will diminish and the process of audience erosion will accelerate. I predict that eventually the oversaturation of sports on television will create an economic implosion which will create such an upheaval in sports that the athletic landscape will be radically altered (probably for the better, because frankly it cannot get much worse).

Just as important as the potential economic impact on the sports world is the sad loss of the kind of great communal moments that only sports can (could) bring. Think about how much less powerful the incredible achievements of the 1980 U.S. Olympic hockey team (which beat the Russians, won the Gold Medal, and helped win the cold war) would be if that amazing story had occurred amidst today's cluttered media scene. For that matter, would Muhammad Ali have been able to become, for better or worse, as significant a cultural character today? Similarly, had Doug Flutie's 1984 miracle "Hail Mary" pass to beat Miami in a rather meaningless game not occurred on a day in which it was the only thing on TV, it would hardly be remembered today as an inspiration for little white guys everywhere (as proof of that, ask any sports fan the name of the well-known Colorado quarterback who a decade later, in a very different media environment, arguably surpassed Flutie's feat to beat Michigan; they probably will not be able to tell you it was Kordell Stewart). Finally, would Tiger Woods's positive impact on race relations not be even greater if he had come around in an age without fragmentation?

This is not to say that sports, under the right circumstances, are unable to still bring a *city* together. In 2004, about 80 percent of Boston TV sets that were on were tuned to the Red Sox finally winning a World Series. In 2005, similar numbers followed in both Boston and Philadelphia for the Patriots/Eagles Super Bowl. Such communal experiences are of priceless value to the long-term well-being of a city, and it is no accident that Los Angeles, probably the nation's most fractured municipality, with no NFL team, happens to be one our most apathetic and troubled as well. Unfortunately, as with so many cultural developments, the Los Angeles of today may very well be the norm of tomorrow.

So, while on very rare occasions some pockets of the country can still enjoy an unifying experience, such huge TV numbers on a national level are now, even for the Super Bowl (which is somehow *ignored* by well over *half* the population), absolutely impossible, and we have all undoubtedly lost a valuable part of our cultural makeup because of it.

As varied and significant as the apparent consequences of media fragmentation already are, the real danger comes from the long-term, largely silent effect of slowly robbing us of a sense of national unity. As with any problem, the first step in combating it is to be aware it even exists. For some reason (perhaps because fragmentation has provided so much entertainment to people that it could hardly seem dangerous), almost no one is sounding the alarm on this one. This is why, while the issue may seem to only be tangentially related to free speech, it is more than worthy of mention within this context.

CHAPTER EIGHT: THE FUTURE OF FREE SPEECH

> *"I believe there are more instances of the abridgment of the rights of the people by the gradual and silent encroachments of those in power than by violent and sudden usurpations."*
>
> —James Madison, fourth president of the United States

Obviously, when I began the process of researching and writing this book, I started with the premise that our free speech rights were being endangered by numerous societal forces. Considering my own personal history with Speech Punishment and what I knew about the perils of speaking your mind in modern America, I knew we had a serious problem. If I did not believe that was true, there would have been little reason to even start this massive project. But as dire as I thought the state of our speech rights was then, I have since learned that the situation is much worse than even I had imagined. This free speech wildfire is no longer just about what curse words you can say on the radio at what hour of the day. It is far more serious and much more widespread than that, and the inferno is undeniably spreading fast. Part of this evolution of thought was provoked by accumulating new information about what has transpired over the past few years, but much of it was as a result of the remarkably rapid escalation of related events that occurred during the actual writing of this book.

You may have noticed I have cited a disproportionate number of episodes from late 2004 and early 2005. This was partly because of a conscious effort to keep the content of the work as fresh as possible, but it was mostly as a result of the very real acceleration of significant developments in the realm of free speech during this time period. In fact, during a remarkable period of just a few days at the start of 2005, an incredible series of important Speech Punishment stories erupted throughout the country.

Nearly simultaneously, Harvard's president was forced to beg for his job after having suggested that men and women may be innately different, the University of Colorado was deciding whether to fire a professor for an outrageous article he wrote over three years before while the governor of the state was inappropriately calling for his ouster, LeMoyne College was wrongly expelling a student for advocating "corporal punishment," a Marine general was being "consoled" by superiors and a major U.S. Islamic group was calling for even further action because Lt. General James Mattis had joked at a conference that "it's fun to shoot some people," and a radio producer and cohost were rightly, though belatedly, fired from their New York hip-hop morning show for repeatedly playing a sick parody song that and made fun of the victims of the Asian tsunami and included racial slurs.

That very same week also saw one of the very few individual cases of *blatantly* wrong Speech Punishment of a public school student. Brad Devlin was suspended for five days from his Florida high school because during his sportscast on the school's TV station he ad-libbed a pretty innocent joke. His teacher had pre-approved a script that said the school's soccer team had "really kicked some booty," and Devlin deadpanned afterward, "I love booty." Kicking him off the broadcast for such a transgression? Maybe. But punishing the student in a way that would significantly and permanently harm his academic record—the equivalent of what he would have received had he brought a knife to school, started a fistfight, or participated in on-campus gang rituals—most certainly should not have been.

I do not believe that this dramatic increase in the number of Speech Punishment–related news stories is simply coincidence or just part of a temporary backlash from Janet Jackson exposing her nipple at the Super Bowl. Instead, a more global view of the facts strongly indicates that the increasing rate of incidents in which free speech has been improperly restricted is evidence that the metaphorical slippery slope I have referred to often in these pages is indeed already at work. What we are witnessing is simply the inevitable quickening of the slide downward once the force needed to overcome the initial inertia has been reached, momentum starts to build, and gravity takes over.

There is no doubt that when it comes to free speech restriction, the threshold of inertia has long ago been overpowered. So now the problem becomes reversing or at least stopping the ensuing slide. As with the laws of physics when it comes to a real slippery slope, the inherent nature of both human beings and our cultural environment are in direct opposition to achieving this seemingly simple but likely unrealistic goal. Usually the only way to stop sliding down a slippery slope is to either plunge all the way down the hill or to crash. It seems that the same may be said about reversing the course of ever increasing speech control upon which we appear inevitably headed.

As illustrative of our free speech predicament as the slippery slope metaphor may be, another image we have also been using may be even more illuminating. With our speech rights being attacked constantly from so many different angles and with their once mighty defense systems being battered and frayed, it seems as if the "fortress under assault" image may be the most accurate representation of the current reality.

In a very real sense, thanks to the purposely unambiguous wording of the First Amendment, free speech has always been sheltered in this country by a wide alligator-filled moat, high fortified walls, lookout perches manned by expert marksmen, and an army of well-armed soldiers/citizens willing to risk their own lives in order to preserve what was always presumed to be sacred. As we have documented in these pages, while many of the soldiers have already been sacrificed in attacks on our free speech treasure, the essence of those rights, though tattered in some important areas, still remains largely intact.

However, there is no doubt that the forces of political correctness have emptied the moat, that the FCC, FEC, lawmakers, and the courts have all helped knock down large portions of the formerly impenetrable barricade, and that our media and substandard educational system have helped to sap the militia of their resolve. With the free speech fortress being relentlessly stormed from nearly every front and with its ramparts now stripped of much of their previously powerful protections, it seems all too obvious that real and lasting damage to the inner core of the castle is all too inevitable.

Like Superman with a kryptonite virus, free speech in this country still looks much the same as it always has, but it is certainly no longer bulletproof and its other superpowers are being quickly diminished if not drained completely.

So what does the future hold? While I have obviously painted an ominous portrait, I still have hope. It is a hope that largely rests in the belief that there will soon be a watershed moment for free speech in this country. That there will be an episode where someone is so blatantly punished by the government for something they said, or where the censorship of an important idea or news story is so dramatic, that the situation breaks through the massive force field of media clutter and becomes emblazoned into the public consciousness (think something along the lines of the Janet Jackson Super Bowl fiasco, only without the nipple and with the backlash targeted in the opposite direction).

With all due respect to the thousands who lost their lives on 9/11, I see this future event as the free speech "equivalent" to that fateful day. The events of 9/11 hardly marked the first time that this country had been hit by terrorists, but it was a moment that had such a dramatic impact that it woke the nation up to the dangers it was facing and caused us to finally get serious about fighting the enemy. While I certainly do not believe that 9/11 was "good" for the country, nor was I remotely "glad" that it happened, there were certainly some very positive developments that transpired because of that national tragedy. Much like 9/11 was the first time that millions of Americans even realized we *had* an enemy, I foresee this free speech "equivalent" as providing this country with a much needed test and potential wake-up call, hopefully without the death and destruction.

When this free speech "9/11" occurs (there is no doubt that it will, the only question is whether the news media will make it as big a deal as they should), there will be basically two possible outcomes to this national test. Under the first scenario, the news media and the public will finally see that an important and unprecedented line has been crossed and that their free speech rights *really are* being *seriously* threatened. Here the outrage (assuming such a thing still exists in this country) is so strong and the reaction is so overwhelming that it fuels a much needed counterattack in defense of our rights. In an ideal world, these circumstances come together as soon as possible so that the pro–free speech forces are still formidable enough to lead an effective offensive.

The other possibility, of course, is that this free speech "9/11" is either muted by the news media because it coincides with something *really* newsworthy (like the death of a former member of the British royal family or the verdict in the trial of a minor celebrity), or, even worse, the public just simply does not react to it in a significant manner. Should either or both of these segments of our society fail their test, the repercussions would likely be devastating.

With the bridge into that dilapidated castle now cleared for safe passage by the forces of censorship, there would be little except self-restraint to keep the government from fully taking advantage of the public's apathy in order to permanently silence dissent. Because we would likely still have enough pro–free speech voices among our elected and governmental officials to at least put up a fight, even I doubt that a failure of our "test" would result in the *immediate* end to all rights to free expression. However, thanks to the fundamental power-seeking nature of government, after that critical point of no return has been passed without an uprising, it would only seem a matter of time before something close to the "Doomsday" scenario would eventually become reality.

Unfortunately, I now believe that this second set of circumstances is more than plausible and possibly even probable. The reasons for my pessimism (other than just my normal "glass is half empty" view of the world) are many. Ironically, the fact that we live in a post-9/11 world is one of them.

There are many reasons why "outrage," as Bill Bennett wrote in his Clinton-era book *The Death of Outrage*, may very well be in greater peril than even free speech. This was the case even before the attacks on our homeland, but now the threshold that must be exceeded before the American populace gets truly exercised about a news event is frighteningly high. Quite simply, because of

9/11 and numerous other never-before-seen epic news events of the past decade or so (O. J.'s Bronco chase and acquittal, Clinton's impeachment, Florida's recount, Paris Hilton's sex video, Jen and Brad's breakup, etc.) we have become dangerously desensitized as a culture.

For instance, had there never been an O. J. trial, the Michael Jackson case would not have seemed relatively puny in comparison. Similarly, in a post-9/11 world, it is far more difficult for increasingly busy and individually focused Americans to feel a prolonged sense of indignation over much of anything. After all, when you have seen the World Trade Towers collapse on live TV thanks to a terrorist attack, someone losing their job, getting sued, or even going to jail for saying something you probably did not agree with just does not rise to the level of creating righteous anger in most people.

I honestly do not think that it is remotely coincidental that just after both the Clinton presidency and the 9/11 attacks that our society's tolerance for previously unacceptable behavior seemed to increase exponentially. Does anyone else find it amazing that U.S. Catholics still attend mass and donate to their church in roughly the same way that they did before the massive pedophilia scandal? Is it not incredible that the audience for the *CBS Evening News*, which was already relatively small, decreased only marginally after Dan Rather's bias, incompetence, and arrogance were fully exposed by "Memogate"? Is it not depressing that Barry Bonds and others like him have suffered almost no repercussions and little loss of prestige or popularity after it has become obvious that their home run records were aided by rampant steroid use?

Because of this rapidly changing cultural landscape I fear that we may no longer be prepared to rise to the occasion and fight for our rights when events eventually call upon us to do so. Many before me have followed similar reasoning to predict the demise of our freedoms and, ultimately, this nation. The prevailing theory among those who envision such a gloomy outcome for this remarkable experiment in democracy is that we the people are much like the cold-blooded frog in a vat of water where the temperature is slowly raised to the boiling point. Since the frog adjusts its body temperature to that of the water it does not realize what is happening until it is far too late for the animal to save itself from being scorched. While the fundamental nature of humanity has always made this scenario logically sound, the desensitization we have recently experienced from this "post-traumatic major news disorder" and the ensuing "death of outrage" has only diminished the probability that our frog will be able to sense what is happening to it.

Amidst this ominous forecast, there could still be a silver bullet in the battle to save our freedom of speech. One of the many "ironies" in the realm of free speech restriction is that so much of it has occurred synonymously with the single most significant development in the history of expression: the invention and expansion of the Internet. Even as there is no doubt that "traditional," "credible," or "broadcast" speech has never been under more duress, there is also no uncertainty that, thanks to the Internet, more is being said and read, in a freer and more diverse fashion, than ever before. While there are certainly many problems for our national conversation that the Internet inadvertently has caused (like making it tougher to separate fact from fiction), it has, at least so far, unquestionably been a victory for free speech. Of course, since in the vast majority of cases very few people are actually reading or hearing what is being said (and usually rightfully so), the triumph must be kept in its proper perspective.

So while the Internet is highly unlikely to save free speech on its own (in fact, it may very well be used as an excuse to justify the further constriction of speech on traditional mediums), it could easily serve as the catalyst for that counterattack to which I have previously referred. The Internet now enables significant forces to communicate, organize, and rally for or against a cause virtually instantaneously and without having to rely on the undependable nature of the "old" media to help spread their word. As long as expression on the Internet is truly liberated (as it is currently, at least in the vast majority of cases), the forces protecting free speech will always have the ability to unite the troops and direct at least a formidable counteroffensive against any violation of speech rights that passes a particular threshold. However, especially since any movement that is associated with the Internet has inherent and understandable credibility problems, this resource is not nearly enough to rely upon alone, especially with the stakes of this fight being so high.

With that said, the most likely role I see for the Internet in helping preserve our speech rights is not necessarily as a direct weapon, but rather serving as a tasty target for the forces of censorship to bite off more than they can chew and inadvertently create enough outrage to spark a powerful and lasting backlash. It seems rather obvious that the next great frontier of freedom likely to be targeted is indeed the Internet itself, and it is the battle over that turf that may very well decide the future of free speech in this country and around the world. There have already been whispers about the government trying to regulate both commerce and content on the Internet (in early 2005 the FEC announced it would start looking at tightening restrictions on political campaigns using the Internet), but when those proposals become serious is when we will likely learn which side will emerge victorious in that seemingly unavoidable clash.

If the government is indeed allowed to cast their censorship net over the vast domain of cyberspace, the great American experiment in free expression will be officially over. If that inevitable initiative is fended off with a decisive victory by the forces of free speech, then a bulkhead against further erosion of our speech rights will have been built and a significant line will finally be drawn. Those who dare to cross this line must suffer severe political consequences so that an unmistakable message/warning is sent to anyone who dares tread on such ground again.

Regardless of when and where the ultimate fight over our ability to freely express our ideas, thoughts, and feelings is finally fought, I plan to be there with the largest rhetorical pitchfork I can find. I hope that you will be there with me along with whomever you can persuade to join the cause for free speech. We owe it to all of those who have died in real battles in order to give us this right, and we will need all the help we can get to make sure their sacrifice was not in vain.

ACKNOWLEDGMENTS

This book could not have been written without the help and support of many people for which I am eternally grateful. They include: Greg Ashlock, Robin Bertolucci, Dee Bliss, Leah Brandon, Sid Comer, Barbara Fouss, Al Gore (for inventing the Internet), Mary Leary, Justin Levine, Janet Lively, Shannon Lopez, Diane and J. J. Macedonia, Brooks Melchior, Kristine Mylls, Jason Nathanson, Merle Robertson, Gerry Sibrack, Sarah Sockolof, Lisa Taylor, Carrollanne Trainer, Robert Trainer, John Yarmuth, Hans Ziegler, and Robert Ziegler.

INDEX